S Is for Saints

By Megan Dunsmore
Illustrated by Lawrence Klimecki

Paulist Press
New York/Mahwah, N.J.

Caseside and interior design by Lynn Else.
Caseside illustration by Lawrence Klimecki.

Text Copyright © 2002 by Megan Dunsmore
Illustrations Copyright © 2002 by Lawrence Klimecki

Library of Congress Cataloging-in-Publication Data

Dunsmore, Megan.
   S is for saints / by Megan Dunsmore ; illustrated by Lawrence Klimecki.
     p. cm.
   Summary: Briefly introduces over fifty Christian saints, including where and when each lived.
   ISBN 0-8091-6693-3 (alk. paper)
   1. Christian saints—Biography—Juvenile literature. 2. Christain saints—Biography—Dictionaries.
[1. Saints.] I. Klimecki, Lawence, ill. II. Title.
BX4653 .D86 2002
282′.092′2—dc21
[B]

2001056009

Published by Paulist Press
997 Macarthur Boulevard
Mahwah, New Jersey 07430

www.paulistpress.com

Printed and bound in Mexico

S Is for Saints

This book is dedicated to Mary, the Queen of All Saints.
—M.D.

To the Church Triumphant and the Communion of Saints,
may they remember us in their prayers.
—L.K.

Hail Mary, full of Grace, the Lord is with thee. Blessed art thou among women, and blessed is the fruit of thy womb, Jesus. Holy Mary, Mother of God, pray for us sinners, now and at the hour of our death.

Amen

Introduction

If someone was so good and so holy that he or she was special, the church may decide that this person was a saint. A saint is someone who deserves our respect and who can help us here on earth with his or her prayers in heaven.

Before making this decision, the church examines the person's life very closely. What did they do, say, and write while alive? Were they so good, so brave, and so holy that they were a hero in some ways? Was the person responsible for miracles, either during his or her life or afterwards?

There are three steps in this examination, like three parts of a test. If the person passes the first part, he or she is called "venerable." If the person passes the second part, he or she is called "blessed." And if the third and final part is passed, the person is officially called "saint." The examination takes time, so some of the "blesseds" and "venerables" in this book may someday be called "saint."

There are many more holy men and women than could fit inside these pages. Some you will know, and others will be new to you. Each one has something wonderful to share about his or her love for God.

St. Anthony
of Padua

Remember his marvelous works that he hath done, his wonders, and the judgements of his mouth.

St. Anthony of Padua

Known as the "Wonder Worker," Anthony was a famous preacher. Many people experienced miracles of healing and conversion after listening to Anthony preach. (Lived from 1195 to 1231, Portugal, Doctor of the Church)

St. Angela Merici

An orphan at the age of ten, Angela saw holy visions. Her visions led her to open schools to educate young girls, and to start the Ursuline order.
(Lived from 1474 to 1540, Italy)

B

St. Brendan the Navigator

St. Brendan

Brendan was a monk who made missionary trips to England and Scotland.
He also sailed the ocean for seven years looking for the "Land of Promise."
Many people believe his journey took him to America nine hundred years
before Columbus! (Lived from about 484 to 577, Ireland)

St. Bernadette Soubirous

B

St. Bernadette Soubirous

Bernadette was a poor and uneducated girl. When she was fourteen years old, she had several visions of the Blessed Virgin. When Bernadette asked the Lady what her name was, Mary answered, "I am the Immaculate Conception." (Lived from 1844 to 1879, France)

C

St. Charles Borromeo

Charles Borromeo was a great reformer for the Catholic Church. He helped restart the Council of Trent, and he revised the catechism of the church. He also helped begin the religious education of young children, or Sunday school. (Lived from 1538 to 1584, Italy)

C

St. Catherine of Siena

Catherine dedicated her life to serving Jesus in those around her. She cared tirelessly for those in hospitals and in prisons. She also worked with both rulers and popes and was an inspiration of faith in action to the people of Siena. (Lived from 1347 to 1380, Italy, Doctor of the Church)

D

St. Dominic Savio

Dominic Savio was a student of St. John Bosco. As a young boy, Dominic formed a club to honor the Virgin Mary. He said that Jesus and Mary were his best friends. He died from tuberculosis when he was just fifteen. (Lived from 1842 to 1857, Italy)

D

Dorothy of Montau

Dorothy had nine children. She showed her husband how to love Jesus
by her own gentleness and humility. After his death, she became a hermit.
She is remembered for her devotion to Jesus in the Blessed Sacrament.
Although the church has not named her so, the people of her country
all consider her a saint. (Lived from 1347 to 1394, Prussia)

E

St. Edmund Campion

Edmund was an underground priest in England. The Queen had outlawed Catholicism. Edmund had to preach in secret. When he was discovered, he was tortured and killed. (Lived from 1540 to 1581, England, one of the Forty English and Welsh Martyrs)

St. Elizabeth Ann Seton

St. Elizabeth Ann Seton

Elizabeth was the mother of five children. After her husband died, she became a Catholic. She started the first American religious community for women. She also helped start many schools for children. (Lived from 1774 to 1821, United States, first U.S.-born saint)

F

Blessed Ferdinand

A prince of Portugal, Ferdinand was a very holy man. He led an army to fight the Moors but was captured. His brother, King Edward, would not pay the ransom to free him. Ferdinand was tortured and held in jail for six years before he died. (Lived from 1402 to 1443, Portugal)

St. Flora

Flora's father was a believer in Mohammed. Her mother believed in Jesus, and she secretly raised Flora as a Christian. Flora's brother tried to make her deny Jesus but she would not. Because of this, she was tortured and killed.

(Died in 851, Spain)

G

St. George

George was a Christian knight in an imperial army. He was martyred in Palestine. Legends say that George saved a princess who was going to be sacrificed to a dragon. He made the local people agree to be baptized. When they did, he killed the dragon. (Died in 303, England)

St. Gemma

Gemma was a beautiful and holy young woman. She had many supernatural visions. She also bore the wounds of Christ (the nail marks of his hands and feet, and the mark on his side where his heart was pierced). Gemma suffered bravely with tuberculosis and died when she was only twenty-five years old. (Lived from 1878 to 1903, Italy)

H

St. Henry II

Henry II was one of the Holy Roman Emperors. He was a great and saintly leader. He gave money to rebuild Catholic churches and monasteries and to start many new ones. (Lived from 972 to 1024, Bavaria)

St Helena

Helena was the mother of the Roman Emperor Constantine. She became a Christian when she was sixty-three and devoted herself to the church. On a visit to Palestine, she discovered the True Cross of Christ. She was known for being generous to the poor and suffering around her.

(Lived from 250 to 330, Bithynia)

St. Ignatius of Loyola

Ignatius was a nobleman who was badly wounded in battle. While healing, he decided to change his life, and he turned his sword over to Jesus. Ignatius began the Jesuit order. He pledged the members of his order to the service of the pope as missionaries. He was also a gifted spiritual director.

(Lived from 1491 to 1556, Spain)

Bl. Isabel

I

Blessed Isabel of France

Isabel was the daughter of the King of France. Many times rich men asked to marry her, but she refused because she wanted to live just for God. She started a monastery in Paris devoted to the Blessed Mother.

(Died in 1270, France)

J

St. Joseph

Joseph was the foster father of our Lord Jesus. A simple carpenter, he trusted in God's word, brought to him by an angel, and raised Jesus as his own son. Loving him like a real father, Joseph passed on to Jesus his own skills, traditions, and faith. (Died in the first century, perhaps in Nazareth)

St. Joan of Arc

J

St. Joan of Arc

Joan was the daughter of a peasant. When she was thirteen years old, she heard voices of saints telling her to save France from the British. She was allowed to lead the French army and won many battles. Then she was captured. She endured months of a grueling trial before being burned at the stake. (Lived from 1412 to 1431, France)

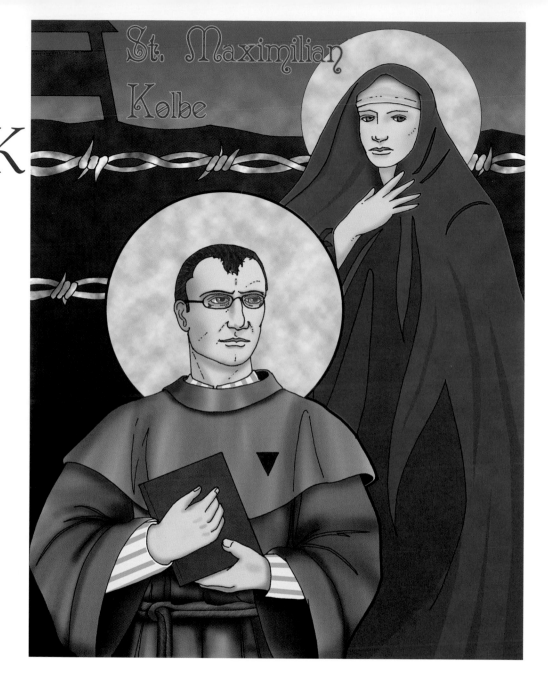

K

St. Maximilian Kolbe

Maximilian Kolbe was a priest who was deeply devoted to the Blessed Mother. During World War II, he was sent to a concentration camp. When some of the prisoners were to be executed, Maximilian offered to die in place of a married man who had children. (Lived from 1894 to 1941, Poland)

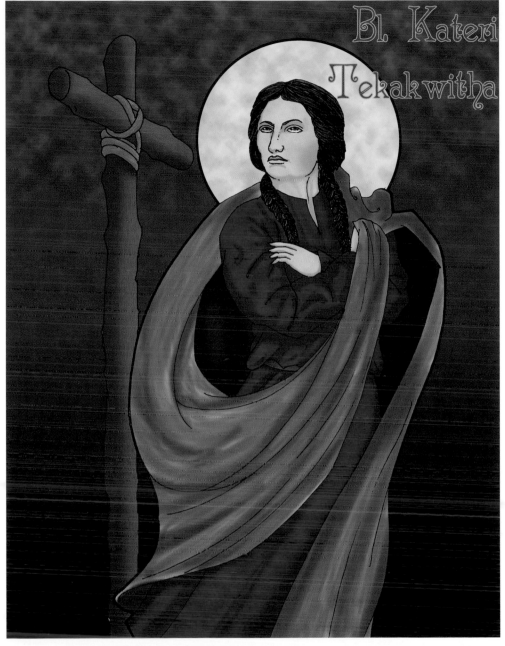

K

Blessed Kateri Tekakwitha

Kateri was an Algonquin Indian married to a Mohawk chief. The tribe
abused and rejected her because she believed in Jesus. She fled and traveled
200 miles to a Christian village near Montreal, Canada. There she lived a
humble life dedicated to Christ. (Lived from 1656 to 1680)

St. Luke

St. Luke

Luke was a physician from Syria. He traveled with St. Paul to preach the
Good News. Luke wrote the Gospel of Luke and the Acts of the Apostles.
Legend says he met Mary on his travels and painted several pictures
of her. (Died in the first century, perhaps in Greece)

St. Lucy

The leaders of Lucy's town tried, as punishment, to have her put in a brothel
because she was a Christian. She couldn't be moved from the spot.
They then tried to burn her and to tear out her eyes, but she
was miraculously protected. (Died in 304, Sicily)

St. Martin de Porres

St. Martin de Porres

Of African and Spanish heritage, Martin de Porres was a Dominican lay brother. He served his fellow Dominicans as barber, nurse, and cook. Tireless in serving the poor, Martin founded an orphanage and a hospital. (Lived from 1579 to 1639, Peru)

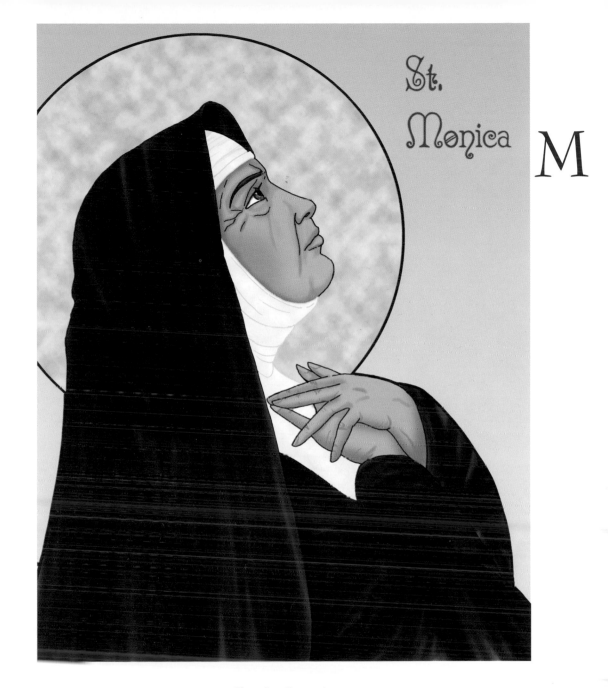

St. Monica

M

St. Monica

Monica was the mother of St. Augustine. She prayed for thirty years that
he would come to know and love Jesus. Her prayers were heard.
St. Augustine became one of the greatest saints of all time.
(Lived from 331 to 387, Numidia, Africa)

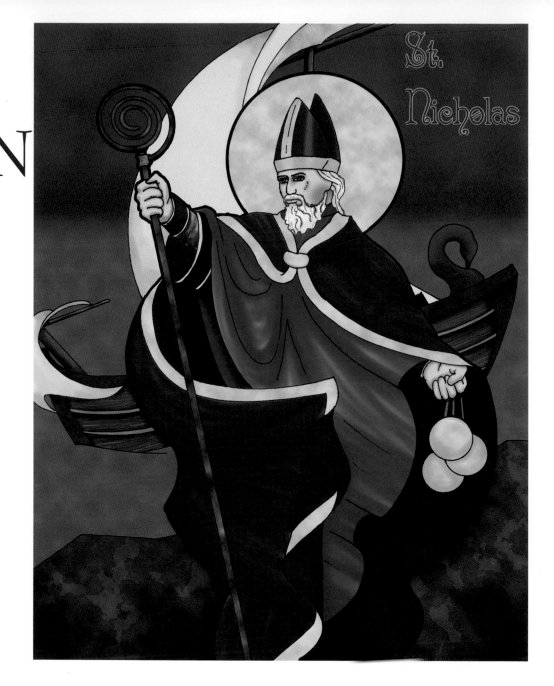

N

St. Nicholas

Nicholas was the Bishop of Myra. He gave away his money and other possessions to the poor. He was so famous for giving gifts that he has become known as Santa Claus. (Died in 350, Lycia)

N

St. Natalia

Natalia was the wife of St. Adrian. Adrian had been put in jail and tortured
because he was a Christian. Natalia bribed a guard to let her join
Adrian in jail. She nursed and comforted him until he died.
Then she escaped. (Died in 304, Constantinople)

St. Olaf II

Olaf was a pirate as a young man. Then he was baptized. He later became the king of Norway. As king, Olaf unified his country by spreading the Gospel. He was killed by his opponents. (Lived from 995 to 1030, Norway)

St. Odilia

Odilia was born blind. Her father sent her away, ashamed of her blindness. She was baptized at age twelve. When the priest touched her eyes, her sight was restored. Her father was shocked by what had happened and allowed her to turn one his castles into a convent. (Died in 720, Alsace)

P

St.

Patrick

St Patrick

Taken as a slave to Ireland when he was sixteen, Patrick eventually escaped to
Gaul and became a priest. He was sent back to Ireland as a bishop and a
missionary. He drove out the pagan Druids and converted the island
to Christianity. Legend says he also drove out all the snakes
from Ireland. (Lived from 389 to 461, Roman Britain)

St. Perpetua

A young mother, Perpetua was thrown in prison for being a Christian. She was very brave and encouraged the other Christians there by her great hope in their salvation. She and another prisoner, St. Felicity, were sentenced to death by being trampled by wild animals in an arena. (Died in 203, Carthage)

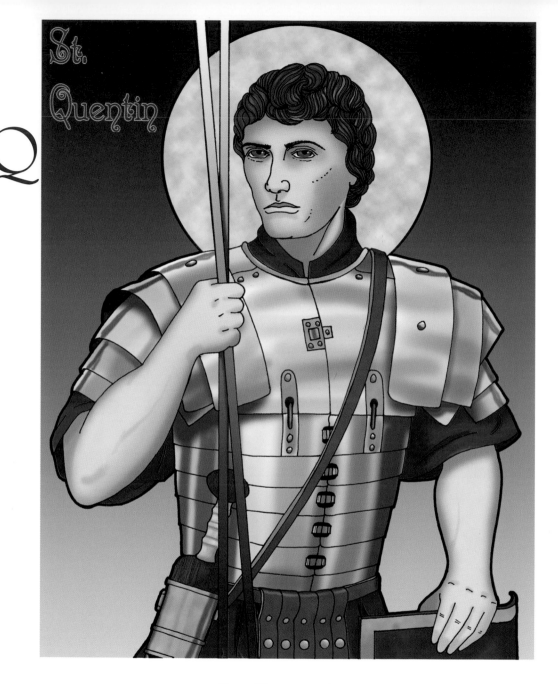

Q

St. Quentin

Quentin was a Roman soldier who converted to Christianity. He became a missionary and was a very effective preacher. Quentin was put in prison by a pagan Roman leader. He was tortured to death. (Died in 287, Gaul)

St. Quiteria

Quiteria was the daughter of a Galician prince. She ran away from home rather than deny Christ. Legend says that she protects against the bite of mad dogs. (Died in the fifth century, Spain)

St. Richard of Chichester

St. Richard of Chichester

Richard was an orphan. He studied in Oxford and Paris and became a Doctor of Canon Law. He was made chancellor of Oxford University and later chancellor to the Archbishop of Canterbury. With some opposition, he was named Bishop of Chichester. He led a holy life and was generous to the poor. (Lived from 1197 to 1253, England)

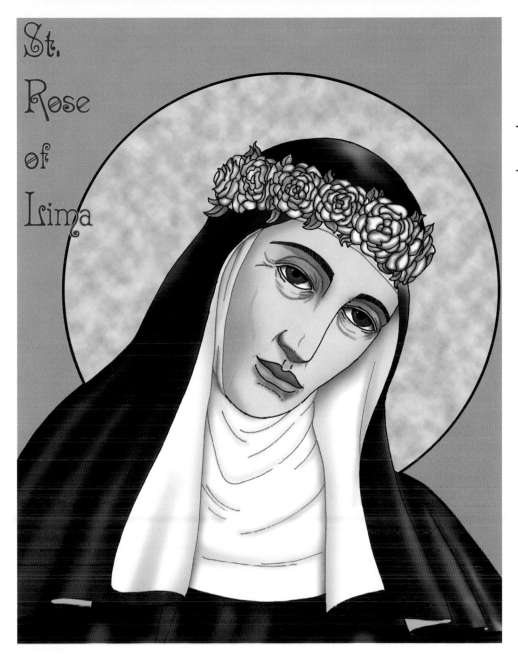

St. Rose of Lima

R

St. Rose of Lima

A Dominican tertiary, Rose chose to live a very simple, very strict life
in a hut in her parents' garden. She had supernatural visions
that caused many people to be encouraged in their faith.
(Died in 1586, Peru, first canonized saint of the New World)

S

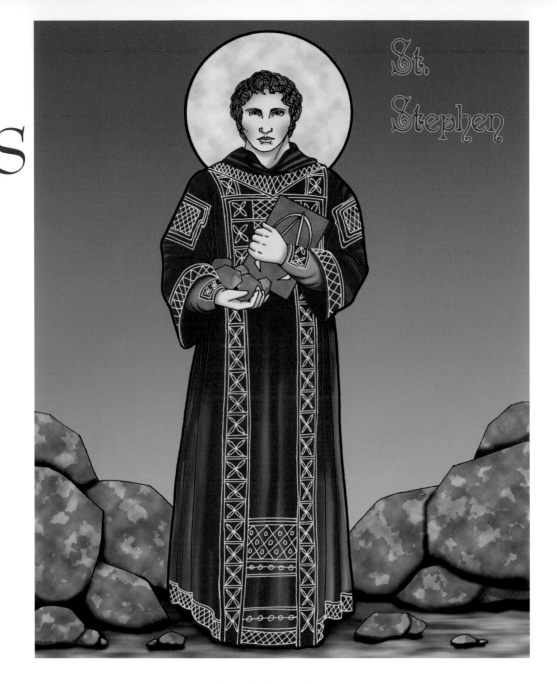

St. Stephen

Stephen, a deacon in the early church, was the first Christian martyr. He was stoned to death while speaking fearlessly about Jesus the Christ. (Died about the year 35, in Jerusalem)

St. Scholastica

Scholastica was St. Benedict's twin sister. With the help of her brother, she founded a convent. She is considered the first Benedictine nun. When she died, St. Benedict had a vision of her soul rising to heaven.

(Lived from 480 to 543, Italy)

T

St. Thomas Aquinas

When Thomas was nineteen, he joined the Dominicans. His family did not approve so they kidnapped him and held him captive in a tower for over a year. Eventually he rejoined the Dominicans. Thomas was very smart, but he hid it so well he was called the "Dumb Ox." He became one of the great theologians of the church. (Lived from 1225 to 1274, Italy, Doctor of the Church)

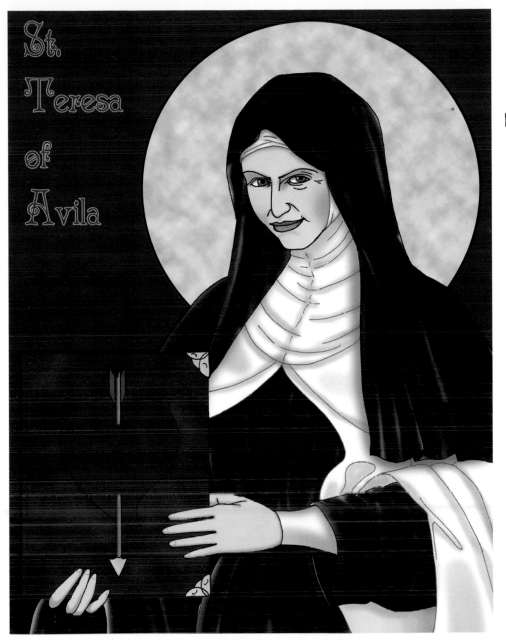

St. Teresa of Avila

Teresa was a holy nun who was known for her sense of humor. She began a reform of the Carmelite order and opened sixteen new convents. She wrote many books about prayer and holiness. (Lived from 1515 to 1582, Spain, Doctor of the Church)

U

St. Ulric

Ulric was the Bishop of Augsburg who set a good and holy example for others. When pagan Magyars attacked and destroyed Augsburg, he encouraged the people to hold on until they could be rescued. Afterwards he helped them rebuild the city and its cathedral. (Lived from 890 to 973, Germany)

Bl. Ursulina

U

Blessed Ursulina

Ursulina had visions and supernatural experiences as a young girl. She lived in a time when there were two popes, and everyone was confused. Led by a vision, she tried to convince the two men, Boniface IX and Clement VII, to reunify the church under one pope. (Lived from 1375 to 1410, Italy)

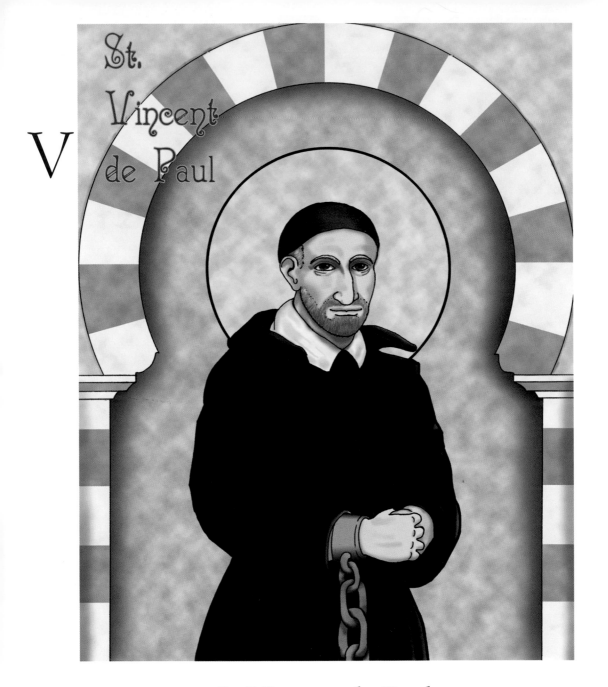

St. Vincent de Paul

Soon after becoming a priest, Vincent was captured by pirates and sold as a slave. He eventually escaped and returned to his work as a priest. He was well known for serving those who suffered, especially the poor, the sick, slaves, and orphans. (Lived from 1580 to 1660, France)

St. Veronica

Veronica wiped the face of Jesus on his way to the cross. Legend has it that
Jesus showed his gratitude by leaving an imprint of his face on
the cloth she used. (First century, Jerusalem)

St. Wenceslaus

Wenceslaus was raised by his Christian grandmother, St. Ludmilla. He became king after an uprising overruled his mother and her anti-Christian plans. He was a just, generous, and holy king who promised his whole life to God. He ruled with Christian mercy and love. (Lived from 903 to 929, Czechoslovakia)

St. Margaret Ward

Margaret Ward helped a priest escape from prison and hid him. She was arrested and was offered her freedom if she would deny her Catholic faith. When she refused, she was hanged. (Died in 1588, England, one of the Forty English and Welsh Martyrs)

X

St. Francis Xavier

Francis Xavier was a follower of Ignatius of Loyola. As a Jesuit, Francis went
to India and Japan. He is considered the greatest missionary since the apostles.
He was so enthusiastic, it was said his heart was on fire for Jesus. Francis
introduced the local people to Jesus by singing to the children. He died
on his way to China. (Lived from 1506 to 1552, Basque Country)

Ven. Anne de Xainctonge

X

Venerable Anne De Xainctonge

Anne De Xainctonge founded the Sisters of St. Ursula of the Blessed Virgin.
They are devoted to the free education of girls and young women.
(Lived from 1567 to 1621, France)

Bl. Simon Yempo

Y

Blessed Simon Yempo

Simon Yempo was a Buddhist monk who became a Christian. He joined the Jesuits as a lay teacher and was martyred. (Died in 1623, Japan)

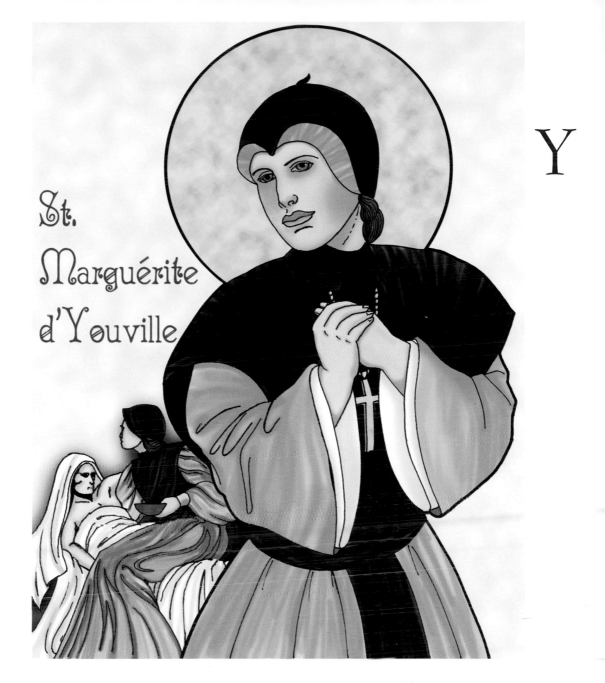

Y

St. Marguérite d'Youville

St. Marguérite d'Youville

Marguérite d'Youville was a widow who worked hard to raise her children. Despite her own poverty, she did many charitable works. She later founded the Grey Nuns and ran a hospital that turned no one away.

(Lived from 1701 to 1771, Canada)

Ven. Zepherin Namuncura

Z

Venerable Zepherin Namuncura

Zepherin Namuncura's father was the chief of the Araucano Indians. He wanted Zepherin to succeed him. A holy and devout boy, Zepherin wanted to be a priest and lead his people to Christianity. He began his studies as a priest, but when he was only seventeen he fell ill from tuberculosis and died the following year. (Lived from 1886 to 1905, Argentina)

St.
Zita

Z

St. Zita

Zita was the servant of a wool dealer. The other servants were jealous of Zita's holiness and hard work. She gave away food and clothing to the poor. Her many miracles finally convinced the other servants of her goodness.
(Lived from 1218 to 1278, Italy)

Patron Saints

A patron saint is a saint who can help us with special problems. If you are having trouble studying, for example, you might want to pray to the brilliant St. Thomas Aquinas for help. Or if you would like to be a doctor when you grow up, you might want to pray to St. Luke. The saints in this book are patrons of the following:

Artists — St. Luke

Blind people — St. Lucy, St. Odilia

Boy Scouts — St. George

Boys — St. Dominic Savio

Bricklayers — St. Stephen

Brides — St. Nicholas

Children — St. Nicholas

Choir boys — St. Dominic Savio

Deacons — St. Stephen

Eye problems — St. Lucy

Fathers — St. Joseph

Missionaries — St. Francis Xavier

French soldiers — St. Joan of Arc

Headaches — St. Teresa of Avila

Interracial justice — St. Martin de Porres

Lost articles — St. Anthony

Maids — St. Zita

Married women — St. Monica

Mothers — St. Monica

Nurses — St. Catherine of Siena

Physicians — St. Luke

Religion teachers — St. Charles Borromeo

Sailors — St. Brendan

Students — St. Thomas Aquinas

Writers — St. Teresa of Avila

Patron Saints of Countries

Some saints help with more than just a single problem. They help whole countries! The saints in this book are patrons of the following countries:

Alsace — St. Odilia

Belgium — St. Joseph

Bohemia — St. Wenceslaus

Brazil – The Blessed Mother, under the title of the Immaculate Conception

Canada — St. Joseph

China — St. Joseph

Czech Republic — St. Wenceslaus

East Indies — St. Francis Xavier

England — St. George

France — St. Joan of Arc

Italy — St. Catherine of Siena

Ireland — St. Patrick

Japan — St. Francis Xavier

North America — St. Rose of Lima

Norway — St. Olaf

Peru — St. Joseph

Portugal – The Blessed Mother, under the title of the
Immaculate Conception

Prussia — Dorothy of Montau

Russia — St. Nicholas

South America — St. Rose of Lima

Spain — St. Teresa of Avila

United States – The Blessed Mother, under the title of the
Immaculate Conception

Further Reading

Butler's Lives of the Saints

Modern Saints Volumes I and II by Ann Ball

Dictionary of Saints by John Delaney

The Making of Saints by Michael Freze

Saints for Now by Clare Boothe Luce

Saints Alive by Hal M. Helms

Mothers of the Saints by Wendy Leifeld

The Twelve by C. Bernard Ruffin

Lives of Saints by Fr. Thomas Plassmann and Fr. Joseph Vann

John Paul II's Book of Saints by Matthew Bunson,
Margaret Bunson, Stephen Bunson

THE CHILD GOD

Ace Books by Louise Marley

SING THE LIGHT
SING THE WARMTH
RECEIVE THE GIFT
THE TERRORISTS OF IRUSTAN
THE GLASS HARMONICA
THE MAQUISARDE
THE CHILD GODDESS

THE CHILD GODDESS

LOUISE MARLEY

ACE BOOKS, NEW YORK

An Ace Book
Published by The Berkley Publishing Group
A division of Penguin Group (USA) Inc.
375 Hudson Street
New York, New York 10014

This book is an original publication of The Berkley Publishing Group.

Copyright © 2004 by Louise Marley.
Text design by Julie Rogers.

First Edition: May 2004

Library of Congress Cataloging-in-Publication Data

Marley, Louise, 1952–
   The child goddess / Louise Marley.— 1st ed.
      p. cm.
   "An Ace Book"—T.p. verso.
   ISBN 0-441-01136-5
   1. Immortalism—Fiction. 2. Women—Fiction. 3. Girls—Fiction. I. Title.

PS3563.A6732C48 2004
813'.54—dc22

                                                      2003063836

PRINTED IN THE UNITED STATES OF AMERICA

10 9 8 7 6 5 4 3 2 1

ACKNOWLEDGMENTS

The author's deepest thanks for insights and inspiration go to Sr. Frances Wink, SNJM; to Dean Crosgrove, P.A.C.; to Nancy Crosgrove, R.N.; and to the Very Reverend Michael G. Ryan, pastor of St. James Cathedral, Seattle. Zack Marley assisted with science questions. The help of Joseph Adam, Kij Johnson, Melissa Lee Shaw, Brian Bek, Jeralee Chapman, Niven Marquis, Dave Newton, and Catherine Whitehead was invaluable. And once again, deep appreciation to June Campbell as first reader.

THE CHILD GODDESS

1

THE JANUARY WIND chilled Isabel Burke's naked scalp as she trudged up the slope through the winter-dry vineyard. Fingers of dormant grapevines caught at her black shirt and trousers. Desiccated leaves crunched under her feet, and the faint fragrance of burning olive wood floated in the crisp air. She paused for a last look at the pastel houses of San Felice, framed by the sere brown folds of the Tuscan hills. This view had comforted her in the last difficult months.

Above her, in front of the Mother House, she could just see the nose of the long black car in the gravel drive. It was time. She adjusted the white band of her collar with cold fingers and resumed her climb.

The long sweep of aging, stuccoed elegance that was the Magdalene Mother House molded itself to the hillside overlooking the vineyards and the village. Once the castello of a noble Italian family, it now housed the priests and novices of the struggling Priestly Order of Mary Magdalene. Isabel had thought of it as home for the past fourteen years, the length of her priesthood. Its gardens lay black and lifeless, but cheerful yellow lights beckoned from its windows. All the ground-floor rooms were alight, the foyer, the r-wave center, the Mother General's office. On the second floor one darkened window marked Isabel's room, empty now.

And at the foot of the broad cement steps, the black car waited for Isabel.

It had all happened too fast. Ordinarily she would have had months to get ready for field work, months to plan and study. Only two days had passed since she'd met ExtraSolar Corporation's administrative envoy, Cole Markham, in the Mother General's office. Two days since she'd learned of the near-alien child taken from her home, transported to Earth, isolated for months in quarantine. Two days of hurried preparation, scanty research, packing. She had bid her fellow priests good-bye, smiled at the novices' curiosity, thanked the staff as they hurried to help her prepare for her flight to the far northwest coast of America.

Isabel could have refused this assignment, but she didn't. It was her penance. And she could never have left the child in the control of people like Cole Markham. She had known that the moment she touched his hand.

The Mother General, Marian Alexander, had summoned her early that decisive morning, two days before. Isabel was just leaving Mass in the tiny chapel behind the castello, chatting with two of her sister priests, when Marian's secretary found her. She circled around to the front of the castello, past the crumbling stonework of the courtyard. An unfamiliar car, long and black, was parked in the drive, gleaming darkly in the pallid sunshine. Isabel went through the double doors and waited briefly in the foyer before Marian put her head out.

Marian Alexander was also bald, like all the Magdalenes. When they could, they wore their black shirts and trousers, the white priest's collar. But often, in their farflung missions, it was necessary to wear other clothes. The bare scalp, the full tonsure, was their sign of community. It singled them out, sometimes inviting resentment from those Roman Catholics who thought the priesthood should be reserved to men. But the Magdalenes persevered.

Marian was much older than Isabel's thirty-six years. The Mother General's thick eyebrows were silver, her pale face lined. Isabel's own slender brows were still dark, but she knew that she, too, had begun to accumulate lines around her eyes and her mouth. They had deepened in the painful year just past, reminding her of her shame whenever she looked into a mirror.

"Isabel, come in," the Mother General said, and Isabel obeyed.

A stranger rose at her entrance. He wore a light suit with pencil lapels and a matching shirt, a fashionable look out of place among the simple wooden shelves of paper books, the racks of disks that crowded Marian's office. His smile was pleasant, but when Isabel shook his hand, a sense of emptiness, a sort of hunger, distressed her. She managed to say, "How do you do, Mr. Markham," and released his hand as quickly as she dared.

"Mother Burke," he said. "I've been hearing great things about you."

Isabel turned to Marian, one eyebrow lifted. "Yes," the Mother General said. "I've been giving Mr. Markham your résumé, Isabel." She sat down behind her desk, and Isabel took a chair. Markham stood where he was, hands thrust into his pockets, smiling his bland smile.

"Would you like to explain, Mr. Markham, or shall I?" Marian said.

He pulled his hands out of his pockets and rubbed them together. "I'm happy to do it, Mother Alexander. Thank you." He smiled down at Isabel as if he were about to give her very good news. "Have you ever heard of Virimund, Mother Burke?"

Isabel linked her hands in her lap and tried not to look away from his face. "One of the expansion worlds, I think?"

"Right, right. I've been telling Mother Alexander, here, that Virimund is mostly ocean, but with a ring of equatorial islands. Moderate climate, no moon. ExtraSolar has established a branch of Offworld Port Force on one of the islands to construct a hydrogen retrieval facility— a power park. For the long-range transports, you know. Fuel cells. Electricity."

He sat down in the chair next to her, leaning forward. She inched back in her chair. "The problem is, Mother Burke," he said. "We found people there."

"People? You mean, human beings?"

He nodded. His face adopted a grave expression. "It seems one of the emigrant ships of the old U.N. found this planet and landed there."

Isabel glanced at Marian. The Mother General was staring at her cluttered desk. Isabel turned back to Markham. "The discovery of a lost colony is a remarkable event, isn't it? But none of this has been in the news services."

"You're right. ESC and Port Force decided it's best to keep this under wraps for the moment. Until we can figure out what's happened. My superior—the General Administrator of Earth Multiplex—is hoping you can help us."

Warily, she asked, "Figure out what? Has anyone communicated with these people?"

His eyelids flickered. "Well," he said. "Not really." The bland smile returned. "That's why we need you, Mother Burke. We need an anthropologist. And we thought a Magdalene would be best, would be . . . would be sensitive to our needs."

"Your needs."

"Yes, yes—confidentiality, you understand."

Isabel folded her arms. "Who are these people?"

He cleared his throat. "Well, it seems—that is, ExtraSolar thinks they were from one of the first ships. A colony from Africa. The Sikassa."

"You're not answering my questions, Mr. Markham. What do you know about them? Their history, their culture—who led them?"

Marian put in, "I told you, Mr. Markham. Isabel is a determined woman."

"Yes, yes. Well, it's difficult, Mother Burke. We're, uh, having trouble communicating with them."

"Has there been recontact?"

Marian Alexander lifted her head. "Recontact didn't go well, Isabel."

"Tell me."

Markham's smile wavered slightly. "You have to understand, no one realized they were there—no city lights, no radio signals. Then when the Port Forcemen saw smoke and so forth, they did a fly-over, and found an inhabited island." He coughed again. "I only read the reports, of course. But there was an incident."

"What kind of incident?"

The Mother General said, "It was a tragedy, Isabel. We don't want it to happen again."

"Someone was hurt?"

Markham sighed. "One of our people died, a man named Garcia. And two of the Sikassa were injured. Our guys didn't know what to do, so they carried them back to the power park, to the infirmary. One of the Sikassa recovered, but the other—ahem—expired."

"This is appalling," Isabel breathed. "How could this have happened?"

"It was most unfortunate," Markham said lamely. "But the hydro workers didn't mean to hurt anyone. They were attacked, spears and knives thrown at them by this gang of children. Caught them by surprise, so they said."

Isabel sat very still. "Did you say—you can't mean—they were *children*?"

He nodded, mutely.

Isabel straightened, her back rigid with indignation. "Let me see if I understand, Mr. Markham. Your workers killed an indigene, a child. And ExtraSolar is keeping it quiet."

"The Sikassa aren't indigenes," Markham protested. "They're Earthers! Emigrants!"

"How long since the emigration? Three centuries? I doubt very much they think of themselves as Earth citizens." Isabel spoke bitterly. There had been other offenses committed by the ExtraSolar Corporation in its rush for expansion, offenses protested by the Global Coalition, by World Health and Welfare, by the Church. She fixed Marian with a challenging gaze. "Why would the Magdalenes become involved with this disaster?"

The Mother General nodded acknowledgment of the irony. She laid her hands on her desk, palms down. "Isabel. There's more."

NOW, ON THE day of her departure, Isabel stepped through the double doors into the warmth and light of the Mother House, wondering how long it might be before she saw her home again. She touched the Magdalene cross on her breast, and offered a petition for patience, for wisdom. For forgiveness.

She stood beside the pile of her luggage and equipment waiting on the marble floor, listening to Markham's and Marian's voices from the office. There was nothing more for her to do. She had attended Mass, the memorial day of St. Angela Merici. She had resisted the urge to pick up the wavephone and call Simon. He would take her call, of course, he would come to her if she asked him. But she wouldn't ask.

The farewell was brief. Marian gave Isabel the Enquirer's Blessing, and kissed her cheek. The driver of the black car loaded her things into the capacious trunk, held the door for her to get in, and they were off. Isabel watched the castello over her shoulder as they wound down the narrow road leading to the village. Only when she could no longer see its tiled roofs did she turn to face Cole Markham, sitting across from her on the cushioned seat.

The driver negotiated San Felice's cramped streets, and picked up speed as they turned west toward the Pisa airport. Isabel asked, "Have you seen the child, Mr. Markham?"

"I've seen pictures," he said. He seemed more tense today. Perversely, Isabel preferred this terse, taut mood to the forced sincerity he had displayed at their first meeting.

"Did she look well?"

"I don't really know anything about children. She looked okay."

Isabel persisted. "No one seems to know how old she is."

"Dr. Adetti thinks she's about ten. But the girl's not saying."

"She's not saying, or no one can understand her?"

He folded his arms. "I don't really know, Mother Burke. Sorry."

"Tell me, Mr. Markham. Was it your idea to ask for a Magdalene?"

"Oh, no," he said. "Nothing to do with me. I'm only an envoy. It was the General Administrator's idea. Gretchen Boreson."

"And why a medical anthropologist?"

"I guess because they want to know how the Sikassa survived without any help from Earth. That's a biological issue, isn't it?"

"It may be."

After a pause he added, "They called Mother Alexander, and she suggested you."

Isabel understood that, of course. Marian would have jumped at the commission, and Isabel, under the circumstances, was the perfect choice to fulfill it. She turned her eyes to the peaceful Italian country-side. It always seemed to her that the land of Italy, the age-worn hills, the old farms, the houses of stone and stucco, knew something, some essential life lesson that she had been in search of since her girlhood.

Markham broke into her thoughts. "What is that on your cross?"

She turned from the view, and lifted the cross in her fingers. "Do you mean the flame?"

"Is that what it is?"

She slipped the cord over her head, and handed him the bit of carved wood. He held it awkwardly in his hand as she pointed to the stylized candleflame above the crosspiece. "This symbolizes our charism," she said. "Our gift, our special grace, is 'to shed light in dark places.' Because our patroness, Mary of Magdala, was maligned by untruths."

"What are these words?"

He handed the cross back, and she ran her finger over the tiny symbols. "It's old Greek," she said. "From the Gospel of Mary. It says, 'Ask what you will.' "

"I never heard of a Gospel of Mary."

She smiled at him. "Many haven't. It came to light at the turn of the twentieth century, but it wasn't authenticated for two more centuries."

"I thought Mary Magdalene was a—excuse me, but—a prostitute."

"Yes, I understand. It was a myth that developed in the western church, and it's what we mean when we say she was maligned by untruths."

He put his head on one side, looking truly interested. "But then what was she?"

Isabel lifted the cross and hung it about her neck again. "She was the first apostle," she said, stroking the cross with one finger. "The first witness to the Resurrection. And the one with the courage to ask the hard questions." She put her head back against the leather seat cushion. "And that's what Magdalenes do—ask hard questions. We are Enquirers. Researchers, investigators—and like our patroness, not always popular."

"I see." He drew breath to speak again, but hesitated.

"Do you have more questions?"

He lifted one shoulder in an apologetic way. "I'm curious about the bald heads."

Isabel lifted her head and ran a hand over her scalp. "The tonsure," she said. "The Magdalenes travel all over the world, the Moon, Mars—places where we don't wear a collar, or vestments. The full tonsure is the Magdalene sign of community."

"You know, Mother Burke—I don't really get the whole priest thing."

Isabel chuckled. "It's not for everyone, Mr. Markham. I could say I don't get the whole ExtraSolar thing, I suppose."

He granted her a dry sound that might have been a laugh. "I guess so. But you're a smart woman. Educated."

"Is that incongruous with religious orders?"

"I guess I don't know exactly."

"In the past, religious orders were often the only way to get an education," she said.

"But not now. And—well." A faint tinge colored his smooth cheeks. "Well—celibacy."

"Yes."

"There are noncelibate orders."

"Yes, there are. It's a choice, one the Magdalenes made at the beginning."

"What's the point?"

"It's about commitment, Mr. Markham." Her smile faded, and sorrow rose in her throat. "And calling." She heard the thickness in her voice, and she turned her face to the window. They were passing one of the ancient ruins that dotted the Italian landscape, stone walls and towers collapsing into the ground. Isabel watched it until the road curved away. So many ruins. So many relics of better times. And not every ruin could be restored.

Her eyes stung, and she pressed her palms to them. It was silly. The winter sun was too weak to make her eyes water. She dropped her hands, and linked them again in her lap. Markham seemed not to notice.

Isabel leaned back and closed her eyes, thinking of the dismaying paucity of information on the Sikassa. The archivist who put the report together had done his best, she supposed, but during the chaotic period between the old United Nations and the era of ExtraSolar's Offworld Port Force, a great many records had been lost or corrupted. Of course, what mattered now was the current situation. It mattered to ExtraSolar Corporation, and it must matter a great deal to this child. It seemed the Port Forcemen, the hydro workers, had happened on an island inhabited only by children. Isabel could not guess why that might be.

She would be appointed the guardian for this solitary little girl, her advocate and protector. The child had been torn from her home and her people, quarantined for months with no one to comfort her. Such loneliness made Isabel's own seem insignificant. Her heart ached for the Sikassa child. ExtraSolar Corporation, she thought, had a lot to answer for.

2

THE SONIC CRUISER sliced through the cloud cover over Seattle and emerged into a drizzling rain, its wings glistening with moisture. Jin-Li Chung and another Port Force longshoreman, Buckley, watched the landing from the shelter of their opensided cart. It wouldn't take long to unload the plane. They had been told there were only two passengers.

Buck lounged in the driver's seat, smoking, one booted foot on the dash. Jin-Li watched the passengers riding the external lift down to the wet tarmac. The man was running a comb through his hair and yawning. The woman beside him, fine-boned and rather small, wore severe black clothes lightened only by a white band collar. Jin-Li recognized the Magdalene tonsure. The priest's bare head shone with raindrops as she stepped away from the lift, until the attendant from the plane caught up with her to hold an umbrella over her head.

Jin-Li stepped out of the cart, brushing raindrops from the beige uniform jacket just as the man hurried past without a glance, eager to get out of the rain. The Magdalene moved more slowly under the attendant's umbrella. As she passed, she looked up, directly into Jin-Li's face, showing clear gray eyes under narrow dark eyebrows. She looked tired. Jin-Li touched fingers to cap in a friendly salute, and the priest smiled, an expression somehow full of warmth and sadness at the same time. Jin-Li watched her narrow back as she crossed the airfield and went into the Port Force terminal.

"Hey, Johnnie," Buck called. "Gonna make me do it all by myself, or you gonna watch the suits?"

"Sorry," Jin-Li said with a little laugh, and turned to the open cargo compartment of the plane, where Buck was waiting to begin on the small pile of luggage.

Buck indicated the terminal door with his head as he handed down the first valise. "Here for the kid, don't you think?"

Jin-Li glanced back at the terminal. The two passengers and the attendant had disappeared. "Orders are not to discuss it, Buck. Last thing I need is more trouble."

Buck picked up another case and handed it down. "Yeah, I know. Sorry. Just curious."

"Yes," Jin-Li said, lifting the cases onto the slatted shelves of the cart. "Me, too."

Rumors had circulated through the Port Force barracks and cafeteria. The child's arrival was supposed to be secret, but it was easy to get assigned to the flight, just a persuasive word to a friend in Dispatch, and so Jin-Li had also been on duty the week before, when the shuttle came in with its mysterious passenger.

The girl's escorts had not been Port Force, but Admin. Jin-Li had known that by their dress, their attaché cases, and the way they ignored the longshoremen waiting to offload the shuttle. There had been three of them, a woman and two men, making a little circle around the girl. But Jin-Li caught a good look as the group crossed the tarmac to the terminal.

The girl was at least as young as the rumors said. She had dark, velvety skin, enormous eyes that flashed white when she lifted her head. Someone had tied her long hair back, and dressed her in an overlarge blouse and a wrap-around skirt that just reached her knees. Her thin legs looked fragile and coltish, and they were just visible through the transparent quarantine suit that enveloped her whole body.

The trio hustled the child into the terminal, the girl stepping awkwardly in the quarantine suit, and disappeared with her through one of the security doors. No Port Forceman had seen the girl since. But Jin-Li, who cultivated acquaintances in every corner of the service, knew where they were keeping her.

The Multiplex in Seattle was home port to all the Offworld stations. R-wave transmissions were received in the dome of Admin, high above the foambrick barracks, the Rec Facility, the three cafeterias. Jin-Li, despite being forced back to Earth in disgrace, was allowed to teach karate in the Rec Fac. The infirmary was sandwiched between the Rec Fac and Admin, and it was there Jin-Li had delivered the boxes and cartons from the shuttle that had carried the little girl. There was no sign of the child, but the inference was not hard to make. No one was being allowed inside. A guard had been posted. And a priority announcement had gone out to all personnel that, for an indefinite period, medical complaints would be handled in a room in the basement of the Rec Fac.

On the day the Magdalene arrived, Jin-Li walked slowly past the infirmary, noting the drawn curtains, the guard lounging beside the door. The child had hardly seen Earth's sun, and had breathed its dubious air only through the filter of the quarantine suit. It was whispered in the cafeterias that there was something strange about the girl, something alien, but no one in the Multiplex knew what it was. Jin-Li hoped the Magdalene would be kind to the child from Virimund.

ISABEL SHIVERED AS she followed Cole Markham through the layers of the Port Force terminal. Even indoors, the air felt chilly and damp on her scalp. The secretary who met them greeted them briefly, stood back to let them pass, then spoke to the door. It closed and locked. She gave Isabel a cool smile, and led the way into a carpeted elevator. A string quartet played over the sound system as they rose five swift flights, and came out into a corridor with muted lights and a series of doors, some open, some closed, each marked with the circled star of ExtraSolar, and a name and title in gilt. At the last door in the corridor, the secretary paused. "Mr. Markham, Mother Burke, could you hold here for just a moment? Our in-house archivist wants a picture."

"I beg your pardon?" Isabel looked around. A man in a suit came through the door, holding a small camera in his palm.

"Just for our records," the secretary said blandly. "And for the media, of course."

The archivist arranged Isabel and Markham on either side of the door to expose the gilt legend. GRETCHEN BORESON, GENERAL ADMINISTRATOR, EARTH MULTIPLEX. The palm cam hummed once, twice, three times. At least, Isabel thought tiredly, the archivist didn't ask her to smile. She didn't feel at all like smiling.

Gretchen Boreson's corner office was elegant, with a thick carpet, a desk made from a thin slab of translucent stone, and pieces of modern art glass arranged in niches. Mullioned windows looked north over the mist-shrouded towers and spires of Seattle, and west to the runways busy with sonic cruisers and short-hop flyers. At one end of the airfield the nose of a space shuttle extended from an enormous hangar, its particle shields opaque in the mist.

Boreson stood up as Isabel and Markham came in. She wore a trouser suit of subdued gray fabric, and perfectly applied cosmetics. Her hair was so white it was almost silver, and it shone in a smooth chignon. She touched it with one hand as she came around her desk. The other hand, manicured and white, she held out to Isabel.

"Mother Burke," she said. "Thank you for coming. How was your flight?"

Isabel, touching Boreson's hand, suppressed a shiver. The white fingers were icy. "The flight was fine. Thank you."

"We're delighted you could join us." Boreson indicated chairs. "Please sit down."

Isabel took the indicated chair, and linked her fingers together in her lap, watching the other woman. Gretchen Boreson's skin stretched tightly over her cheekbones. Her pale blue eyes gave Isabel the feeling she was looking into an empty sky.

The administrator resumed her seat. She picked up an r-wave transmission wand and tapped it lightly on the pale stone of her desk. Isabel felt her attention focus, like a beam of light narrowing and intensifying, with herself at its center. "You understand that we have a situation here, Mother Burke," she said.

"I've read the archivist's report, Administrator."

Boreson nodded, and touched her lips with one silver-polished nail. "Children," she said. "It's very sad. We feel it's our duty to do something about them."

"Administrator, I realize you weren't there, on Virimund. But there will have to be an explanation for why a child died."

"Dr. Adetti—the power park physician—did all he could, Mother Burke. No one intended for the child to be injured. But our people were attacked."

"They should not have approached the indigenes in the first place, Administrator. That's expressly forbidden in your charters."

Boreson nodded again, and tapped the wand. Its rhodium tip gleamed. "Of course. But it was well-meant. And you realize, the Sikassa are not indigenes. They're Earth citizens."

"Perhaps they no longer feel like Earth citizens."

The transmission wand tapped. "That's possible."

"And they must have believed they were abandoned. Forgotten."

"Even so—our people were only curious."

"Your people," Isabel interrupted, "murdered a child. This much we know."

"It seems to have been unavoidable," Boreson said.

"They should have been warned not to attempt contact."

"It was most unfortunate," the administrator said, her voice sharpening. "Our information said the planet was uninhabited. We had no way of knowing."

"Does that excuse what happened?" Isabel's jaw tightened. She drew a careful breath, and touched her cross. "Why were they armed, Administrator?"

"What if they hadn't been armed? They might all have been killed!"

"By a group of children?"

Markham shifted in his seat and cleared his throat. "The thing is," he said, "as regrettable as it all was, it's done now, and we have to try to smooth things over."

Isabel ignored him.

Boreson flicked him a glance, then transferred the wand to her other hand, rolling it between her fingers. Her voice was level. "We need Virimund, Mother Burke."

"We? Do you mean ExtraSolar?"

"Not only ExtraSolar." Isabel saw the soft wrinkling of her lips as she spoke, the fissures that marked her cheeks beneath her cosmetics. The Administrator was not a young woman. Lines at the corners of her eyes ran improbably upward, evidence of the surgeries that had given her face its smooth appearance. Isabel saw an involuntary twitch of the risorius muscle at the side of Boreson's mouth, and she wondered if the older woman was more nervous than she seemed. "By we," Boreson went on, "I mean Earth. All of us. The long-range transports are essential to the expansion effort, and they need the hydrogen the power park will produce."

Isabel unlinked her fingers, made her hands relax on the curving arms of the chair. Beyond the mullioned windows a cruiser rose from the port, its curving nose piercing the clouds that blanketed Puget Sound. Two black flyers hovered out of its way, waiting their turn at the airspace.

Boreson toyed with the transmission wand, the veins on the back of her hand vividly blue against her white skin. "If Earth—" She waved the wand at the world beyond the windows. "If the nations of Earth want to expand, we need bases, we need food sources, we need—"

"Cash," Markham put in.

She nodded. "Mr. Markham is right. ExtraSolar wants to fulfill the charters given to it by the Coalition, and by World Health, but for that we need to be profitable. We spent a lot of time and money finding a planet where we could put a hydrogen power park. Virimund is almost all ocean. It's perfect."

"And you didn't know the Sikassa were there."

"No one did!" This was from Markham, and it had the indignant ring of truth.

Boreson interrupted. "Unfortunately, some who oversee the charters think the Sikassa should be treated as indigenous. I don't agree, and I was hoping you wouldn't, either."

Isabel drew a deliberate breath. Penance, she reminded herself. But she hated being manipulated. She rose and went to the window, looking out past the striations of rain to the glass and steel towers of the city. "Administrator," she said mildly. "Think of it. The Sikassa have lived on Virimund for three hundred years. More than ten generations."

The flyers had landed. Suited men and women climbed out, and Port Force longshoremen set to work around the aircraft. Isabel thought she recognized the stocky figure of the one who had met her own plane, the one with the long, heavy-lidded eyes. It had been a pleasant face. It had been the only friendly face she had seen today. She put one finger against the cool glass, and a damp spot formed where she touched it. She turned abruptly to Gretchen Boreson and Cole Markham.

"What is it you expect me to do?" she asked. "And why in heaven's name did ExtraSolar take this child from her home? Surely your people could see that their action compounded the offense already committed."

"Dr. Adetti did what he thought was best." Boreson's voice was tight. "Remember, there is fault on both sides."

"We don't know enough to judge that. The study should have come first."

"Look, Mother Burke." The administrator stood up, and came around the desk with quick, short steps that gave the impression she was about to fall down. She stopped beside Isabel, bracing herself with one hand on the wall. The muscle jumped again beside her mouth, rippling the thin skin of her cheek. "We secured an extraordinary empowerment provision from the charter governments to allow us to study this child and her people," Boreson said. "Your guardianship of her is stipulated by that provision. By helping us, you will be helping the girl. We need to understand what's happening on Virimund. What has already happened." She waved her hand at the towers and domes and spires of the city beyond the Multiplex. A narrow beam of sunshine lanced through the cloud cover to brighten the rooftops. "We didn't know the Sikassa were there, we truly didn't. And there's still no sign of anyone else except this group of children. But ExtraSolar needs what Virimund has to offer."

"It's a lot to ask of one person."

Boreson nodded and, to Isabel's relief, stepped away from her. "If you need an assistant, you have only to ask."

"Have you spoken to this child yourself?"

Boreson's shake of the head was dismissive. "No. I understand she doesn't speak much English. And I'm afraid I'm not good with children."

"What made you think of the Magdalenes, Administrator?"

Boreson's delicately tinted lips curved slightly. "I believe the Magdalenes are still trying to establish themselves. We thought you might need us as much as we need you. And your Mother General told me you would be perfect. She was quite eager for you to accept."

Marian Alexander, of course, had her own agenda. Isabel knew very well how ambitious she was for her order, how much she wanted to prove its worthiness to Holy See. And Isabel, returning from Oceania with a stain on her soul, had provided Marian with the ideal answer to ExtraSolar's request.

"I'd like to see the girl now," Isabel said.

Boreson, with the same quick, falling steps, moved back to her desk and fitted the transmission wand into its receptor. She spoke into it briefly, and then turned her chilly smile on Isabel. "They're expecting you in the infirmary," she said.

"The infirmary?" Isabel asked. "Is the child ill?"

Boreson's features froze, just for an instant, but the moment of stillness made Isabel's neck crawl. "No," Boreson said. "Not so far as we know. It seemed the safest place."

"Who has been caring for her?"

"There's a nurse. And Dr. Adetti sees her every day. Naturally her health is of prime concern to us."

"Naturally," Isabel murmured.

"But, Mother Burke—the more time that passes, the more money we lose. We have men and women on Virimund, equipment, supplies. They're ready to begin." She laid down the transmission wand with a little click. "Can you try to work quickly?"

Isabel looked out the window again, away from the tightly stretched features of Gretchen Boreson and into the soft grayness of the January day. "Please take me to the child," she said.

3

OA SHIVERED DESPITE the garment they had brought her. She didn't like it. It scratched at her elbows and neck, and smelled strange. Her hair caught on its fastenings. She would have preferred her arms to be bare, but this gray place was too cold for that. She had arrived in a chill drizzle, and now, even indoors as she had been ever since, the air felt damp. They had brought things for her feet, too, that made her feel clumsy. She felt as if she would fall, or step on something and not know it. On the ship she had gone barefoot, become familiar with the odd materials of its floors, hard or spongy, slick or textured. The ship had been warmer.

The food was odd, too, almost without odor. There was a kind of pale, soft bread, unfamiliar fruits, a variety of meats that were bland on her tongue. But she was hungry, and she ate. She had noticed on the ship that if she ate all of something, the same food would appear again. No one touched her, or showed her their faces except through thick glass or translucent masks, but they noticed what she ate. She didn't understand that. Since the tatwaj, no one had cared whether she ate, or slept, or bathed. Or lived.

*Oa remembered the day of the tatwaj. The pricks of the bone nee-
dle and the sting of the ink blended in her memory with the column of
thick white smoke rising from the bonfire. The people of the three islands
swayed in the great circle, singing, naming the ancestors. And then there
was the counting. And the weeping. She remembered the smell of the
wind from Mother Ocean, the smell of her own mother's skin, the scent
of her tears.*

Oa pushed the tray away and got up to wander in an aimless circle
around the space she was trapped in. The bed fit against one wall, covered with smooth sheets and fat pillows. A low table and two hard
chairs filled the opposite corner. As on the ship, everything was made of
materials that were not real, and smelled of machines. There was no
wood. There were no vines, or leaves, or feathers. A great mirror filled
one wall, shinier than still water. The opposite wall held more glass, a
square of blank gray with buttons beneath. There were pictures on the
walls of things for which Oa had no names, in her own language or in
the language of Earth. Sometimes she felt like one of the little tree
lizards of her home, slithering round and round in her cage and finding
no way out.

Doors opened from her central room into three smaller rooms. One
held a bed like her own, though it had no sheets or blankets. The second had a tub for bathing and a toilet, like the ones she had learned to
use on the ship. In the third a high padded table waited beneath the
thing she hated most of all.

She knew its name. She had become acquainted with it on her long
journey, when Doctor first sent its nasty feelers crawling and nipping
over her body. It was called a medicator, that humming machine that
dripped with tubes and wires. Its touching and probing set her shaking
with horror, as she had trembled before the forest spiders of Virimund.
It was the worst part of being here. Every day Doctor came in, wearing
his crinkly suit with its plastic mask and slick gloves and booted feet.
He made her lie on that cold table and he set the spider machine to
crawling over her body. Oa suspected the spider machine was searching
for her soul. If that was its purpose, she would never be free of it.

On the ship, Oa had been kept in one room with blinking lights and
a narrow bed that folded down from the wall. Even then she longed for

the touch of natural materials, familiar textures. She missed the aroma of drying vines and sweet wood, the close warm scents of the anchens' nest. The days on the ship had seemed to go on forever. At first she saw only Doctor. She couldn't understand what he said to her, and she didn't know how to speak to him. Then, after a time, a ship lady brought her a reader, and pantomimed how to use it. There were three books for it, miracles of pictures and sounds and squiggly marks that told how the sounds should be made. Oa looked at the books, and listened to the words, and began to learn.

She understood now that she had been carried to Earth. The long journey on the ship had ended with a short, noisy trip on something called a shuttle. She was wrapped in one of the crinkly suits, far too large for her, and she was brought here, to a room called infirmary. She still saw Doctor every day, and had her reader and her three books. One of the guards who stood outside infirmary brought her a box with an assortment of strange objects. She slipped it through the quarantine bubble, saying she wanted Oa to have something to play with. Toys, the guard said. So Oa wouldn't be lonely.

The guard wasn't allowed to come into infirmary. Only the man called Doctor and the people who cleaned were allowed inside, and they always wore the crinkly suits. They made her wait in the empty room, sitting on the bare mattress of the bed, while they washed the floors and walls. She couldn't come out until they were done, and then the smell made her eyes sting.

Oa puzzled over the things the guard had brought her. The toys.

There was a tiny ship like the one she had made her journey in. There was a paper book with blank pages, and a box of colored sticks that smelled a bit like food but tasted very bad. There was a plastic baby, dark like Oa, but plump, with a lot of stiff hair on its head. Oa lifted its gaily colored clothing and found there was nothing at all between its dimpled legs. It was blank there, smooth and empty. It made Oa shiver with revulsion.

There was an assortment of little mechanical objects. Oa figured out that the pieces fit together to make different shapes, but she didn't see the point. The only toy she liked was a soft, fuzzy creature with button eyes and stubby arms and legs. It had no fingers or toes or claws. She didn't know what it was, but it was somehow comforting to hold. When she squeezed it against her, it grew warm from the heat of her body.

What Oa really wanted was more books, to learn more words. But she didn't dare ask for books. Anchens knew better than to ask for anything from people. Anything given to an anchen came at a cost.

Someone had brought a basket from the island. Bibi, or perhaps Ette, had dropped it in the meadow when they seized up their spears and knives to defend the kburi. Oa knew the people on the ship had put it through a machine, because she could smell it, but the woven vines had been soaked in Mother Ocean, and the salt tang still clung to them. Sometimes when her homesickness was at its worst, when she found herself tortured by the shocked face of Nwa as he fell, she sniffed the tang of salt and seaweed and fish, and remembered.

When she wasn't remembering, Oa prowled the little rooms, or curled up on the bed with her back against the wall, holding the fuzzy toy, waiting for something to happen. Anchens knew how to wait. Sometimes she called out to Raimu-ke, but she worried that Raimu-ke couldn't hear her so far away. The ship lady, through the glass, had showed her a picture of their journey, and talked about stars, and worlds, and space. Oa didn't understand all of it, but she grasped that it was a long, long way, much farther than the distance between the island of the anchens and the three islands of the people.

Oa wondered if those who kept her here knew she wasn't one of them. Maybe they didn't know about the tatwaj. When she began to understand what they said, when the words began to form ideas in her mind, the man called Doctor had asked her how old she was. She held up her arms for him to count, but he didn't seem to understand. They must not understand, or they wouldn't bring her food, and toys, and books. Yet they let the spider machine crawl over her every day. It made no sense to Oa.

She pulled the sweater tighter around her shoulders. Sometimes she thought she had not been warm since she left Virimund, since they took her in the awful noisy flyer that stank of fear and anger, and then up to the ship, which smelled of nothing. She huddled on the bed, the fuzzy toy nestled close in her arms. It, too, was not-real, but it had picked up the scent of a person. A child, perhaps. She buried her face in its plush body.

*   *   *

ISABEL WAS SURPRISED at what Gretchen Boreson had referred to as the infirmary. It looked more like a small hospital, with a waiting room, several treatment rooms, each with a medicator, and a small inpatient ward, three single rooms and a tiny lounge. All the rooms were deserted now, dark and empty, except for the inpatient ward. Outside the building, three armed Port Force guards clustered under the eaves, out of the rain. Inside, one woman stood guard before the quarantine bubble that had been erected around the door to the ward. A long window opened on the room, obviously mirrored on the opposite side. Isabel and Boreson and Markham stood before it, looking in on the child.

Someone had tried to turn the little lounge into a bedroom, with a small plastic table and two child-sized chairs, and a bed fitted into the corner. A wavephone receptor and wand hung on one wall, antenna glistening. A large reader was built into the opposite wall. A small portable reader lay on one of the chairs. A doll and an assortment of mechanical playthings were lined up in a neat row on the table.

The girl crouched on the bed, her back to the corner. She wore a vivid pink sweater. She held a brown teddy bear, her face buried against it. All Isabel could see of her were thin legs, sharp knees, a cascade of kinky black hair. A child, snatched from her people, transported through space, without concern for her welfare. Isabel trembled with fury.

"Why is she still in quarantine?" she asked in a tight voice. "It's been more than fourteen months! Surely if she had any sort of communicable illness, the medicator's taken care of it?"

She felt, rather than saw, Boreson and Markham glance at each other. Boreson said, "We wanted to be certain."

"How can you not be certain? Who has been examining her?"

Boreson said, "The doctor's on his way now."

"But you know what he's found."

"I'm not a doctor, Mother Burke. Dr. Adetti says he's still assessing."

The girl lifted her head as if she could sense their presence. Her great eyes glittered under the lights, irises dark against astonishingly clear whites.

Isabel put her hand to her throat. "So young," she breathed.

No one else spoke. Isabel watched the child unfold her legs, pull her hair free of the pink sweater, and climb off the bed. She laid the teddy bear carefully on her pillow, and walked toward the mirrored window.

Isabel turned abruptly to the guard. "Let me in." The guard nodded.

"Wait, Mother Burke," Boreson said uneasily. "Wait for the doctor."

"You really should," Markham said. "A few more minutes can't hurt."

Isabel ignored them. "Open the door, please," she said to the guard. The Port Forceman's eyes kindled, and Isabel knew the woman had been waiting for someone, anyone, to do something for this child.

"Mother Burke," Boreson began again.

Isabel spun to face her. "Administrator," she said. "Am I to be the girl's guardian?"

Boreson glanced sidelong at Markham, as if for help. "Yes, of course, but—"

Isabel turned again to the guard. "If you please."

The guard pulled aside the flap of the quarantine bubble. Disposable sterile suits hung from a dowel, their plastic masks and empty feet drooping like corpses on a gibbet. The guard took one down and held it out.

Isabel shook her head. "Maximum quarantine protocol is six months," she murmured. "We're well past that." The guard's lips curved and she spoke to the door hastily, before anyone else could intervene. It swung open.

Isabel smiled her thanks. She stepped through the bubble and into the ward, leaving Boreson and Markham sputtering behind her. The door closed silently, and she and the child were alone.

The girl turned from the false mirror to face her.

Isabel smiled, and said simply, "Hello, Oa. Did I say your name right? Oh-uh? My name is Isabel. I've come to talk to you."

The girl neither shrank back nor came toward her. She stood, her full lips slightly apart, her eyes bright with—fear? Suspicion? Isabel opened her hands, showed her empty palms. "Will you talk with me?"

The child's thin hand lifted to her face to mime a mask over the nose and mouth.

"Ah," Isabel said. "Yes, I see." She took a step closer. "No, I won't be wearing a mask."

Now the girl's fingers lifted to her head, where her abundant hair sprang from her scalp like a black fountain. Isabel chuckled, and she mimicked the child's gesture, touching her own naked scalp. "No, it's true. I have no hair at all. Perhaps I seem very strange to you."

Silence stretched in the room. The sounds beyond the walls seemed to grow louder, the fans, the ventilation, the hum of carts and trucks on the street outside. Isabel watched the girl, waiting. The child's hair was a glory, a deep, shining black. Her skin glowed like chocolate satin. Her willowy limbs promised that she would be tall when she grew up. And how old must she be now? Ten, perhaps eleven, Isabel thought. Certainly no older. She still had the flat chest and narrow body of childhood. She was six or eight centimeters shorter than Isabel.

"Oa," Isabel said. "Can you understand me? Do you understand my words?"

The child's voice was high and sweet. "Oa understands," she said.

Isabel hardly breathed. The girl, walking as if her shoes didn't quite fit, moved forward, stopping an arm's length away. The length, Isabel thought instantly, of a blow. The child's nostrils flared as if she were testing the air, and Isabel kept very still as the girl's hand rose, reached, came slowly up to Isabel's breast. She leaned forward, a movement full of caution, and she put her forefinger on the Magdalene cross.

She looked up into Isabel's face, and she said, with a wide flashing grin like the sun shining through winter clouds, "Oa likes it."

OA HAD NEVER seen a person with no hair. The elders of the people sometimes had gray hair, and some of the crones had very thin hair like the moss that hung from the nuchi trees, which padded the anchens' nest. But she had never seen anyone whose head was utterly naked.

The woman in black had arching thin eyebrows as dark as Oa's own, and delicate bones in her face. Her eyes were clear and light like a tidepool at dawn, and her bare head was a graceful shining curve, with slight shadows here and there. Oa was somehow pleased that she wore no mask. It seemed to mean something, yet it was as incomprehensible as being served a food she liked.

When she went close to the woman called Isabel, there was no cloying scent to offend the nose, nothing to interfere with the fragrance of clean skin and sweet breath and good nature. When Oa opened her nostrils, the woman didn't step back, or look at her with distaste. Her eyes glowed as if she understood.

No one else seemed to understand. They didn't like her doing it, but Oa couldn't help it. How could she know, if she didn't smell the person, what they were like, what they intended? When one of the people was angry, a sharpness came to the breath, a whiff of acid rose from the skin. But this one—called Isabel—smelled as fresh as a newly sprouted nuchi leaf.

And when she touched the pretty ornament Isabel wore around her neck, the lady took it off and handed it to her so she could hold it, stroke the carving, smell real wood at last. And all the while, this woman called Isabel stood smiling at Oa as if she were a person.

"If you like it, Oa," the woman called Isabel said with that gentle voice, "I will give it to you. A gift. And later I will explain to you what it means."

Oa's back stiffened. Could she have been wrong? Gifts from people were dangerous. What could she want, this Isabel? What would she want of Oa? To use her body, perhaps? Or was it about the medicator, something about the spider that kept sucking and sucking from her body, never satisfied? Or perhaps some new torture, something Oa couldn't yet imagine.

She thrust the little carving back into Isabel's hands.

ISABEL FROZE, HER cross in her fingers. What had she done, or said? She hadn't touched the girl, she had been very careful in handing her the cross. But the child pulled away, scurried backward across the room to fold herself onto the bed, her knees pulled up, her head buried against them, her hair tumbling to her ankles.

Isabel wished she could call back her words. A gift. She would remember. A gift was something not to be trusted, not to Oa. Isabel had thought, because of the toys ranged on the table . . . but no. There must be something else.

"Oa," she said softly. "I'm sorry. My friends and I give gifts to each other, and it doesn't mean anything. The person who receives the gift can say yes or no, and it's all the same."

For a long moment neither of them moved. Then Isabel saw how the child's fingers sought the buttons of her sweater. Her hair had tangled in them. She didn't look up, only blindly struggled, her hair pulling tighter and tighter. Isabel said softly, "Oa? Will you let me help you?"

The child's fingers stopped moving. Her whole body froze.

"I would never hurt you, Oa. I promise you. May I help you with your sweater?"

The girl didn't answer.

Isabel leaned wearily against the wall. She should have known it wouldn't be easy. She eyed the row of toys on the table, the little mechanical bits stuck together in various configurations. It looked as if the reader was the only thing the girl used. Her room was as pristine and neutral as a hotel room—a hospital room. Through the open door Isabel saw the exam bed with the medicator poised above it, the long thin tubes of its syrinxes drooping over the paper sheet.

"Oa," she murmured. There was no answer. "Oa," Isabel said again, even more softly. "I will leave my cross for you to look at. If you want to." She moved to the table to lay the cross on it, and then, following her hunch, she placed it on the chair beside the little reader instead. "I'll go now," she said. "But I'll come back. I came a long way to see you." No answer.

Isabel felt Markham and Boreson watching her through the mirrored window. She raked the glass with an angry gaze, and then turned her back on it to call to the guard to release her.

4

THE DOOR DIDN'T open.

Isabel knocked again, two sharp raps. Behind her, Oa looked up with wide eyes. Isabel waited a moment, then turned on her heel and strode to the mirrored window.

She put her hands on her hips and glared into the silvered glass. "What's happening?" she demanded. "Open the door, please."

The little speaker on the wall beside the window crackled as someone turned on the intercom. Oa jumped at the sound, making the bed creak. Isabel supposed the speaker had not been used since Oa's arrival. This further evidence of the child's isolation fueled her anger.

"Mother Burke." Even through the speaker, Gretchen Boreson sounded tense. "Dr. Adetti has arrived. He's coming in."

Isabel stepped back. Oa had knocked her teddy bear to the floor. Isabel crossed the room to pick it up and set it beside the child's knee. "Don't worry, Oa," she murmured. "I'm sure I can deal with the doctor." There was no response. The girl curled around herself again, and lay unnaturally still. Isabel recognized the coping mechanism, one she had seen once or twice in Australia among children who were victims of violence. But surely no one here at the Multiplex, or on the transport, had been violent with Oa. Isabel's jaw tightened. There were all too many ways to hurt a child.

A few seconds passed before the door opened and someone stepped through from the sterile bubble. It was a tall figure, in the pencil-lapelled suit that seemed to be an ExtraSolar uniform, and swathed from head to toe in a transparent accordion-paper quarantine suit. The reverse airflow hissed into the quiet room until the door closed.

Through the mask Isabel saw black hair, a black mustache. Dark expressionless eyes flicked over her, on to Oa, back to her. His voice, muted by the mask, was deep and slightly hoarse. "Dr. Burke?"

Isabel folded her arms. "I prefer Mother Burke, if you don't mind. You're Paolo Adetti."

"Dr. Adetti. Yes."

"Oh, of course. Doctor." Isabel indicated the door with her chin. "And you're planning to imprison me as well?"

"No one is in prison here," Adetti said. He stood stiffly, his arms straight at his sides. "I certainly would have preferred to meet under more congenial circumstances."

"No doubt. Try to imagine how I feel." Isabel's fingers tightened on her arms. "Are you going to open the door for me, or not?"

He eyed her. "I'm told you were offered a suit. You chose to violate the quarantine."

Isabel's head began to ache. In Tuscany it must be midnight at least. She felt too weary to sustain her temper.

She turned her back on the doctor, and went to one of the orange plastic chairs, settling into it with a sigh. Slight as she was, she barely fit.

"Dr. Adetti, you've had this child in your custody for fourteen months," she said. "Eight months past the most stringent quarantine recommendations. There's nothing in the archivist's report to show that she has a contagious illness. Surely the medicator has run tests for antibodies and antigens, bacterial infections. You yourself had direct contact with Oa when she was injured, and you haven't become ill. Neither have any of the hydro workers who touched her or the other Sikassa child."

"This is out of your area of expertise, I believe," Adetti said sourly.

Isabel rubbed her eyes with her fingers. "I know enough to understand that ExtraSolar took a young child from her home, subjected her to the risks of a long space journey, and continues to isolate her here. She needs company. She needs to see friendly faces, perhaps meet other children. She needs a bit of kindness."

"No one has been cruel to her," Adetti said.

Isabel stared at him. "You don't find any of that cruel?"

"It was necessary."

"Why? What are you afraid of?"

"It's not a question of fear, Mother Burke, but of caution."

"Tell me what you're being careful of, then. This is a poor way to begin a working relationship."

"You might at least have observed quarantine protocol."

"It's ridiculous. You could have lifted it months ago."

"I have my reasons."

Isabel closed her eyes briefly, asking for patience. "What are your reasons, Doctor?"

"I'll explain, in time."

Isabel rose from the little chair. She stepped close enough to Adetti to see his eyes through the clear plastic. "Your reasons, Doctor, or I will refuse this assignment. I will refuse to serve as the girl's guardian, and your extraordinary empowerment provision will be voided."

He made a sound that might have been a laugh. "You can hardly reject the job at this point," he said. "By coming in here without protection, you've guaranteed a good long stay."

"Try me." Isabel gave up trying to moderate her tone. "You can find a pretext to lock me up, I suppose. But if you do, I'll make absolutely certain you have to explain it to someone."

He paused, as if considering. She regarded him with narrowed eyes. "Dr. Adetti. You wouldn't dare cut me off from communication with my superior. You don't have the authority. You're part of a public organization, overseen by the regents of World Health and Welfare. Do you want to risk a lawsuit?"

From the intercom they heard Boreson's anxious voice. "There's no need for that," she said tightly. "We can work things out, Mother Burke."

Isabel glanced over her shoulder at the mirror. "Not without the medicator reports."

Adetti folded his arms. "They won't change anything. You can stay here, with the child, or we'll set up another room if you prefer. But you're not going out until I've cleared you."

"You can't silence me forever, Doctor. And I want those reports."

He moved to the door, and stood looking back at her. "I'll have them sent over."

"Today, please."

"As you wish." He spoke to the door and it opened.

"Dr. Adetti—all of them."

"There are dozens," he said. "They'll take you days to read."

Her lip curled. "Well. Then I'll be grateful to you for providing me with plenty of time."

He grunted, and went through the door into the quarantine bubble. The guard stepped back to let him pass, glancing at Isabel with a face full of apology. Isabel gave her a wry shrug.

When the door closed, she went back to the chair and sat down. "Oa, I'm afraid you've acquired a roommate. I hope you won't mind."

There was silence for several minutes, and then the girl began to uncurl her body. She unthreaded her tangled hair from the buttons of the sweater. With a rustle of bedclothes, she straightened her back and tucked her feet under her, eyes fixed on Isabel. Isabel thought she had never seen a child capable of such stillness.

She let her head fall back against the top of the chair, and closed her eyes. It had been a long, long day. Despite her bravado, she supposed Adetti and Boreson could keep her in isolation as long as they liked. She didn't really mind. There was no other place she wanted to be at the moment. She would need her valises, though, and her equipment. She could put the time to good use, and keep an eye on the child at the same time. Absently, she put her hand up to touch her cross, and then she remembered. She had taken it off.

A soft noise made her open her eyes. Oa had climbed off the bed and moved to the chair where Isabel had laid her cross. The girl picked it up, and came to stand before Isabel, presenting the carved wood on her small pink palm. "A . . . gift," she said.

*   *   *

IT SEEMED TO Oa that the slender bald woman confronted Doctor without any fear. Isabel must be strong in some way Oa could not recognize. She was too small to fight him with her hands or her feet. She had no knife, or even a stone to throw. She must have some other power. If Oa had stood up to him in that way, he would have snarled at her, dragged her into the little room with the spider machine to strap her to the high table again. People hurt anchens when they were angry.

Oa remembered Mamah weeping while Papi dragged Oa down to the beach. The night had been clear and warm, the air full of the salt fragrance from Mother Ocean, the spicy scent of nuchi. The brilliance of the stars mocked Oa's misery.

The tatwaj was over. Her skin stung from the needle, but her arm hurt much worse where Papi's hand gripped it. His lips pressed hard together, a thin line of fury. When Oa cried out, he released her arm and backhanded her across the cheek. She slammed to the ground, the pastel sand of the beach grinding into her face, her hair. Mamah had screamed, a high kooning that stopped abruptly, as if someone had put a hand over her mouth.

Oa was too shocked to weep. Papi had never struck her before. He pulled her up from the sand and shoved her into the canoe next to Bibi. Stunned and silent, she gazed back at him as one of the elders rowed the canoe out of the bay. Papi stood on the beach, his back to the water, refusing to watch his daughter disappear.

When the canoe reached the island of the anchens, the elders made Oa and Bibi climb out. The girls stood together on the beach as the boat bobbed away through the surf, leaving them. Oa remembered how the waves washed their ankles with foam, and how her cheek stung from Papi's blow.

Not till the canoe disappeared into the darkness did the anchens— the other anchens—come down to the beach. They led the newcomers into the forest, Oa rubbing at the circle of purple fingerprints on her arm, Bibi weeping great gulping sobs. Oa never saw her papi again.

And now the woman called Isabel sat in the not-wood chair with her hands together in her lap, her pale face drawn. When Oa held out the cross, she smiled, and little lines curved around her mouth and wrinkled her eyelids. "Thank you, Oa," she said.

Oa sniffed. She detected no scent of anger or fear rising from Isabel.

Oa wanted to touch her, to see if her skin was as smooth as it looked, her white hands as soft. Oa hadn't touched anyone in a long, long time. Doctor had touched her, at first, but his hands had been hard and cold. And he had worn gloves. Isabel didn't have gloves.

It occurred to Oa that Isabel didn't yet know about her. Would she be the one to understand what Oa was, to figure it out? And what would happen then?

Oa laid the cross carefully in Isabel's open hand, then dashed back to her bed. She put her back to the corner, and clutched the fuzzy toy to her chest. She waited.

THERE WAS NOTHING for Isabel to do but wait, as well. She didn't look into the mirrored window again, or try to call anyone through the door. She put the cross around her neck, and sat absently gazing at the wall, where a framed print showed varicolored horses galloping across a white field. Her eyelids drooped, and she let them fall.

She startled awake at the crackle of the speaker. "Excuse me," a voice said, one Isabel had not heard before. "I'm sorry to disturb you. I have your valises."

Isabel stood up with difficulty, finding her muscles stiff from travel and tension. Her voice was scratchy when she spoke. "Do you have my equipment cases, too?"

"I don't, but I think I can get them for you."

"Can you? That would be a great help."

"I'll just put these in the bubble, and go back for the other things."

Isabel crossed to the mirrored window, where she could see only her own tired face. "Who are you? I would like to say thank you."

The silver of the mirror dissolved, deliquescing to clear glass. The window became a real window, showing the corridor beyond, the external windows facing into the Multiplex and the darkness of the early evening. Oa gasped.

A longshoreman faced Isabel through the glass, the friendly face she had seen at the airfield, with long, heavy-lidded eyes and a slow smile. "I'm Jin-Li Chung."

Isabel smiled back. "I'm Isabel Burke. Thank you, Jin-Li."

"You're welcome." The longshoreman's black hair was very short, and streaked with silver. "Mother Burke. Jay Appleton is on guard now. Tell him to call me if you need anything else."

"Thank you," Isabel said again. "I will."

Just as the glass silvered, becoming a mirror again, Paolo Adetti loomed in the corridor. The speaker was still on.

"You, there!" Adetti rasped. "Are you the one who brought Dr. Burke's things? Who gave you permission to clear the glass?"

Isabel closed her eyes, listening, imagining the confrontation on the other side of the mirror. She heard Jin-Li Chung's mild response. "Mother Burke wanted to speak to me." Adetti snarled something dismissive. There was a click as he turned off the speaker, and then silence.

Absently, Isabel wandered back to the table, and stood rubbing her bare scalp reflexively, wondering what Paolo Adetti wanted.

SHE LEARNED LITTLE more that day. Someone brought blankets and sheets to make up the bed in the empty room. There was an observation camera suspended from the ceiling, but Isabel thought it didn't matter. Let them watch her if they liked. Jin-Li Chung returned with her equipment, and the medicator reports arrived in the form of a box of disks in plastic sleeves, dozens of them. Isabel found her reader and set it up, but she put the disks aside to look at in the morning. She needed to sleep. She had left San Felice more than thirty hours ago.

A meal appeared, brought by someone in a quarantine suit who also made up the beds and brought extra towels for the tiny bathroom. Oa seemed accustomed to the routine. She ate her supper, washed herself, and when the lights dimmed, she climbed into the bed with the teddy bear in her arms. Isabel was half-asleep herself by the time she pulled on pajamas and brushed her teeth. She hesitated in the doorway to the little room that was to be hers, at least for tonight.

"When I was young, Oa," she said sleepily. "My mother always tucked me into bed at night. I would do the same for you, but I'm afraid you would misunderstand."

The child's eyes showed white in the gloom. She whispered, "Oa sleeps now."

"Yes. Isabel sleeps now, too. I wonder if you would prefer my door open, or closed?"

There was no answer. Isabel couldn't think of another way to ask. She could hardly keep her eyes open. It would all have to wait until tomorrow. She said, "Well, then. Suppose we compromise? I'll leave it half-open. Good night, Oa. Sleep well."

As she slipped into her own room, she added under her breath, "God bless you."

JIN-LI TAUGHT A karate class in the Rec Fac, then showered and went to the cafeteria for a late dinner. Buckley was there, lingering over coffee and watching a sports video on the big screen set into the wall. He muted the sound as Jin-Li approached.

"Hey, Johnnie," he said in a low tone. "You get a look at the girl over there today?"

Jin-Li set down the tray and slid onto the bench across from Buck. The cafeteria was almost deserted. Jin-Li had the last hot meal to be served for the night, a fish casserole. "It's nothing to do with us, Buck."

Buck grinned. "Yeah, but you're the curious type, Johnnie. We all know that."

Jin-Li eyed him. "Apparently you are, too."

He laughed. "Yeah, well, she's an offworlder and all. And Matty Phipps says that Adetti is really interested in her—I mean, medically, not the other way."

"Who's Matty Phipps?"

"Crew from the transport. You know, the guys that stay awake while everyone else is in twilight sleep."

"Yes. I know."

The fish was good, and Jin-Li ate with a healthy appetite while Buckley watched the play on the screen. When the casserole was gone, and Jin-Li pushed the plate away, he said, "You did see her, didn't you, Johnnie? How does she look?"

"I caught a glimpse," Jin-Li said with a shrug. "She seems well."

"Yeah, but, I mean . . . they're saying there's something really strange about this kid. Something weird."

"I wouldn't know anything about it, Buck."

He pushed aside his coffee mug and leaned across the table to whisper, "They say this Dr. Adetti is over there at the infirmary all the time, every day, and the ice queen, too. And now this priest is here. Gotta be something going on."

"Sounds like it." Jin-Li stood up.

"Come on, Johnnie. You always know everything! What's happening?" Buck stood, too, and followed as Jin-Li deposited the tray in the recycle bin, and walked to the door. When they were outside, he fished for a cigarette and lit it. "Come on, Johnnie. Nobody's around."

Jin-Li laughed. "Nothing to tell. Sorry."

"I promise I'll keep the secret."

Jin-Li sobered. "Port Force gave me a second chance. I don't want to blow it." They had reached the barracks building. " 'Night, Buck. See you in the morning."

He waved the lighted cigarette in exasperation. "You're just not a sport, Johnnie."

"I know it. Not a sport at all."

Buck had been right, Jin-Li thought, climbing the stairs. Adetti spent a lot of time at the infirmary, or poring over medicator reports, or huddled with Boreson and Markham. None of them inspired much trust in Jin-Li. And it would be interesting to meet Matty Phipps.

5

OA DIDN'T LIKE sleeping alone. The anchens had slept in a comforting tangle of arms and legs, hearing the murmurs of the others die away as forgetful sleep stole over their nest, and the buzzing of insects and the faint chirping of night birds filled the darkness. On the ship, and here in the infirmary, Oa often lay awake for hours, listening to the alien sounds around her. But the presence of Isabel, this lady of the shining bare scalp and soft, weary smile, soothed her. Isabel's eyes shone like sunshine through clouds, and her scent was transparent as a mountain breeze.

On this night, moments after Isabel went into her room, leaving the door neither wide open nor fully closed, Oa slept.

She dreamed of the island. She knew it was a dream, because Nwa and Micho were still alive. Nwa, who they called Nah-nah because he was so small, and Bibi, and one-eyed Ette, tall Micho, and the others knelt around the kburi, chanting the song of the ancestors, begging Raimu-ke to help them. To work a miracle.

Oa woke, and lay wondering for the thousandth time if Raimu-ke could hear her over such a great distance. Or if she was even listening.

But sometimes Raimu-ke listened. She had listened to Lili.

Oa remembered the day Lili returned to the people. The tide was receding, and the anchens had been digging for pishi in the shining wet sand. Oa opened one and shucked out the tender meat with a bit of stone. She was just about to put it in her mouth when Lili came running out of the forest, shouting, holding up the end of her ragged skirt to show the blood markings. Lili danced and cried and waved the bloody flag of her triumph. Oa's fingers went limp, and she dropped the meat of the pishi into the sand. Like everyone else, she stared at Lili in stunned silence, hardly believing in the miracle.

Only Micho, who always knew what to do, remembered to start the signal fire. While Lili pranced along the beach, celebrating, the anchens scattered into the forest to find the green wood and wide fronds of nuchi leaves to make thick smoke. When it billowed above the beach, a wavering white column against the blue sky, the anchens slipped into the trees. They left Lili alone on the beach, weeping with joy and relief, watching the horizon.

Lili had not been on the island long. She had not acquired one of the crude marks they inked on each other at their private tatwaj, the one they held before Raimu-ke. When the canoe came, Lili splashed out through the surf, calling to the elders. She never looked back at the island, and none of the anchens called a farewell to her. Lili was a person now. She would not have answered.

WHEN THE LIGHTS brightened in the Multiplex, Isabel opened her eyes to the depressing sterility of the small room, with its generic white walls, beige plastic sink in the corner, only a padded, wheeled stool for furniture.

Her equipment was where she had stacked it, her two modest valises waiting in a corner. She sat up, yawning and rubbing her scalp with her fingers. Someone would be coming in soon, no doubt, with breakfast, and perhaps with plans for the day. Adetti would come, and Gretchen Boreson. She needed to decide what to do.

She rummaged in a valise for her toothbrush, and then bent over the sink to wash her face and brush her teeth. She tried not to be aware of the camera set into the ceiling, its amber light winking at regular intervals. There was no sound from the outer room. She would say her prayers first, and afterward, she could set about organizing a work space.

From the second valise she took out her little foam kneeling pad, and a crucifix on a stand. She wheeled the stool to an empty corner, and covered it with a white embroidered cloth. She set the crucifix on the cloth, and the pad on the floor beside the stool. She found her box of miniature candles, blessed for her by Marian, and lit one. She flicked on her portable reader, and keyed it to the liturgical calendar. She smiled to see that it was the memorial day for St. John Bosco, the great educator. Perhaps it was a good omen.

She knelt on the foam pad, made the sign of the cross, and began the devotions with which she had started every day since her novitiate.

SAINT MARY OF MAGDALA,
PATRONESS OF THOSE WHO ASK,
AND WHO STRIVE TO FOLLOW IN YOUR FOOTSTEPS,
GUIDE ME, YOUR UNWORTHY ACOLYTE, TO SHINE LIGHT IN THE DARK
    PLACES.
HELP ME TO REVEAL THE TRUTHS THAT ARE HIDDEN BY LIES.
IMBUE ME WITH YOUR STRENGTH, YOUR WISDOM, AND YOUR
    PATIENCE.
DISPERSE THE SHADOWS OF DECEPTION,
AND LET RIGHTEOUSNESS AND PEACE SHINE OVER YOUR PEOPLE.

She spoke the ritual with her eyes closed, her hands linked. For so long, these words, their intention and their rhythm, had carried her to a perfect haven of peace and contemplation, a level of mind and spirit no temporal trouble could disturb. Since Simon, that sanctuary seemed beyond her reach. But she kept trying.

The prayer finished, she knelt on, concentrating on the cross, on the sacrifice it represented, on the beat of her heart, on the flicker of the tiny candle that represented her calling. Nothing. She felt nothing. The voice of her soul, which had commanded her since she was fifteen years old, had fallen silent.

The slight squeak of the door broke her concentration. She glanced up, and saw the dark face of the child from Virimund peering around the doorjamb. At her movement, the girl jumped back, out of sight.

"Oa! It's all right. Would you like to come in?"

No answer.

Isabel made the sign of the cross, silently repeating her petition for patience and wisdom. Then she rose, tucked her traveling kneeler beneath the bed, snuffed the candle between her thumb and forefinger. She went to the door, and looked out into the larger room.

The child stood before the mirrored window, one hand on the shining glass. Her narrow shoulders, covered in the awful pink wool sweater, hunched as if she were cold.

"You didn't know it was a window, did you?" Isabel said lightly.

Oa dropped her hand from the mirror, and held it behind her back.

Isabel strolled up to stand before the glass. "It's a trick, I'm afraid. A trick so people can look in at us without being seen themselves." She looked down and saw the flaring of the girl's nostrils. They were delicately formed, little dark wings with pink undersides. "Do I smell different to you, Oa?"

Oa considered this. "Isabel—" she began. One hand waved slightly in the air, as if grasping for the right word. "Isabel is smelling like—like air."

"Air." Isabel smiled. "I think I like that. Air." She left the mirror and moved to the table, saying easily, "And what do you smell like, then?"

A long pause. Oa followed her at a little distance. Her feet were bare, and they whispered against the gray tiles of the floor. "Oa smells—" She turned one palm up, a cup of shell-pink with a tracing of dark lines. "Empty."

"Empty?"

"Empty. Nothing inside."

Isabel sat down. Empty. What a sad choice. She hoped the answer meant only that Oa didn't understand the word, but there was a sadness in the great dark eyes—indeed, an emptiness—that oppressed her. Her eye fell on the portable reader that lay on the other chair. She picked it up and held it out. "Oa. Will you show me your reader?"

That sudden white smile blazed, lighting the girl's face. Apparently the child felt on certain ground over the reader. She accepted the instrument, and flicked it on with a deft touch.

"Who gave it to you?" Isabel asked.

Oa grinned again. "Ship lady," she said. She thought for a minute, one finger pressing into her cheek. "A gift," she finally added.

Isabel smiled back at her. "How nice, Oa. The ship lady gave you a gift."

The reader came to life, and began to reel off a series of pictures. A clear voice read the text beneath them. Oa held the screen so that Isabel could see it, and recited with the voice while the book played. "Dog," she said. "Cat. Child. Mother. Father. House."

It was a reading primer, and she had memorized it.

"The child plays with the dog. The dog runs after the cat." Oa spoke every accent and emphasis in perfect imitation of the narrator. Isabel listened. Her heart sank when Oa recited, "No one is inside the house. The house is empty."

For ten minutes, Oa spoke in unison with the narrator, right to the final sentence. ". . . after school, the children are hungry. Mother gives them milk and cookies." She flashed her white smile once more, and laid the reader down.

"Thank you," Isabel said. "I enjoyed the book."

"Oa has two more books," the girl said.

Isabel was about to ask to see those as well, but she was interrupted by the opening of the infirmary door. Oa retreated to her bed as a quarantine-suited guard brought in two trays of eggs and rice and juice that he set on the table in front of the row of toys. Isabel asked, "Could I get some coffee?"

The guard hesitated at the door to the sterile bubble. Again Isabel heard the hiss of the airflow, and wondered whom Adetti was trying to protect. It wasn't Oa, certainly, not with a reverse quarantine. In any case, the medicator would have inoculated her against any diseases she lacked antibodies for.

The guard said, "I could ask—all I know is they gave me the trays. Someone brought them over from the cafeteria."

"Oh, never mind, then. I understand. Jin-Li said I should ask—"

"Jin—you mean Johnnie? Oh, sure, Mother Burke. Listen, I'll tell Johnnie."

"Only if it's no trouble. You must be Jay."

"Right. Jay Appleton. I'll look up Johnnie for you."

"Thank you, Jay."

The guard withdrew, and Isabel drew her chair closer to the table. It was too small for comfort, but it was all she had. "Are you hungry, Oa?"

Oa took a step toward the table, glancing at Isabel with a little furrow between her brows.

"You know the word, don't you?" Isabel urged. "It was in your book. Hungry. Wanting food." She touched her stomach and smiled. "I'm hungry."

"Yes," the girl said. "Yes—Oa is hungry."

Isabel hesitated, and then said, as gently as she could, "Can you say, 'I'm hungry'?"

The girl dropped her eyes. Her head drooped. The fragrance of hot rice and scrambled eggs filled the room, and the muscles in Oa's slender throat worked as she swallowed saliva.

"Never mind," Isabel said. "It doesn't matter. Oa and Isabel are both hungry. Let's have our breakfast together."

ISABEL WAS IMMERSED in the medicator reports when Paolo Adetti and Gretchen Boreson arrived. She had set up her reader on the low table, with a chair in front of it, and she slid the boxes of disks beneath it. Her computer she parked on the smooth plastic surface of the exam bed in the empty surgery, pushing the medicator to one side. Periodically she left her reader and went to the computer to make notes or look up a reference file. With her things unpacked and her equipment set up, the little infirmary seemed more like a home. Isabel brought out a sweater of her own, black, but a smooth Italian merino. She laid it out to give to Oa. The girl sat on her bed, the teddy bear in her arms, her eyes gazing at something Isabel couldn't see.

When the mirror cleared, the change in light made Isabel look up. Gretchen Boreson stood in the corridor. She wore a black suit that made her skin look pale as milk, and her lips were painted scarlet. Earrings of some red stone hung from her earlobes, trembling, catching the light. Even through the glass, Isabel could see the tic that marred the administrator's tight features, and she felt a swell of sympathy. She rose from her chair and went to the window.

"Good morning," she said.

Boreson held a black silk scarf in her hand, and she pulled it through her fingers, pleating it, smoothing it, pleating it again. "Good morning, Mother Burke." The speaker made her tone thin. "I'm so sorry about—" She gestured at the space beyond the glass. "About this situation."

"I have most of what I need." Isabel smiled. "Oa and I are getting to know one another."

"But, you know, there were lovely rooms all ready for you at the guest suites. I'm sure you'd rather be—"

Paolo Adetti came to stand at Boreson's shoulder. Without the mask, Isabel saw that his complexion had the charcoal undertones of Sicily, and his black eyes were stony. "I see you got your equipment," he said.

"Yes."

"Good. Fine. Well, I'm coming in now to run a medicator test on the girl."

Isabel's back stiffened, but she made an effort to keep her voice level and her face noncommittal. "Not now, I think, Dr. Adetti."

"I have work to do, Mother Burke. I won't interrupt you. It won't take long."

Isabel pursed her lips, as if considering. Then she said calmly, "No, I think not, Dr. Adetti. I'll finish these existing reports first."

"You can go right ahead. But I need some readings today," he insisted. "There's not a great deal of time . . ."

Isabel looked away from him deliberately, turning her face to Boreson. "Administrator, as Oa's guardian, I prefer not to have her disturbed until I've completed my preliminary evaluation."

Boreson's tic worsened, tugging at her cheek and distorting her eyelid. "Ah, Mother Burke, I'm sure Dr. Adetti's presence won't interfere—"

Isabel was shaking her head. "No," she said, letting her voice sharpen. "Not today. Probably not tomorrow." She gave them both a cool glance. "I'm sure you don't want to endanger the extraordinary empowerment provision—or have a report reach the press that ESC officials put their own interests ahead of this child's."

She saw the fire blaze in Adetti's black eyes, and his chin jutted. Boreson put her white, sharp-nailed fingers on his arm, and murmured something Isabel couldn't catch.

Isabel nodded. "I'll let you know, shall I? And I do appreciate your patience until then."

She turned away from the window and walked with deliberate steps into the small surgery where her computer waited. She spoke to Oa from the doorway.

"Oa. Come here, will you? I want to show you a book I have on my computer."

Isabel held the door as if she had every confidence Oa would do as she asked. She held her breath. For an uncomfortable moment, she thought the child might not respond.

Oa didn't move quickly, but she did move. Bit by bit, she straightened her legs and slid down from the bed. She didn't look at the window, but her awareness of Adetti's presence showed in every muscle, in her gaze that fastened on Isabel with a kind of desperation. The walk was no more than five steps, but it seemed to take forever. Isabel stepped back, and Oa, bless her, walked straight into the small surgery.

Isabel directed a warm smile at Boreson and Adetti, and shut the door.

SHE READ THE first medicator reports with great care, absorbing every detail of Oa's physical condition, her blood counts, her heart and respiration rates, her temperature, oxygen saturation, electrolyte levels, hepatic function, everything. Her immunity indices, after the first test, leveled. She had recovered from her initial injury, the burn from a shock gun, with remarkable speed. All other indications were within normal ranges.

Isabel compared the first ten reports, and then the first fifteen, searching for a reason that Adetti would have subjected the girl to multiple analyses. She already understood that Oa's fear of the medicator would not have forestalled the ESC physician . . . but the testing took time, and analyzing the results took time. What was he looking for?

She glanced up at Oa, who was bent over the computer, using the touchpad to page through *A Child's Garden of Verse*. Oa's lips moved as she followed the narrator's voice, a little behind, but managing most of the words. It was a marvel, truly. The girl had taught herself to read with one little reader and three books. She was bright, without doubt. And so what was the matter with her?

Isabel's doctorate was in anthropology. She knew a good bit of medicine, but it was the sort of hands-on knowledge needed in the field. There had to be a secret buried in the numbers and symbols in the medicator reports; but by the time she reached the thirtieth, she knew she would not be able to uncover it on her own. Whatever it was, she felt certain that even Adetti had not yet found the answer.

She needed help to solve the puzzle. She needed Simon.

6

SIMON EDWARDS SAW the pictures of Isabel with Cole Markham, taken outside the office of the General Administrator of Earth Multiplex. They flashed across the networks with a brief statement about ExtraSolar sparing no effort or expense in meeting the requirements of its charters. The info-bite said nothing about what the Magdalene was to be researching, but it went on for a full three sentences about the role of the Magdalenes as Enquirers, the variety of their studies, their reputation for honesty. Simon smiled at that. He knew how Marian Alexander chafed under the disdain of the older orders, the male orders. Especially the Jesuits. Marian must have leaped at the chance for Isabel to pursue a high-profile commission. He wondered what it entailed. A brief search on the networks turned up nothing more, which meant no one was talking. Perhaps no one had yet asked. But then why was the photo being offered?

Simon thumbed off his reader and left his desk to stand by the wide picture window, looking out over the gardens of the World Health and Welfare offices. The networks reported rain in Seattle. Here in Geneva, a fragile sunshine glistened on the icy lake and set last night's fresh snowfall sparkling on the roofs and gardens of the city. The long sun-baked days he and Isabel had spent together in the Victoria Desert seemed to belong to another life.

Simon felt Isabel's absence as a physical loss, even now. It was as if, he thought with dark humor, someone had taken a rib and left a great gap in his chest. His work couldn't fill it. His wife Anna, though she was willing to try, couldn't fill it.

He didn't know how to reach Isabel. She refused to have her own wavephone number, and rarely carried one even in the field. It didn't matter in any case. She had made it clear she didn't want to see him. She had vanished without a farewell, leaving no doubt that she meant their separation to be final. He had tried, and failed, to understand the compulsion that ruled her life. Now he struggled simply with acceptance.

Poor suffering Anna, mystified in her own way as he was in his, hovered on the edge of his awareness, there whenever he opened his eyes to see her, eager to repair their marriage. Distantly, he understood he was being cruel to her. He didn't mean to be, and he didn't want to be, but he couldn't help it.

He turned away from the window. He was due at a meeting of the directors that couldn't start without him. He left his office, nodding to his secretary and his aide as he passed their desks, and turned down the broad corridor to the boardroom, trying to fix his mind on the discussion ahead. There were a number of crises demanding his attention, all more serious than his personal troubles. Months had passed since he left Australia, since the morning he woke to find Isabel gone. But then, Simon reflected, like stubbing your toe or scorching your tongue, pain was often disproportionate to the gravity of the injury.

He managed a silent laugh at his own expense before he turned into the boardroom.

OA TREMBLED EACH time Doctor appeared in the window that she now understood was not a mirror. She made herself small in her corner, and listened to Doctor argue with Isabel.

Three days in a row, Isabel won the battle, and Doctor went away with the strange pale woman whose face jerked and crawled as if insects wriggled beneath her skin. Since Isabel came, Oa had not once had to submit to the spider machine. The second day, Isabel went into the central surgery where the medicator lurked, and she did something to the machine, something bad. Oa sniffed a complex perfume of anger and triumph as Isabel came out.

"There, Oa," Isabel said. "That will need some repair."

Oa crept to the little room and peered in. The machine's looping wires and tubes now hung free, trailing to the floor.

Isabel came to stand beside her. "I broke it. They can fix it, but it will take time."

"Fix?" Oa's lips and tongue struggled with the new word.

"Yes, fix. Repair. Do you know what a wavephone is, Oa?"

Oa pointed to the wavephone on the wall.

"That's right." Isabel's smile made Oa think of sunlight flashing on the face of Mother Ocean, or the glow from the nuchi shell lamps of the people. "That wavephone doesn't work. Someone broke it so I couldn't use it." Isabel's smile faded, and she looked tired again. "And I don't need the medicator. What I need to know, only you can tell me."

"No more spider machine?" A surge of hope washed over Oa. If there was no more spider machine, maybe Isabel wouldn't find out.

"Not for now."

"Oa is not liking it."

"I know." Isabel sat down in one of the not-wood chairs. It was too small for her, and her knees poked up beside the low table. "Do you know, Oa, I have dozens and dozens of medicator reports. They tell me a great deal about your body, but they don't tell me very much about you."

The brief flare of hope died in Oa's breast. She wished Isabel wouldn't go on.

Isabel rubbed her hand over her scalp. "Do you think you could tell me some things, Oa? Some things about your home, or your parents. About the island, and the other children."

Oa knew the word "parents" because it had been in the books. She knew it meant "mother" and "father" together. She knew the word "children." In fact, she understood almost everything Isabel said to her. Isabel spoke clearly, and not fast.

Oa dropped her eyes to her toes. She would have liked to tell Isabel, tell her everything. She had not talked to anyone in a very long time. But she was afraid.

Oa remembered a night when a boat had come from the people, not after the tatwaj, but just a night. Some men had been drinking beera, which the people made with fermented fruit. The men decided to come to the anchens' island. The anchens' nest was too close to the shore, and they were caught by surprise. They were sleeping, and the men found them.

The men were young and wild, in the first fire of their manhood. It was tabu for them to use girls of the people. But Bibi and Ette and Oa and Likaki were only anchens.

Micho tried to fight them off, because he was the tallest, but he was too thin and weak. The men hit Micho until he didn't get up anymore. The men didn't care if Micho ever got up again, because Micho was not a person. But afterward, Oa and the others grieved for Micho just as if he were a real person. She supposed that was because they were only anchens and didn't know any better. They buried Micho's body beneath the kburi, near Raimu-ke.

Oa cried for days afterward. She remembered how her throat hurt from sobbing and her eyelids burned with her salt tears. It was no comfort to her that Micho was not a person. Even though he was an anchen, he was brave and sweet and kind. It hurt more to lose Micho than it hurt when the men used her body.

"Do you understand my question?" Isabel pressed gently.

Oa whispered, "Yes. Oa understands."

"But you don't like to talk about it?"

Oa tugged at the ends of her hair.

"Suppose we start with something easy," Isabel said. "Can you tell me how old you are?"

Oa trembled. Doctor hadn't understood. Would Isabel understand? Oa wished she would not. But Isabel was a person, and Oa was an anchen. It was the way things were, the way the ancestors had made them both.

She shrugged out of the pink sweater and held up her arms.

*   *   *

ADETTI'S INITIAL EXAM notes mentioned tattoos on both subjects' arms, the living child and the dead, but his chill description had not prepared Isabel. Oa's slender arms, trembling as if with cold, were littered with tattoos, row upon ragged row. Columns of black symbols marched up her forearms, over her wiry biceps, her thin shoulders. They stretched beneath her cascade of curly hair, and down the other side, right to the wrist. There looked rather like the markings on playing cards, like the suit of diamonds. Some were evenly drawn, but some, Isabel saw, were crude, as if the materials were inferior, or the hand that drew them unskilled. And so many! Dozens, at least.

"Oa!" Isabel breathed. "What do they mean?"

Tears flooded the child's eyes. She dropped her arms, and hung her head in a posture of humiliation. Of submission.

"Oa, what's wrong? How have I upset you?"

But Oa couldn't, or wouldn't, answer.

IT WAS AFTER she had reached the end of the reports that Isabel disabled the medicator.

The information changed very little from one scan to another, even less than one might expect from any single patient. She double-checked on her computer to be certain the medicators were estimating normal ranges correctly. She dug through her resource files for any hint of illness, of allergic reaction, of adrenal or other insufficiency, of low organic functions. Only two details of Oa's medicator reports seemed curious. There was a bit of wear on her teeth, which Isabel supposed could be put down to the foods the Sikassa consumed on Virimund. The other was stranger, the charts of her hormone levels. Body chemistry was beyond Isabel's scope, but it seemed to her that some fluctuation would be natural. If the medicator reports were correct, Oa's hormone levels never varied, not from the very first scan to the most recent. Isabel had no idea what that might mean. There were other things, too, that she simply didn't have the knowledge to puzzle out. Finally, frustrated, she went to the wavephone on the wall. She would have to call Simon. He could tell her what it all meant.

She discovered the wavephone's rhodium antenna had been snapped in two. Sabotaged. She was cut off.

She stared at it for a long moment, shocked. Then she turned on her heel and marched straight into the surgery. She ripped the connections out of the medicator, broke the scan mechanism, pulled the connecting cord between the syrinxes and the screen. When she was done, she glared up into the ceiling camera.

And now, she couldn't persuade Oa to explain the tattoos, and she couldn't bear to see her hanging her head, tears slipping down her cheeks.

The girl's passivity was part of the puzzle. The child had lived alone on an island with only a flock of other children for company. Would she not demonstrate more independence? That she had initiative was clear, since she had taught herself to read. That she had a good mind was obvious. But she wouldn't answer the simplest personal question, and Isabel couldn't think how to gain her trust.

Oa at least accepted the Italian sweater, so much softer and warmer than the one she had been wearing. She allowed Isabel to help her with her other clothes, too. There was a box of things, dresses, pants, a jumpsuit, a pair of soft pajamas. It seemed she had been sleeping in her clothes. Isabel persuaded her to exchange her too-short dress for a pair of fleecy trousers and shirt. She encouraged her to put aside the ill-fitting shoes for a pair of thick socks. When she gave her the sweater, she said, "This sweater was made in Italy, where my home is, Oa. It makes me think of my home, and my friends."

She watched Oa pull the sweater over her arms, hiding the ragged rows of tattoos. The girl lifted the hem of the sweater to her nose and inhaled. Isabel watched her, smiling. "What does the sweater smell like?"

Oa tipped her head to one side, considering for a moment. Finally she said, "Sweater is smelling like Isabel."

Isabel laughed. "I suppose it must. I've worn it many times."

Oa wrapped her arms around herself, hugging the black wool close to her body. With her eyes on the floor, she said, "Oa likes it. Is it—" Her eyes came up cautiously. "A gift?"

"Yes," Isabel said, feeling a quiet triumph at this small sign of progress. "It certainly is. It's a gift. A gift to Oa from Isabel."

The white grin flashed. Oa's fearful mood seemed to have fled. She made a little dancing circle of the room, fluid and graceful on her slender legs. When she twirled back to her bed, Isabel was glad to see she didn't put her back to the corner, but sat on the edge, her legs dangling over the side, her long-toed feet just touching the floor. It was a small thing, but Isabel took it as an encouraging sign. She pulled her chair close, and leaned back in it, crossing her legs at the ankle.

"I have an idea, Oa. Suppose I tell you some things about myself."

The girl's eyes brightened. "Stories?"

Isabel chuckled. "I guess you could call them stories. True ones, though, not like in your books." She paused, raising her eyebrows. "Is it all right for me to tell you how old I am?"

The child nodded. Isabel linked her hands together. Apparently there was nothing wrong with mentioning age if it was her own. "Well. I'm thirty-six years old. My mother and father lived in a lot of different places when I was young, so I grew up all over the world—France, and North America, and Egypt, and Italy. My father was a diplomat. He died a few years ago, and now my mother lives in a city called Rome. I have one brother and one sister."

None of this seemed to bother the girl. "I'm a priest. Oa, do you know what that is?" Oa pointed at Isabel's cross. "Yes, that's the symbol of my priesthood. I took the vows of the Priestly Order of Mary Magdalene fourteen years ago." She gave a short laugh. "My parents weren't too happy about that. They didn't think women should be priests."

Still Oa watched her, head tilted to one side, tugging on strands of her hair. She didn't appear to be disturbed by any of these confidences. Isabel ventured further, "I'm also a medical anthropologist. That means I ask a lot of questions. I study how people live."

Oa dropped her hands. She went very still.

Isabel stopped talking. She barely breathed. Something had changed. She watched the child struggling with something, and wished with all her heart she knew what it was.

At last the girl said, her voice very faint, "Isabel is studying Oa?"

Isabel took her cross in her fingers before she answered. She looked directly into the girl's liquid dark eyes. "Only," she answered firmly, "only if it's all right with Oa. Only if Oa gives her permission."

ISABEL WOKE LATE that night when her door slid open, its rubber seal whispering on the tiles. She turned her head on her pillow. Oa stood in the doorway, framed by the dim glow of the night lighting, her eyes flashing white. She crept to Isabel's bedside and crouched there, her arms around her knees.

For some moments Isabel thought she would say nothing, but then, in her high, slender voice, the child said, "Oa gives per-mission. Per-mission to Isabel."

Isabel let her breath out in a long sigh. She drew her hand out from beneath the coverlet, and extended her open fingers toward Oa. The girl looked at her hand, pale in the darkness, and then, hesitantly, put her own dark fingers into it.

As gently as she could, Isabel closed her hand around the child's.

An immense darkness swept over her at the touch, a bottomless grief that was almost unbearable. Isabel closed her eyes, letting it flow through her.

She found, in a moment, that it was not an absolute darkness that immersed her. A flicker of hope brightened the shadows of Oa's mind. There was a sense of love, and faith, and tenderness. And underlying all, in the midnight sea that was Oa's soul, was the bedrock of pure courage, the stuff of which great spirits are made.

Isabel murmured, "Thank you, Oa." And she sent a private, silent thanks to her patroness for this small step forward.

7

THE WORD WAS out about the damage the Magdalene had done to the infirmary's medicator. A man who had been posted at the infirmary laughed about the incident to a group of friends at the Rec Fac, in Jin-Li's hearing.

Paolo Adetti was not a popular man. The longshoremen and technicians, the clerks and secretaries of Port Force, had heard the rumors from Virimund. A secretary in purchasing had talked to her brother on Virimund via r-wave, and the word spread. The secretary's brother told her that two people had died on the ocean planet after an altercation on one of the hundreds of small islands. Everyone at the Multiplex, it seemed, knew now that one of the dead had been a native child.

Gossip boiled through the ranks. Matty Phipps had been reassigned to the Multiplex, a reward for serving a long voyage. Jin-Li sought her out in the Rec Fac. Phipps was a broad-shouldered woman with a strong jaw and wispy red hair. She was watching a program on the big screen in the lounge, her boots off, her long legs propped on a table.

Jin-Li waited till the program ended to settle into a chair near her. "Are you Phipps?"

The woman looked up. "That's me."

Jin-Li put out a hand to shake. "Jin-Li Chung."

"Jin—what did you say your name is?"

Jin-Li smiled. "Everyone calls me Johnnie."

"I get that! Johnnie it is, then." Phipps grinned, her freckled cheeks creasing, and put out her hand. "Matty."

"Just thought I'd say welcome," Jin-Li said. "I teach some classes here in the Rec Fac, so if you have any questions . . ."

"Thanks. I might take a class. For now, I'm still resting up."

"Right. You were on the Virimund transport, weren't you? Interesting."

Matty Phipps sighed and stretched long arms over her head. "More like boring. Long, long trip, that. Everybody in twilight sleep."

"I guess that's what it's like for crew. I went to Irustan, a few years ago," Jin-Li said.

"Irustan," Phipps said, shaking her head. "That's a two-year trip."

"But I was in twilight sleep the whole time," Jin-Li said. "Woke up enough to eat meals, do the circulation exercises. That was it."

"Best that way, believe me. Nothing to look at, not a lot to do." Phipps waved a broad, freckled hand. "I did two voyages, back to back. Nuova Italia and then Virimund. Thought I'd go nuts, frankly. Great if you're antisocial. I've had enough."

"What kind of work did you do onboard?"

"Maintenance and supply. There was plenty of work, just got lonely. Only three crew and the officers to talk to." She laughed. "And not a one of 'em played a decent game of Go. You play Go, Johnnie?"

"No, sorry. I could learn, I guess." Jin-Li leaned back in the chair. "Ever see the girl? The one ESC brought from Virimund?"

Phipps's grin faded. "Yeah." Her voice grew hard. "That damned doctor kept me running with his lab supply requests, I can tell you. And the poor kid! Fourteen months in space, and he kept her awake the whole damned time."

Jin-Li straightened. "Awake?"

"You got it. Shut up in quarantine the whole voyage, wide awake, with only Doctor fucking Adetti for company." She winked at Jin-Li. "Well, and me, once in a while. Through the glass, anyway. I couldn't stand the thought of this little girl all alone. She didn't speak much English, but I slipped her a reader and a few disks to pass the time. She figured 'em out right quick, too!" Phipps shook her head, her eyes clouding. "Hope she's doing all right. I haven't heard a word about her since we got here."

Jin-Li stood up. "She has somebody with her now. It's a Magdalene priest."

"Well, I hope she gets her out of there," Phipps said. "Rotten business, keeping her locked up in quarantine all those months. She sure didn't look sick to me."

"DR. EDWARDS, THE people at Earth Multiplex assure me the child is being well cared for."

Simon leaned back in his chair and frowned at ExtraSolar's liaison to World Health. He had been asking hard questions, and getting very few answers. He had finally demanded a face-to-face, and Hilda Kronin had come to his office.

"Why is she being kept under wraps?"

"I'm told Dr. Adetti is examining her." Kronin shifted nervously in her seat.

"Look," Simon said. He leaned forward, his elbows on his desk. "ESC is going to have to explain why they brought this girl away from her own world. Otherwise, I'm going to recommend official censure, and that's a very public event."

She put up an anxious hand. "No, no, Dr. Edwards, that isn't necessary. Cole Markham called me this morning from Seattle. He assures me ExtraSolar has satisfied the requirements of the charters. They acquired an extraordinary empowerment provision from the regents, and they brought in a medical anthropologist to sort out the child's situation."

"What does that mean, sort out the situation?"

Kronin shook her head. "I'm so sorry, Dr. Edwards. I'm not a scientist, so I can't explain it well. But, you know—" She waved the same hand in an apologetic gesture.

Simon let his eyes stray to the view of Geneva beyond the window. Lowering gray clouds promised more snow by evening. The bitter weather suited his mood.

The liaison said hesitantly, "I suppose they mean, you know, understand the child's background. What happened on Virimund. And why."

Simon watched the light change from pale gray to a deeper ash as the layers of cloud shifted over the city. It was almost evening, when he would go home to Anna, and they would spend the long empty hours carefully not talking of anything that mattered. "Why don't you try to make me understand what happened, Hilda," he said. He felt his temper rising. It was good, somehow, to feel an emotion that was not sadness. He steepled his fingers, and focused his gaze on them. "Tell me about Virimund."

"Well, it was complicated . . ."

"Of course."

"The hydros took a flyer out over the islands and saw movement, what looked like people on a beach. They decided to check it out. Only one island. No one knew, you understand . . ."

"Virimund was supposed to be uninhabited."

"Right, right. And even after weeks, no one had any idea. There were no lights, no radio communication, nothing. It was a complete surprise to our people."

"But they saw someone . . ." Simon prompted.

"They were just curious," she said defensively. "And after the—the incident—our people have stayed strictly away."

"Okay," Simon said. He flexed his fingers. "Now tell me why the physician assigned to the hydrogen installation—" He glanced at the reader inset into his desk. "Adetti," he said. "Paolo Adetti. What made him decide to bring this little girl back with him? And why was it allowed?"

The woman breathed a wilting sigh. "I can only tell you what they've told me. I'm supposed to forestall censure, and a World Health investigation. I'm doing my best, believe me."

"I know you're trying, Hilda."

"They told me the children attacked the hydros when they landed.

Two children and one of the workers were injured. One child and one man died, but this girl survived. Dr. Adetti discovered, I guess, that she had some communicable illness, so he put her in quarantine."

"But why bring her to Earth?"

She spread her hands. "I'm afraid they didn't think I needed that information. I'm sorry."

"And what's her status now?"

"I'm sorry," she repeated. "I just don't know."

"Well, it can't go on much longer. Not without an accounting."

She nodded. "I know. But that's why the anthropologist is there. She's a Magdalene priest," she offered, with a hopeful raising of the eyebrows.

Simon pushed away from his desk and went to stand at the window, looking out over the peaked roofs of the city to the lake. The old fountain had shut down, but he knew where it was. Anna was working near the lakeshore, teaching in a school for refugees. He felt a spasm of sorrow for her. Her steadiness, her persistence, the same qualities that now drove a wedge between them, were taken as great virtues by her colleagues in the school.

He forced himself to turn his eyes back to Hilda Kronin. "Make it clear to your people," he said, "that we understand perfectly why they called in a Magdelene." He avoided saying Isabel's name. Surely even this minor diplomat, this nervous woman, would hear something in his voice, some hint of his feelings. He cleared his throat. "This was a public relations move, Hilda, a transparent ploy to garner public approval. Unless some solid information comes out of it, it won't be enough."

She stood, eager to leave. "Right, Dr. Edwards. I understand."

"I'd like to make it easy for you," he said. "But we have to be clear on this."

"Thanks. I'll try to explain it to them."

"It's best to be straight out with it. Diplomacy is all well and good, but we have a child to consider, and apparently an islandful of them out on Virimund."

"I know it. Thank you." She made a hasty exit, and Simon turned back to the austere winter scenery.

His secretary looked in the open door. "Dr. Edwards? Do you want anything?"

"No. Not now," he said. What he wanted, he could not ask for.

JAY APPLETON TOLD Jin-Li that the priest had asked for coffee.

"We could just get it from the cafeteria," he said, waving at the big institutional pots at the end of the line of hot tables.

"But she's from Italy, Jay. Bet she likes her coffee strong and fresh. Think it would be all right if I could find her a small machine and some good coffee?"

Appleton grinned. "Figured you'd say that. But you don't fool me, Johnnie. You just wanta see what's happening."

Jin-Li laughed, but showed up on Jay's next shift at the infirmary, carrying a small espresso maker, wheedled from a friend in the cafeteria, and a pound of freshly ground coffee.

Jin-Li spoke into the comm mike. "Mother Burke? It's Jin-Li Chung here. May I clear the window?"

The priest's light voice answered almost immediately. "Of course, Jin-Li."

The silver deliquesced to show Isabel Burke standing beside the window, dressed as before in black. Her white collar glistened in the harsh light. She nodded to Jin-Li. "Hello."

The girl from Virimund came out of the side room, peering shyly past her curtain of kinky hair. She wore an oversize black sweater and loose fleece trousers.

Jin-Li held up the espresso maker and the foil bag of coffee. "I heard you like coffee."

Isabel Burke laughed, a warm sound even through the little comm system. "I love it! It's my weakness. But how did you know?"

Jin-Li shrugged. "Oh—we talk, you know. In the cafeteria. In the Rec Fac."

"What a kindness! I've really missed my little vice. I hope you didn't go to any trouble."

"Not at all. I'll send these in with your dinner trays."

"Thank you for being so thoughtful." She hesitated, and then said, softly, "Jin-Li—I don't mean to take advantage of you when you've already been so helpful—"

"Yes?" Jin-Li encouraged.

The priest glanced to her right, to the closed door of the infirmary. Jin-Li gave a slight nod. Jay was on the other side of the sterile bubble.

"I'm quite cut off here," the priest murmured. "This is my fourth day, and I haven't been able to speak to anyone. I could really use a wavephone."

Jin-Li glanced at the wavephone mounted on the wall.

The priest made a wry face. "It's not working," she said. "Disabled, actually."

Jin-Li eyed the spare furnishings of the infirmary, the guarded bubble. It was a risk. But the infirmary had been turned into a virtual prison. It was worth taking the chance. "See what I can do," Jin-Li said. "I'll be back soon, Mother Burke."

"Thank you," the priest said again, and she smiled in farewell. She had a wonderful smile, which made her eyes seem to light from within. People probably did favors for Isabel Burke often, just to see her smile. Jin-Li smiled back, touched the control to restore the mirror, and went off in search of a wavephone.

8

DOCTOR'S EYES BLAZED with fury over the broken spider machine.

Oa trembled, but Isabel faced Doctor through the not-mirror without fear. Her slight shoulders were squared. She even smiled, not her lovely, lamplight smile, but a cool curving of the lips.

Oa had started to tell Isabel things, things she remembered. Then Isabel told Oa things, about her home, about her prayers, about her work. It was a trading of memories, like the trading of mats and pots and blankets among the three islands, or of cutting stones and baskets among the anchens.

It started when Oa knelt beside Isabel's bed in the night. The faint light shone softly on Isabel's bare scalp, and her clear gray eyes were bright in the darkness, reflective, like the shimmery flanks of fish in Mother Ocean. Her hand was warm, and strong, though it was so slender. Oa clung to it, so grateful for the touch of skin that tears burned in her eyes, and she tried not to worry that it was a person's skin, and not an anchen's.

She started with "parents."

"Parents live on people's island," she whispered. She could feel Isabel listening. "Papi is making shahto." It was a relief to speak of Papi again. The anchens had always spoken of their papis and mamahs, sitting at night around their fire. "Papi is taking nuchi vines to Mamah. Mamah soaks vines in Mother Ocean and stretches them on sand—so." Oa stretched out her free arm to demonstrate. "Then Papi—" Again she demonstrated, weaving her hand back and forth to show the braiding, though she didn't have a word in English to express it. "Is making vines together. Is making big knots. Knots is against forest spiders." She sighed. "Anchens are not making shahto."

Isabel lay quietly for long moments. Oa let her eyes drift up to her face, to see if perhaps she had fallen asleep, as the anchens so often did while they were remembering. But Isabel's eyes were open, glistening with reflected light. Finally, she said, "Why, Oa? Why do the anchens not make shahto?" She didn't sound angry, or shocked, or anything other than curious.

Oa sighed. "Hands too small," she said. "Vines too hard. And—" She swallowed, the memory making her shiver. "Forest spiders are coming," she finished in a whisper.

"Oh," Isabel said, as if she understood.

But could she? These people lived in ships, or in rooms like this, with floors that were slick and objects that were made by machines. And except for the spider machine, Oa had seen nothing like a forest spider, or any creatures at all, since she left the world of Mother Ocean.

"Isabel is making shahto?" she breathed, daring to ask a question.

Isabel seemed to think for a time before she answered. "I don't know your word," she said finally. "I live in a house, with other women priests, and with girls who want to be priests."

"Oh," Oa said, in imitation.

Isabel squeezed her fingers gently. "I'm going to tell you all about my house, Oa. But suppose we get you back into your bed first, and I will sit beside you while you fall asleep."

Oa's breast filled with gratitude. It was almost as if Isabel were an anchen. She must not think that, must not allow herself to hope. One day Isabel would understand, and then everything could change. But it would be so easy . . . and it had been so long . . .

WHEN OA SLEPT at last, Isabel still sat beside the bed, her legs crossed at the ankles, her back against the wall, pondering. She watched the child's slender chest rise and fall, long lashes fluttering gently as she dreamed. What did Oa of Virimund dream, Isabel wondered. Of the shahto made by her father? Of the forest spiders that, in her mind, had given their name to the medicator? Or would she dream of something she longed for, something she yearned to have or to do? Isabel's heart ached with pity.

She had worked with many children in Australia, and among the refugees from the east who crowded into Italy. Some were starving, or orphaned, or abused. They could be withdrawn, frightened, clinging, rebellious. But Oa mystified her, with her flashes of intelligence, of laughter, her retreats into silence, her refusal to speak of herself in the first person. And Isabel sensed that Oa was keeping some deep secret, something of desperate importance, at least to her. Isabel had framed her questions carefully, trying not to provoke the fearful reaction she had seen before. What, she wondered, did the child mean by the word "anchen"? She struggled with it as she went to her own bed, yawning. When her eyes closed, she still had no answer.

She woke late the next morning, and hurried to set out the crucifix, arrange her foam pad, light her candle. Just as she was kneeling, ready to begin her devotions, she heard Oa's soft step at her door. She glanced over her shoulder.

"Oa? Would you like to come in?"

The child's hair was tangled from sleep, and she had pulled Isabel's black sweater on over her pajamas. She stepped inside the small room, and stood looking at the little crucifix.

"You can touch that, if you like," Isabel said. She held it out. Oa took it in her hand, frowning over the carved figure on the cross, tracing the thorny crown with one dark finger.

When she handed it back to Isabel, she said, "Raimu?"

"Raimu?" Isabel repeated. "I don't know that word, Oa."

Oa took another step, and then knelt beside Isabel, with a nod to the crucifix and the burning candle. "Raimu," she repeated. She shrugged, and spread her hands.

Isabel smiled at her. "Perhaps later you can make me understand, Oa. Right now I'm going to say my prayers. Thank you for joining me." She turned to the cross and the candle, and began, speaking slowly and clearly, hoping the child could understand some of the words.

SAINT MARY OF MAGDALA,
PATRONESS OF THOSE WHO ASK . . .

Isabel paused at the end of her devotions, eyes closed, searching in the silence for the source of her inspiration. It was not there, or she couldn't find it. She sighed, and snuffed out the candle. "We had better get you dressed, Oa," she said. "I think they're coming today to fix the medicator." She rose to replace the crucifix and the kneeler. As she turned to the door, she glanced up at the little camera in the corner, its light blinking at her like an unfocused eye. She murmured, "Do you suppose they enjoy my prayers?"

Oa's eyes moved from Isabel to the camera and back. Isabel wasn't sure she understood. But as they left the room, she saw that Oa glanced once more up at the camera. Isabel was sure she saw a quick, defiant blaze in Oa's dark eyes. She hoped they—whoever was watching—had seen it, too.

WHEN JIN-LI CHUNG spoke a cheerful greeting over the comm system, Isabel and Oa hurried out into the central room. The longshoreman was at the window, a wrapped package in one hand. A big redheaded woman was there as well, wearing a huge grin as she looked through the glass.

Oa exclaimed, "Ship lady!"

Isabel turned to see Oa's flashing white smile, a hand lifted in greeting to the redheaded woman. Isabel nodded to their visitors, laughing. "Good morning, Jin-Li," she said. "I gather Oa knows your companion."

The redheaded woman leaned closer to the glass. "Hey, kiddo," she said in a deep voice. "It's good to see you." She turned her eyes to Isabel. "Mother Burke. I'm Matty Phipps. I was crew on the transport from Virimund."

"So I understand," Isabel said. "You were kind to Oa."

"Mother Burke—" Jin-Li began, and glanced to the left, where Appleton stood, arms crossed, eyes watching the corridor.

"I think you should call me Isabel, Jin-Li."

Jin-Li's long eyes gleamed briefly. "Thank you. Isabel. Matty tells me the doctor kept Oa awake the whole journey."

Isabel felt the smile fade from her lips, and her skin went cold. "He kept her awake? You mean, all those months, alone in quarantine . . ."

"Right," Phipps said. Isabel saw the anger in the big woman's eyes, in the set of her long jaw. "Whole ship in twilight sleep except crew, Adetti, and the little girl."

A chill fury tightened Isabel's cheeks and prickled across her scalp. She gripped her cross. "Fourteen months," she breathed. She turned and gazed at Oa.

The child had taken her customary place, scrunched on her bed, the teddy bear in her arms. Her eyes searched Isabel's for reassurance. Isabel tried to smile at her, but her lips were stiff with anger. Fourteen months, alone, with only Adetti for company, and occasional visits from the ship lady. And still the child had not broken.

She turned back to the window, and her voice dropped. "Jin-Li. Do you have it?"

Jin-Li Chung held up the wrapped package. "I can send it in with your breakfast."

"Adetti?"

"Hasn't arrived at the Multiplex yet. But soon."

"Better not wait for breakfast then. Please ask Jay if he would bring the package in now, Jin-Li. I don't want this child to spend another day as a prisoner."

*   *   *

"ISABEL?" SIMON COULD hardly believe his ears. When his secretary had announced the call, he had been certain she was mistaken. "Isabel, aren't you in Seattle?"

"I am," she said. He heard the deep note in her voice. She was angry.

"Tell me," he said. He saw her in memory, the smooth scalp, the clear gray eyes, the set of her jaw when she lost her temper. He wished she had used a video phone.

"I have to be quick," she said. "They'll cut off the call if they know I'm making it."

"You mean—ExtraSolar? They're not letting you—"

"Simon. I can explain all that later. For now, listen, all right? You have to hear this."

She spoke swiftly, and Simon listened. He soon understood why she was angry, and why she had called. It wasn't for him, not a change of heart, but for the child. Still, foolishly, his heart lifted.

Within half an hour he had Hilda Kronin in his office again. Within an hour, he had invoked the authority of World Health and Welfare to demand an accounting from Paolo Adetti, Gretchen Boreson, and ExtraSolar Corporation over the treatment of an indigenous child from Virimund. Within two hours, Simon had a sample of medicator readouts from Adetti's examinations of the girl. By afternoon he had sent a terse report of events as he understood them to Marian Alexander at the Magdalene Mother House in Tuscany, and his secretary had booked his overnight flight on the sonic cruiser from Geneva to Seattle. He left his office early, needing to explain the situation to Anna, and dreading it.

She asked, as he knew she would, "Why you, Simon? Why does it have to be you?" Her voice was high and light, and when she was upset, it tended to shrill. She pressed her fingers to her mouth as if she knew it.

Middle age was not dealing kindly with Anna. The gray in her once lustrous brown hair had faded it to a muddy color Simon had no name for. Her skin, once lustrous and smooth, had grown sallow. She worked too hard, of course. And Simon, though he was the same age as his wife, forty-two, had the sort of wiry body that changed only slowly with the passing of years. Sometimes he felt her eyes on him when he was

dressing, a look of vague resentment that he stayed lean while her figure thickened. He touched her hand, filled with a pity that did nothing
to restore the affection between them. He was deeply sorry to have hurt
her, and filled with added compunction over the joy he felt, despite
everything, at being called to Isabel's side.

"Anna," he said. "I'm the advisory physician. It's my job to super-
vise disadvantaged populations. This girl falls into that category."

"You have people who could go in your place."

He hesitated. It was true, he could send someone else. But the medicator reports hinted at something very strange about the child, something that fired him with curiosity. "You know, Anna," he said slowly.
"I want to go. This is why I do this work, why I've always done it, because I think I have something important to offer."

"I don't know what else I can do, Simon." Anna pushed aside the pa-
pers before her, and rested her head on her hands. She looked exhausted.
He had come home to find her immersed in a stack of rewritable flexcopies, struggling with the school budget. Even in her unhappiness, she
would return to the problem, would wrestle with the numbers far into
the night. It was her nature to persevere, to grapple with a problem far
past the point where a less stubborn person would have surrendered. It
was both her strength and her weakness. When she woke tomorrow, her
eyes would be shadowed with fatigue. He knew he was not helping, and
he tried to speak gently.

"What do you mean? There's nothing for you to do."

She lifted her head and fixed him with a gaze full of misery. "You
know what I mean, Simon. I can't fight this. I can't even understand it."

He gazed down at her, wishing he could speak some words of comfort. He wished she didn't look so—defeated, he decided, was the
word. As if she had lost a battle.

"You don't need to fight anything," he said.

She gave a bitter laugh.

"I'm sorry about all of this, Anna. But whatever this ESC physician
is up to—Adetti, his name is—it's going to take someone with authority
to take him in hand. To force ESC to an accounting."

"It sounds as if you've already decided the case, Simon. Or *she*
has." She spoke the pronoun as if it burned her mouth.

He set his jaw. There was no time for an argument. "I'm trying to reserve judgment." He bent to pick up his valise. "But they've been keeping Isabel—"

Anna winced at the name, and dropped her head again. He made himself put a hand on her shoulder.

Anna knew, of course. She had guessed, and he had admitted everything when she asked. She had listened to the recitation, her face drawn with pain and anger. She had asked a few questions. She had said nothing of her fury and resentment, but they had been plain in her clouded eyes and her tight voice. When she offered him forgiveness, he had said something, stumbled over some hollow expression of regret and shame. He had been in pain himself.

None of this could help Anna now. "I'm sorry, Anna. ExtraSolar has kept Isabel cut off from outside communication for almost a week. I need to find out why."

The beep of a car horn sounded from the street, and Simon reached for the door handle.

"You could have at least let me drive you to the airport," Anna said, her eyes bleak.

"It's not necessary," he said. "My aide is already here."

"You did that purposely," she grated. "To shut me out."

"No," he said firmly. "I didn't. It was arranged for me."

"Simon, wait—we should talk."

He shook his head, and leaned to kiss her cheek. It felt cold and dry against his lips. "There's no time now, Anna. I have to catch this flight. I'll call you from Seattle."

She leaned against the doorjamb to watch him climb into the car. She didn't say anything further. "Get some rest," he called before he closed the door. She just shook her head, her lips compressed. When the car turned the corner, she was still there, outlined by yellow light from the foyer, an unremarkable, solitary figure.

JIN-LI HAD FINISHED a class, had a brief meal in the cafeteria, and was getting ready for bed when the room comm buzzed. "Chung here."

Matty Phipps's voice sounded tinny over the speaker. "Johnnie? Not in bed, are you? Something's on down at the infirmary—can you come down? And hurry."

The Seattle night was cold and damp. Shreds of gray cloud filtered the moonlight and drifting patches of fog shrouded the waters of Puget Sound. Jin-Li pulled on a Port Force jacket and followed Phipps at a trot through the complex of barracks. Phipps had said only, "Adetti's at the quarantine room," as they dashed through the Multiplex. It was after eleven, and the Rec Fac was dark.

Phipps was right. A van was drawn up before the infirmary entrance, and inside, lights were on. The shuttered blinds on the external windows were closed, but the lights made silhouettes of people walking back and forth inside.

"Moving them," Jin-Li muttered.

"That's what I thought," Phipps said. They slowed their steps as they approached the building. There was no one in the van that they could see. They strolled past the entrance, hands stuffed in their jacket pockets. "I don't know what we can do," Phipps said. "But I didn't want that girl to just disappear."

"Right." Jin-Li scanned the street. Nothing moved. The sounds of the city filtered through the Multiplex, an occasional siren, motor noises, faint and distant bursts of music and laughter. There was no sound from the infirmary, but they could see three people outside the quarantine bubble. As they walked by, another light went on beyond the bubble. They supposed the priest and the girl had been awakened. They reached a corner, and leaned against a wall in a pool of shadow, watching the silhouettes moving against the light inside the building.

"What can we do, Johnnie?" Phipps asked in a low voice.

Jin-Li straightened, and took a last look at the infirmary. "Matty, you stay here. Keep an eye out, and don't let them see you. I'm going to get a cart."

IMMEDIATELY AFTER THE evening meal, Isabel had felt unaccountably, irresistibly sleepy. She thought perhaps it was the excitement of speaking to Simon, after all the months of silence. He had sounded just as she remembered, his voice even, matter-of-fact, giving away none of his feelings. She had spoken as fast as she could, afraid the call would be ended at any moment. She had outlined the situation, told him of the mystery surrounding Oa, promised him copies of the medicator reports. They said good-bye without saying anything personal, but as she broke the connection, her heart hammered in her ribs. She passed three sheafs of hardcopies through the quarantine bubble to Jay Appleton, to be given to Jin-Li Chung, and she waved her thanks to the longshoreman through the window.

The rest of the day passed unremarkably. Adetti didn't come. Gretchen Boreson stopped by to speak to Isabel through the window, but she didn't press her, as she usually did, to allow the doctor to conduct more medicator tests. Cole Markham had been at her elbow, and he avoided Isabel's eyes. She and Oa had eaten dinner together, and when she saw that Oa, like herself, was yawning, she decided they might as well both be in bed.

She helped Oa into the flannel pajamas and smoothed the covers over her. It seemed that Oa was asleep before she reached her own room. She left the door half-open, and fell into her own bed without even brushing her teeth. Sleep was a heavy hand pressing her down, blurring her thoughts. Simon, she thought. Simon will take care of it. Tomorrow.

When she woke, her mouth was fuzzy and dry, and her head ached. She blinked against the brightness of the lights. It seemed to take a long time to wash her face, brush her teeth, and pull on her clothes. There was no sound from the outer room, and she supposed Oa, like herself, had slept long and hard.

Isabel rolled the stool away from the wall, and took her kneeler out from beneath the bed. She was just setting the flame to the candle for her morning devotions when the thought struck her. She glanced at her reader.

It was the Memorial of the Japanese Martyrs. And it was ten in the morning. She had slept more than twelve hours.

A rush of adrenaline cleared her mind. She thrust herself to her feet, and threw open the door to her room.

The covers on Oa's bed were thrown back, the pillow askew. The teddy bear lay on its plush tummy on the floor, its stub of a tail pointing at the ceiling.

"Oa?" Isabel cried. She ran to the central surgery, but it was empty except for the broken medicator. She took two steps to the little bathroom, and pulled that door open. Empty. She whirled, seeking someplace, anyplace, the child could be hiding, even looking under the bed, going back into her own room as if Oa might have slipped past her. Oa was not there.

Isabel strode to the door and banged on it, calling out, "Guard! Guard! Who's there? What's happened?" No one answered.

9

JIN-LI PARKED THE cart in the alley that separated the five-story Admin building from the low-roofed infirmary. The two of them watched as a tall quarantine-suited figure emerged from the infirmary, carrying a small form wrapped in a dark blanket. Steady rain streaked the infirmary's dimly lit windows and slicked the dark streets. A black van, with tinted windows and no insignia, was waiting in front of the infirmary. The driver jumped out, shielding his face from the rain with one hand and opening the back door with the other. The man in the quarantine suit slid into the back seat with his burden, and the driver shut the door. No one else appeared.

"Just the girl, then," Phipps muttered.

"Yeah." Jin-Li waited until the van's engine started, and its lights came on, before starting the cart's light motor.

"Bastards."

"No argument." The van began to move, passing their alley, picking up speed as it moved toward the Rec Fac.

"Better keep a good distance."

"I will." When the van had passed the Rec Fac, Jin-Li let the cart roll down the sloping alley and into the street. There was no other traffic, nothing to hide behind. The cart, its headlights off, chugged through the murky streets, following the van's amber taillights. The windshield wipers slapped left and right, spraying rainwater. The van's taillights flashed red when the driver applied the brakes, and Jin-Li slowed the cart.

Phipps leaned forward, peering into the darkness. "Where do you think?" she growled.

"Don't know." Jin-Li swung the cart around a corner. The black van was making a right at the next intersection. "Looks like they're leaving the Multiplex."

"Bastards," Phipps repeated.

Beyond the restricted streets of the Multiplex, other traffic appeared. The van turned west toward the Sound, and then took a sharp right up a steep entrance into a six-lane throughway. Jin-Li turned on the cart's headlights, and tried to blend with the light nighttime traffic. Theirs was the only Port Force cart, but trucks, cars, other vans whirled past. The little motor whined, struggling to keep up speed.

Phipps gave a short laugh. "Like riding in a can-opener."

"I know it. Hope the battery holds up."

"Got a spare?"

"Yes. Have to stop to change it, though."

Phipps grunted. "Keeping my fingers crossed."

They cast each other a look of relief when the van took an exit from the throughway. It turned left when it reached the surface street, and drove north along the darkened waterfront, following the curve of the bay. Jin-Li doused the headlights again, and concentrated on the van's taillights. In moments it came to a stop before a controlled-access gate.

"Who lives there?" Phipps asked, gesturing with her long arm. Beyond the guarded gate a thicket of residential towers rose into the mist. Discreet lights set into the landscaping picked out their silhouettes and gleamed on exaggeratedly tall windows and miniature scrollwork balconies.

"Mostly ESC executives. Nobody else could afford those apartments." Jin-Li parked the cart at an unmarked curb that was masked by the drooping branches of a tall cedar.

They climbed out, and stood in the rain, watching. A guard leaned from a lighted booth to talk with someone through the van's open window, then moved to a control board. The long iron gate slid silently back on well-oiled wheels, opening just enough to admit the van. It closed again, just as silently, as the van disappeared between two of the towers, taillights winking out one by one as it turned and disappeared.

Jin-Li and Phipps stood impotently beneath the cedar tree. Cold raindrops dripped past their caps and down their necks.

"That's it," Jin-Li said glumly. "Far as we can go."

And Phipps growled, "Bastards."

OA OPENED HER eyes to a dazzling brightness, and squeezed them shut again. Something had happened. She had slept hard, with no dreams. Her head ached, and the light that blazed in her eyes was too bright, not the light of her room at the infirmary, her room with Isabel.

She heard Doctor's voice, and someone else's, a woman's. She had woken to some new place. Some new power, greater than Isabel's, had moved her while she slept.

For a long time she lay without moving, wishing it was a mistake. Perhaps when she opened her eyes a second time, she would be back in the familiar cramped room, with the reader on the chair and the fuzzy toy. And Isabel.

But she knew it was not a mistake. This was not the infirmary. The woman's voice was not Isabel's. The scratchy blanket that covered her was unfamiliar, and the brilliant light burned even through her closed eyelids.

She waited for the dull ache in her head to recede. Her throat and mouth burned with thirst, and she was too hot under her blanket. When the voices stopped, she waited for the space of a few breaths, and then, cautiously, she lifted her eyelids.

A more different place than the infirmary Oa could not have

imagined. Sunlight poured through tall windows, glittered off a bay of gray-green water, shone on white mountains in the distance. She lay on a couch upholstered in an unlikely gold color. A white woven fabric covered the floor. There were chairs and tables everywhere, real wood chairs and tables, and a variety of large and small objects for which Oa had no name, a riot of colors and shapes.

Slowly, she sat up, letting her bare feet touch the carpet. Its spongy softness invited her toes to sink into it. The view of water and sky and mountain also invited her, tantalized her, mocked her lack of freedom.

Trying to make no noise, Oa stood. She took one careful step forward, and then turned to look behind her.

It lurked in the farthest corner of the room, its black looping tubes and silver syrinxes poised as always over a white-sheeted bed, awaiting its chance. A spider machine. And this one, Oa could guess, had all its parts intact.

She backed away, toward the tall windows, as far from the medicator as she could get. She tugged her tangled hair, wondering where she was, how she had gotten here, what was to be done with her. She turned toward the wind-ruffled water of the bay. It looked cold. She pressed her hands to the glass, and that was cold, too. She leaned her forehead against it, letting it cool her brow, and she called out to Raimu-ke, silently, desperately, for help. She supposed Raimu-ke was lost to her. And now, Isabel was lost to her, too.

A door opened behind her, and she tensed. Her nostrils flared, hoping to detect Isabel's clean, airy scent, but what she caught was something cloying and spicy, something not-real. Definitely not-Isabel. Someone was moving toward her. Oa's legs felt weak, and she began a slow slide to the floor, her cheek grazing the chilly glass, her hands gripping, and then losing, the sill. She folded in on herself, her head on her knees, her arms around them, making herself as small as possible. If only she were brave, like Isabel, standing up with her shoulders straight and her eyes bright. But she was too small, and too afraid, and now, again, utterly alone.

The voice was brittle. "Good morning!" it cried. "You're awake! Look, I have some lovely muffins here, and milk. Children like milk, don't they? Come now, don't huddle there on the floor! You'll get dirty. Come and eat something."

Now Oa knew who it was. She had never been in the same room with her, but she had heard her voice, and seen her face. It was the pale lady with the white hair, the one whose face twitched and quivered. She sometimes came to the infirmary with Doctor to look at Oa through the not-mirror. There had been something ravening in her face, a deep and intense hunger as if she wanted to bite Oa, taste her flesh, sip at her blood the way the spider machine did.

Oa tightened her grip on her knees. There was nowhere to run.

"Come now, honey. Come drink your milk. We're going to have fun, you and I!" The pale lady's voice grated like stones scraping together. "Come on, now," she said more sharply. "I know you understand me. Don't make me come and get you. You're too old for that."

Oa's head snapped up. Did she know? Had she guessed?

Slowly, Oa released her knees. She put her trembling hands on the windowsill and stood up, still looking out at the bleak vista of cold water and icy peaks. Oh, Raimu-ke, she prayed. Help me. Help me. Slowly, slowly, she turned around, and put her back to the window.

The pale lady was not dressed in a quarantine suit.

She wore a dress of midnight black. Her hair, white and shining as the mountains, was pulled tightly back from her face. Her lips were a kind of vibrant pink that was lovely on the fish in Mother Ocean and somehow revolting on the pale lady's mouth. Her cheek jerked at irregular intervals, a spasm that distorted her pink lips and tugged at her eyelid. Her hand, hovering over a tray with glasses and plates, also twitched and trembled. She tried to smile with her jittering mouth as she sat down on the gold couch. The tray waited between her and Oa, on a low round table with a raised edge.

"There, now," the pale lady exclaimed. "Isn't that better? Come now! Let's have breakfast together, just us two girls!" She nudged a glass forward with one finger. Oa understood she was afraid to pick it up, afraid her shaking hand would spill it. "Drink it up, won't you? Let's be friends. You can call me Gretchen." The ferocity of her pink-lipped smile made Oa's stomach turn.

But she was thirsty, so thirsty. It was making her head ache more. One of the glasses held something blue-white, unappealing. The other held some kind of fruit juice. Its fragrance drew her. It didn't look as if the pale lady was going to come after her, or even as if she had strength for it. She was very thin, and she had bony white fingers, the hands of a skeleton.

Warily, Oa walked across the soft carpet, keeping the low table between her and the pale lady. She bent to pick up the glass of juice.

Gretchen watched her hungrily. Oa pulled back her hand.

Gretchen's trembling lips parted. "Come on, Oa," she hissed. "The juice is fine. Drink!"

Oa's thirst overwhelmed her. She watched to see if the lady would get up, reach for her. She didn't. Oa put out her hand again, picked up the glass. The juice was red and tart, tasting of sunshine and soil. She drank it all, and set the glass back on the tray.

Gretchen snatched up the glass with her sharp white fingers. She turned it upside down, letting the drops Oa had left trickle past her vivid lips. She put a finger inside to wipe up two or three more, and then she sucked her finger clean. She put her tongue out, and licked the rim of the glass, inside and outside, all the way around. Oa stared at her, mystified.

Gretchen set the glass down at last, and rose. Oa took a step backward, but Gretchen was no longer looking at her. Instead, she glanced around the room. "I think you have everything you need," she said offhandedly. "There's a bathroom just through there." She pointed to a side door. "I guess you should brush your teeth and so forth. I'll be back later."

She crossed the room, the narrow high heels of her shoes making no sound on the thick carpet. She passed the medicator without glancing at its array of drooping wires and tubes, its lifeless readout screen, its scanning hood. She disappeared through the door, and Oa listened to the snick of the lock. It was a familiar sound. She had learned it very well on the ship.

SIMON FOLLOWED COLE Markham through the carpeted corridors of the Multiplex, and up to the General Administrator's office. Markham was new to him, but Gretchen Boreson was not. He remembered her as an intense, driven woman with a quick mind and a burning ambition. He was shocked, when he entered her office, to see how thin she had become, to notice the tremors that marred her features. Then he saw Isabel, and for the moment, he forgot everything else.

She stood by the mullioned windows, her slight figure framed by the rain-blurred view of the city. "Simon," she said. "Thank you for coming."

He stood still for a moment, drinking in the sight of her. Her collar gleamed white against her black shirt. The carved wooden cross with its twisting flame hung on her breast as always. Her eyes—her magnificent eyes—shone like gray crystals in her slender face.

"Isabel," Simon said huskily. "Are you all right?"

Boreson stepped forward before Isabel could answer, holding out her thin white hand. "Dr. Edwards," she said. "It's always a pleasure to have you here in Seattle."

Isabel's eyes flashed something, and Simon turned abruptly to Boreson. "What's the meaning of all this, Administrator?" he demanded.

Boreson's extended hand trembled. She withdrew it hastily, and pressed it to her stomach. "Dr. Edwards, I had hoped . . ."

He cocked one eyebrow. "Evidence suggests that ExtraSolar has committed actionable offenses against Mother Burke and against a child, in direct violation of its charters. To say nothing of the guidelines set up by World Health and Welfare."

"We can explain," she protested. "There are reasons for everything. There's been a misunderstanding."

"Misunderstanding? You mean you did not restrain Isabel Burke against her will? You did not transport an indigenous child away from her home world without demonstrable cause? If not, then, yes, there has been a misunderstanding." The anger Simon had been containing made his voice hard. He was ready for a fight.

Boreson, though, was not strong enough. Faintly, she protested, "She's not indigenous," before her face colored, and then paled, leaving her skin white as paper. She groped for her chair. Her trembling hand did not quite reach it, and she stumbled. The muscles of her cheek jerked, and jerked again.

Simon and Isabel both stepped forward, but Simon was closer. "Administrator. Sit down. You don't seem to be feeling well." He helped Boreson into her chair, and touched her wrist with his fingers. It was icy cold. He glanced up at Isabel, and she raised her eyebrows and gave a slight shrug.

Cole Markham, his forehead creasing with concern and confusion, said, "Administrator? Shall I call your doctor?"

Boreson shook her head, and pressed one palm to the side of her face, as if to stop the spasms. "No, Cole, don't do that. I'm just tired."

Simon glanced around the office. In one corner was an ornate brass coat hanger holding a black fur coat. "Mr. Markham, get the Administrator's coat, will you?" he said.

Markham brought the coat. Simon helped Boreson into it, watching her closely as he did so. The spasms in her face seemed random, sometimes jerking her eyelid almost closed, sometimes pulling up the corner of her mouth. Her hands shook as she thrust her arms through the sleeves.

She settled in her chair, the fur collar close under her chin. After a moment, her color improved. Simon said, "Administrator, surely you realized the events here at the Multiplex would attract the scrutiny of World Health."

"Dr. Adetti will be here in a moment," Boreson said. "He can explain the situation. We thought—that is, he made the decision to bring the girl here, to Earth, where she could be properly examined. And—and protected. Cared for."

"Cared for? Was there no one on Virimund to care for her?"

"Please, Dr. Edwards, just wait for Dr. Adetti. He was there, and he explains better than I can. I'll have some coffee sent in, shall I? And we'll just wait for him."

Simon watched her shaking hands tug at the coat, pulling it tighter. Her eyes met his, and then slid quickly away. She made a vague gesture. "I'm sorry, Dr. Edwards. I've been tired lately. Cole, ask Cecilia to bring in some coffee, will you?"

Markham hurried out of the office, and Simon turned again to Isabel.

She put out her hand. With a wry smile, he took it. "It's good to see you," he said inadequately.

"Simon." She squeezed his fingers a fraction of a second before she released them. "Thank you so much for being here." She glanced over at Boreson, who sat with her head tipped against the headrest of her chair, her trembling eyelids closed. Isabel murmured, "They've taken Oa away, and they won't tell me where she is."

He could hardly tear his eyes from her. Her nearness frustrated him. He felt such a strong desire to touch her, to fold her in his arms, that he almost took a step back, away from the magnetic pull of her slender body. Instead, he folded his arms across his chest. "Do you have the rest of the medicator reports?"

She waved at a small pile of cartons and luggage waiting by the door. "In my things."

"Good." He glanced over his shoulder again at Boreson. "There's something very unusual about this child, Isabel. Something—"

Isabel watched him with a familiar intensity. Whenever anyone in their care was in trouble, was in danger—especially a child—he had seen this look. "She's all right, isn't she, Simon? Healthy?"

"I think so. I should know more soon."

Gretchen Boreson stirred, and opened her eyes. Simon turned to face her. "Administrator? When can I see the child from Virimund?"

Boreson said stiffly, "I don't really know. That decision will be made by Dr. Adetti."

"Adetti!" Isabel spat the name. "Simon, do you know what Adetti did?"

Boreson said, "Mother Burke . . . please . . ."

Isabel touched her cross. With the deep note in her voice, she said, "He kept her awake, Simon. The whole journey. Fourteen months in space, and no twilight sleep. He put her under the medicator so often she's terrified of it. He kept her awake with no one for company and nothing to do but be examined like a bug on a slide!"

The secretary came in with a coffee service, and they fell silent while she arranged cups and spoons. When she had left, closing the door behind her, Simon said, "Administrator Boreson, I can hardly believe that you would sanction such behavior. Did you know?"

Boreson fidgeted, playing with a coffee spoon. "I didn't know he intended that. Perhaps it wasn't good judgment on Dr. Adetti's part—but the situation is unique. We're struggling with it, too, you understand."

"Bring her back," Isabel said simply.

Boreson looked up at Isabel with an ice-blue gaze, and her voice was cold. "Dr. Adetti feels she's better off where she is."

"You contracted with the Magdalenes for me to study the girl. Let me do my job."

"Dr. Adetti says you have interfered with his work."

Simon cleared his throat. "He had the girl for fourteen solid months," he said. "I would judge he's had his chance."

Boreson tapped the spoon against her desk. Her color had improved, her thin cheeks tinged with pink. "Dr. Adetti says he needs just a little more time. We didn't realize—" Her eyes swept Isabel again. "We didn't realize that Mother Burke would try to interrupt his research. We will contact her Mother House and cancel our contract."

Isabel said, "Do have any idea what you're doing to this child? Do you care?"

Boreson pursed her bright pink lips. "She is being looked after."

"I—" Isabel began.

Boreson lifted her chin. The skin of her throat pulled in vertical lines. "ExtraSolar received an extraordinary empowerment from the charter regents. Because of this extraordinary situation. In fact—" A gleam of triumph brightened her eyes. "In fact, we've applied for approval to bring two more subjects here from Virimund."

"Subjects!" Isabel exclaimed. Simon touched her arm.

Simon said firmly, "We will take this to a review board, Administrator."

Boreson stiffened. "You don't have that authority."

Simon favored her with his coldest smile, the one he saved for head nurses and recalcitrant bureaucrats. "But I do," he said. "I have the authority of public opinion. World Health carries a lot of weight with the media."

Boreson stood up. She turned the spoon in her fingers, and it caught the light, sparkling in her hand. "ExtraSolar has observed all regulations regarding this child. She is not, in fact, an indigene, but the descendant of a colony long believed lost. We are fulfilling our responsibility to the expansion movement to fully investigate the fate of that colony and its descendants."

"Good," Simon said mildly. "You can say all that to the review board."

The administrator dropped the coffee spoon onto her desk with a rattle of silver on wood. "I don't like being threatened, Dr. Edwards," she said, with a flash of her old intensity.

He let his smile fade and his own voice grow cold. "And I don't like being manipulated," he said. "Isabel, I'll help you carry your things down. Administrator—" He nodded to her. "I'll be in touch."

10

A WEAK SUNSHINE briefly overcame the rain. Isabel tipped her face up to feel it on her cheeks, breathing deeply of the damp air. Simon stood beside her on the sidewalk as they waited for a driver. Boreson's secretary stood with them, twittering something about linens in the guest suite. Isabel didn't listen. She would have preferred a hotel or apartment away from the Multiplex, but she wanted to stay close, hoping for word of Oa.

Simon didn't speak until they were in the car, with the partition to the driver's compartment closed. "The World Health office will find a room for me by tonight," he said. "You'll have to put up with me till then."

"Of course," Isabel said. She gave him a rueful smile. "You look tired, Simon." She thought how ordinary his face was, really, lean, slightly lined, with deep furrows framing his narrow mouth. Those furrows deepened when he smiled, making her irrational heart turn over. It made no sense, of course. But there was nothing rational about falling in love.

He answered her smile with a weary one of his own. "I'm all right," he said. "But I didn't sleep much on the plane. Anna was upset when I left."

A fresh wave of guilt made Isabel's cheeks hot. "Anna knows . . ."

He nodded, his face grim. "She guessed. And I couldn't lie to her." He lifted a shoulder in a deprecating way. "Anna is a remarkably persistent woman. It's one of her assets."

"Oh, Simon. I'm so sorry. About hurting Anna—about everything. I'm sorry I didn't say good-bye to you. I just had no words for it."

He put up one hand. "Don't, Isabel. There's no need. I understand."

She twisted her hands together. "Simon, Oa must be terrified. We have to find her."

"I'll call the Seattle office, but what I told Boreson was true. They'll have to bring the regents together, and for that they have to go through channels."

"How long will it take?"

The car rolled to a stop in front of a foambrick building. Thick rhododendron bushes flanked its glass doors, and an awning bore the circled star logo. Simon said tiredly, "It can take days, sometimes even weeks, to convene a review board."

Isabel's heart sank. "Oh, no, Simon. What can we do?"

"First, I'm going to look at the rest of the medicator reports. Try not to worry, Isabel."

"I can't help it." The driver opened her door, and she climbed out, saying over her shoulder, "She's just a child, and she's alone and frightened." A doorman hurried out to help the driver unload the car, a porter following with a rolling dolly. Isabel watched to make sure that none of the cartons were left behind, and then followed the doorman up the steps. "And I don't know what they might do to her. I don't even know why they want her."

"I don't think she's in danger," Simon murmured as they followed the porter across the faux-marble lobby. "They need her, or at least they believe they do. They won't hurt her."

"There are different kinds of hurt, Simon." She tried not to see the look that crossed his face, the reminder of his own hurt, and hers. She had to concentrate on Oa.

*   *   *

OA KNELT TO sniff the white carpet. It had that machine smell, the not-fragrance that was now familiar to her. The little bathroom had white towels and bits of white pottery. There was a round mirror on the wall, with a scalloped silvery edge. Oa touched the glass, and put her ear to it, but she couldn't tell if it was a trick.

She circled the big room, looking at the pieces of bright glass that rested on every surface, in every niche. One was a transparent oblong with yellow and blue blobs suspended in it, looking a bit like blurry fish. Another, slender, with slashes of scarlet and gold, reminded her of sunsets over Mother Ocean. There were others, all different shapes and colors. None seemed to have a purpose.

When she drew near the medicator, she stopped and turned to re-trace her steps. She trailed her fingers along the cold glass of the tall windows. The sunshine had given way again to the dreary, endless rain-fall. Did it always rain like that here, she wondered? Perhaps the sun of Earth was not very strong.

She looked out over the choppy gray waters of the bay. There were floating craft there, but they were oddly shaped and clumsy-looking, not the sleek, swift canoes of the three islands. These not-canoes were tall, with shahto built right on their decks. They had no oars that she could see and they floated aimlessly to and fro, to and fro, going nowhere. To the north, she saw a building with a great white cross on it, and another with a sort of wheel at the top. She wondered what they meant.

She had been foolish to think things could be different, to think things could ever change. Probably Isabel knew, now, that Oa was an an-chen. That she was a not-person. Probably Isabel had let the pale lady take her, bring her here, where the spider machine worked. Perhaps Oa would never see Isabel again. Something hurt in her chest at that thought, and the pain spread up into her throat. She crouched beside the window to rest her forehead on the sill, closing her eyes as she thought of Isabel.

Oa remembered the airy scent of Isabel's skin, the sweetness of her breath. She remembered the touch of Isabel's hand in the darkness, warm fingers closing around Oa's as if they were anchens together. Or people. She thought of Isabel's house with all the women in it, the priests, and the girls who would be priests. She remembered Isabel kneeling before the tiny flame of her candle, and her prayer that began, "Saint Mary of Magdala . . ."

When Oa stopped remembering, she opened her eyes and stared out over the gray water to the white mountains. She didn't even have the fuzzy toy now. Oa had nothing.

When Doctor came to make her lie down under the spider machine, she found herself wishing the spider machine would take all her blood, take away her mind, suck out all her feelings. She hardly noticed that Doctor no longer wore a quarantine suit, that his bare fingers were cold and hard. It didn't matter.

ISABEL AND SIMON spread the medicator reports on the table, the couches, the chairs, the floor of her suite. For two hours, Simon pored through them, while Isabel unpacked her things in one of the two bedrooms and then stood by the window, holding Oa's teddy bear. The little soft, inanimate thing felt lonely in her hands. She set it in the windowsill, face turned out to the flat roofs and narrow streets. The rain had closed in again. She could barely make out the outlines of the Seattle hills rising beyond the Multiplex. It lent a feeling of intimacy to the room. If she hadn't been so worried about Oa, it would have been a perilous feeling, she and Simon alone together. But at this moment, Oa was all she could think of.

In the late afternoon, she ordered coffee and a plate of sandwiches. When they arrived, she set them on a small side table and went to touch Simon's shoulder.

"Simon, you'd better take a break. You must be exhausted."

He was bent over a sheaf of flexcopies laid out on a chair. "You're right," he said, straightening, rubbing his back. "In any case, just as you said, the figures hardly change."

"What do you think is happening?" Isabel poured coffee for both of them as Simon came to sit across from her. Isabel avoided Simon's eyes, aware of their closeness. "Oa is well, Simon, isn't she?"

"I don't find anything to indicate otherwise." He took a sip of coffee, and leaned back with a sigh of fatigue. "Your instincts were right about the hormone levels. They're remarkably stable. And look at this—" He reached behind him to snag one of the flexcopies, and ran down it with his forefinger. "This designation—" He tapped an entry that was a mix of letters and numbers. "It's an antibody the medicator doesn't recognize. Monoclonal, apparently, so I would guess it's a specific immunological response, undoubtedly to a virus native to Virimund. It could be the reason Adetti kept the girl in quarantine. You were with her for four days, right?"

Isabel nodded.

"We should test you, too, see if you've developed the antibody."

"There were hydro workers exposed, at the Virimund power park."

Simon shook his head. "I saw all their scans. They're routinely transmitted to World Health in Geneva. I didn't see this." He reached for a sandwich. "All the imaging data is missing, by the way. Chemical spectroscopy might have already identified the virus, but Adetti kept some things back."

Isabel had a sandwich on her plate, but she couldn't eat it. She drank coffee, looking away from Simon to the streaks of fresh rain on the windows. "Adetti's fixed on his own purpose. He doesn't see Oa as a human being."

"No," Simon said. "I'm sure he doesn't. He sees her as an opportunity."

Isabel set down her cup, and looked into Simon's eyes. "For what, Simon? What in God's name does he want with her?"

"I don't know. Whatever it is that's strange about her, he plans to profit from it." He shook his head slightly. "He's not much of a scientist, I'm afraid. It looks like he kept doing the same tests over and over, hoping the answer would fall into his lap by chance. Hoping the medicator would do his job for him." He sighed and rubbed his eyes again. "Ambition without ability. It's a damned disaster waiting to happen."

"And Gretchen Boreson?"

Simon shrugged. "I imagine he's convinced her there's profit in it. ESC always needs cash, always has big plans. There's nothing wrong with that, essentially. But the way they achieve it is what organizations like World Health have to monitor." He laughed a little. "Big business is both a curse and a blessing, Isabel. They work wonders, sometimes, and feed a lot of people. Profit is a powerful motive, but it's a danger-ous one."

"Oa isn't a business," Isabel said bitterly. "She's a little girl. We were just making progress—she had begun to talk to me, and to trust me—I allowed her to trust me! She will think I abandoned her." She stood up, moving away to the window. She picked up the teddy bear from the sill and hugged it to her. "We must find her, Simon, and soon. We must."

JIN-LI PUT IN a long day unloading a shuttle and transferring its cargo of rhodium to the insulated storage bay. The containers were small and heavy, and it took several trips to finish the job. When the last container was in the storage bay, Jin-Li shut the door with a bang, and went in search of Matty Phipps.

Matty was in the cafeteria, hollow-eyed with lack of sleep. She lifted a freckled hand in greeting. "Johnnie. You as tired as me?"

"Yes." Jin-Li slipped into a chair opposite. "Did you locate the priest?"

"I haven't seen her, but I found the driver who took her from Ad-min to the guest suites. Got a buddy over in the garage. She had some-body with her, too, he said."

"Who?"

"I don't know, some man. Not too tall, little bit older."

"Not a priest?"

"Well, apparently not. No collar." Phipps grinned. "Has hair."

Jin-Li smiled a little. "Lots of priests have hair, Matty."

"Yeah, I know. But this Magdalene . . . don't you find it sort of strange?"

Jin-Li shrugged. "I don't know. Everyone takes their own path, I guess."

"Yeah, I guess. Just seems like she gave up a lot."

"We need to tell her where the girl is."

"Sure, Johnnie. But she won't be able to do anything about it."

"Maybe she will. If we help."

"That's a secure complex," Phipps said, shaking her head. "And we don't know which building she's in, either."

Jin-Li frowned, thinking. "The question we need to ask is why they moved her. And why, after ExtraSolar brought the Magdalene here, they're keeping her away from the girl."

"Oh, that's an easy one."

"It is?"

"Sure. They thought they could hire this Enquirer, then use her to cover their asses. They didn't know she'd have a mind of her own."

"That makes sense, Matty. She stepped right in the middle of whatever's on."

"Yeah." Phipps leaned forward, her pale blue eyes intent. "And listen, Johnnie, I watched that bastard for fourteen months. He's obsessed with the little girl."

"Obsessed? You mean, sexually?"

"No, no, that's the strange thing. He examined her constantly, had her under the medicator every damn day. Yet he never touched her, not skin to skin. Frankly, if I had thought it was something else, I would have reported him to the captain. But he wore a quarantine suit every time he went into her room. I know, because he kept me on the hop replacing them!"

"So he won't harm her," Jin-Li said slowly.

"Well, he didn't in all that time," Phipps said, leaning back now, crossing her arms. "But who knows when the poor kid reaches the end of her rope?"

They sat in silence for a few more minutes. Jin-Li's eyes were dry with lack of sleep. Dinner had tasted like sawdust. "Come on, Matty. Let's go over to the guest suites. See if we know anyone in housekeeping."

SIMON SPENT THE evening on the wavephone in Isabel's suite. She paced, listening to his side of the conversations, marveling at his patience with the web of bureaucracy he was trying to pierce. They had been at it for hours, and it was dark beyond the window, a dark that came early to this rainsoaked northern city.

When Simon finally put the wavephone back in its cradle, he sighed and rested his head in his hands. "Isabel, there's nothing more I can do tonight. The regents are agreeable to the review board, and they'll convene it as soon as the members can get to Seattle. But apparently the extraordinary empowerment provision allows Adetti and Boreson to isolate the child. They claimed there were concerns about contamination and infection, both to her and to others."

"It's not true." Isabel's voice scraped in her throat, and she told herself she must drink some water. She tried to think when they had eaten.

"I know," Simon said wearily. He stood up, and came to join her, looking out into the sodden, joyless night. She noticed, with mingled sadness and relief, that he stood an arm's length away. "You know, Isabel, the medicator is a great tool, but it's only a tool, and only as effective as the people who use it. Adetti's not much of a physician."

"I don't suppose they send the best doctors to the expansion worlds," Isabel said. She managed a small smile at Simon. "We need them too much here."

He gave a dry chuckle. "Where we make them fight political battles."

"Yes. That, too." He gazed out over the flat roofs of the Multiplex, and she watched his profile, the strong line of his jaw and throat. His hair had just begun to gray at the temples. Her fingers tingled with the desire to touch it, to smooth it back from his cheek. She tore her eyes away, back to the stacks of hardcopies and flexcopies scattered across the table.

Isabel knew Simon to be an intuitive diagnostician, a perceptive researcher, and a tireless worker for the rights of his patients. She had seen him put in twelve-hour days in the camp clinic in the Victoria Desert, and then spend hours more talking to Geneva and other World Health offices around the globe, summoning support, money, supplies. He had worked that way for years, and in her own field, so had Anna. They had lived apart as much as they had lived together . . . but that was no excuse. Isabel knew that if she had not been the direct cause, she had at least been the catalyst in the disintegration of Simon's marriage. And now, though she regretted it, she couldn't undo the damage.

She said, "It's late, Simon. I'll call for some dinner." And Oa? she wondered. Would someone bring Oa dinner, and would Oa feel like eating it? Did she have her sweater, and her socks, the little things that had made her comfortable? Isabel went to the house comm to order, but it was mostly for Simon. Her own stomach roiled with tension, and she doubted she could eat anything.

Fifteen minutes later, the door to the suite buzzed, and Isabel spoke to it. As it swung open, she moved to the table to clear a space for the tray, hearing Simon's polite murmur behind her, and two voices respond. Isabel straightened, and turned to see two white-coated people standing in the suite, one holding a tray with covered plates, the other a carafe and cups.

"Jin-Li!" she exclaimed. "And—Matty, isn't it? Matty Phipps?"

Phipps laughed. "You can call me 'ship lady' if you want to!" she said.

"Mother Burke, could you order the door to close?" Jin-Li said in a low tone. "We're not really supposed to be here."

11

IT SEEMED TO Oa that the spider machine's appetite would never be satisfied. Its microneedles sucked at her wrists, her elbows, her knees, her temples. Its black legs trailed over her face and her chest and made her tremble with horror. Isabel had said there would be no more of it. But Isabel was not here. There was only Doctor.

Oa closed her eyes and retreated into memory.

The anchens found a new nest, after Micho was killed. It was a place of entwined branches and arching roots, a shallow bowl of leaves and moss that they reinforced as best they could. They had tried many times to weave vines, pulling on the thick thorny stems until their fingers bled. If three worked together, they could manage to twist the vines into thick braids, the plaits shading from green to brown as the air leached away the color. The stems stiffened as they dried, and the corner knots became impossible.

Oa remembered her father's big hands bending, forcing, swiftly twisting the vines to make wall mats and floor mats, to make the roofs of shahto that kept out any raindrops that slipped through the forest canopy. Shahto kept out the forest spiders, but the anchens had only their nest. They had better luck with nuchi bark, soaking it in the surf, pounding it with stones to soften it. They made sleeping mats of the pounded bark, and spread them in the nest, snuggling together at night like abandoned fledglings.

They took turns watching for the forest spiders, crying the alarm when one minced out of the forest on its long, jointed legs. But sometimes the watcher fell asleep. Once, in their old nest, Oa had woken to feel a forest spider crawling up over her hair and onto her face, its legs like needles, its forward eyes glowing amber in the starlight. She had frozen with horror, whimpering in her throat. Micho heard her, and leaped up, seizing one of their digging knives, striking the spider down before it could sink its fangs into her throat. He speared the spider, and flung its body as far as he could into the forest. All the anchens huddled around Oa, stroking her, comforting her. They all knew the forest spider's bite.

When Doctor released Oa from the spider machine at last, she crept to the long gold couch and curled up in one corner. She tucked her forehead against her knees, and wrapped her arms around her ankles. She still wore the pajamas from the infirmary, with the black sweater pulled tightly around her, more for comfort than for warmth. Night was coming again, and there was still no sign of Isabel.

Gretchen came in after Doctor left. She tried to get Oa to move, to uncurl her body, to join her over a tray of food. She shook her by the shoulder. "Come on, honey, come on now. Eat. Drink something." Oa tried to cover up her icy, desperate scent by burying her nose in the black wool of her sleeve, breathing the calm fragrance of Isabel. Eventually Gretchen went away, leaving a bowl of soup to chill on the table.

Beyond the locked door, crockery clinked, doors closed, water ran. Past the tall windows the sky darkened. Brilliant lights like tiny white fires burned in the buildings and the streets, flamed from the tops of the great towers like bonfires on the hilltops of the three islands.

When the sounds quieted, and Gretchen didn't return, Oa slowly unwound herself. She got up gingerly, wincing as she straightened her stiff knees. The room lights had dimmed, though the one on the ceiling camera still winked its warning amber. The chairs and couches and tables cast thick shadows on the white carpet. Oa went to kneel beside

the windowsill. The rain had stopped, leaving tracks on the glass like
tear marks. The strange crescent shone dimly white in the night sky.
Moon, they called it. Virimund had no such Moon, but Oa had read
about it in her books.

Even now, the not-canoes floated back and forth in the bay, blazing
with lights strung in looping patterns over their spread sails. What were
they doing there, on the night-dark water? Perhaps there were fish to
catch. Perhaps the people had islands to visit. But they seemed only to
drift, going nowhere, crossing and recrossing the bay.

*Oa remembered a feast day, long ago. She was very small, having
passed no more than four or five tatwaj. Canoes came from all the three
islands, and there was roasted fish and steamed pishi and hot nuchi
milk spiced with honey. The people sang, and danced, and went in and
out of shahto, giving gifts and receiving them. It was the feast of the ancestors, a time to sing the songs and tell the tales.*

*The anchens struggled to remember the songs and stories. In the
evenings, the anchens sat on the great boulder on the northern side of
their island, with the waves of Mother Ocean splashing up to their toes
as they sang the songs of the three islands.*

*Oa remembered the mildness of the evening air, the brilliance of the
stars, the deep song of Mother Ocean, the treble voices of the anchens
reciting memories. Kikya spoke of Raimu-ke. Kikya claimed to remember Raimu-ke, and the others pretended to believe him.*

Oa crouched by the sill for a long time, until she began to get cold,
and then, slowly, she stood. Isabel had not come. Isabel was not coming.

Oa wandered back to the couch, and curled up under the blanket.
The soup Gretchen left had grown a skin of pale yellow, with bits of
vegetables and rice poking from it. The bread had gone dry and hard.
Oa drank a bit of water, but ignored the rest. She lay for a long time
staring out at the white lights of the alien city. Before she finally fell
asleep, she sent one feeble, hopeless prayer into the night. At least, she
prayed to Raimu-ke, at least send me Isabel.

SIMON SHOOK JIN-LI'S hand, and then Phipps's. Isabel invited them to
the table, hastily clearing stacks of flexcopies and slumping piles of

disks from the chairs. They all sat. Isabel watched Jin-Li's heavy-lidded eyes assessing Simon. A tired grin creased Phipps's freckled face.

"I'm glad to see both of you," Isabel said. "But—" She spread her hands. "I can't imagine what you're doing here!"

"Same thing as you, I bet," Phipps said stoutly. "Trying to help the kid."

"We followed," Jin-Li said. "When Adetti moved her."

Sudden hope flamed in Isabel. She leaned forward across the table. "You know where she is? Can you take us to her?"

"Careful," Simon said. Isabel flashed him a look. "We can't just break in someplace."

Jin-Li's eyes gleamed. "Not possible, in any case. They took her into a complex of condo towers down by the water. With a guarded gate. And we don't know which building."

"Tell us what happened," Isabel said. She wanted to rush out, to bash down someone's door, but she knew Simon was right. She tried to tell herself that one more night would not matter. But it did. It very much did.

"Please, Jin-Li, Matty, as long as you're here, do eat something." She stood to divide the fish casserole into portions, using saucers to make enough plates. In the bathroom sink, she rinsed the cups they had used earlier, dried them on a hand towel, and poured coffee. Phipps smiled her thanks and took a plate.

Jin-Li accepted a cup of coffee, saying, "Matty knew they were up to something, so we went to the infirmary. It was late, almost midnight."

Isabel said, "They put a sedative in our food."

"I guessed that." Jin-Li nodded. "It was Adetti who carried her out, I think."

Phipps said, "Bastard," and then her freckled cheeks flushed. "Sorry, Mother Burke."

Isabel managed a small laugh. "It's the right word, Matty."

Jin-Li went on, "He wore a quarantine suit. We followed them out of the Multiplex, down to the condo towers. Had to stand and watch the guard let them in."

"Do you know who lives there?" Simon spoke quietly, eyes fixed on his steepled fingers.

Phipps said, "Yeah. I asked my friend in transportation services." She pushed her fingers through her rough red hair and said triumphantly, "The General Administrator lives there. Great apartment, apparently. Big windows, wonderful view of Elliott Bay and the Olympic Mountains. Very, very expensive."

WHEN GRETCHEN CAME in again in the morning, Oa was already kneeling beside the window, watching the slow morning light brighten the vista of sea and mountain and city.

"Good morning!" Gretchen cried.

Oa turned, still on her knees.

Today the pale lady wore a brown suit, with pleated trousers and a tie at her collar. She carried a fresh tray of food, and Oa, though she hated to take anything from her, was ravenous.

"Come now, honey," Gretchen said, stretching her scarlet lips in a rictus of a smile. "You come right over here and sit with me, and we'll have some breakfast. You must be hungry this time! Come on, now, come on. I don't want to have to drag you." She laid the tray on the table before the gold couch, sitting down, patting the cushion beside her. "Come on, now, honey."

Oa stood up slowly, and took small, wary steps toward the table. The fragrance of yeast bread and sugar drew her to a basket full of tiny golden-crusted rolls. A bowl held sliced rounds of some soft white fruit with a yellow rind. Her stomach clenched with hunger.

She didn't sit on the couch, but knelt beside the table. It didn't seem to matter to Gretchen. She pushed the tray closer to Oa, her smile fading, the skin of her cheek twitching and distorting her mouth. Her left hand twitched, too, and she gripped it with the fingers of her right. She watched Oa pick up the juice glass.

Oa remembered what Gretchen had done before with her empty glass. She set the juice down without drinking.

Gretchen opened her mouth as if to urge her again, but though she caught a noisy breath, she didn't speak. She put one of her bone-thin fingers between her teeth, and fixed Oa with a look of hunger. There were snakes on the islands who watched their prey just that way, heads and eyes very still, mouths open.

Oa didn't want to eat or drink in front of Gretchen, but she was too hungry to resist. She took one of the rolls from the basket, and bit it in two.

It was fresh, sweet as if it had been drenched in honey. Her eyes closed involuntarily at the relief of it. Her mouth flooded with saliva, and she swallowed. She didn't see the white hand coming toward her until Gretchen's sharp-nailed fingers were right in her face. One scarlet nail caught her cheek and scratched it as the woman tore the half-eaten fragment of sweet roll from her mouth.

Oa's eyes flew open, and she fell back, away from Gretchen's reach. She lay on her back on the carpet as Gretchen Boreson thrust the bread into her own mouth and swallowed.

A drop of warm blood rolled down Oa's cheek. Gretchen stood abruptly, reaching for her. Her hand wavered toward her face, and her painted lips parted. Oa tensed to wriggle backward, but Gretchen was too fast for her. She swiped at Oa's cheek, smearing her fingertip with blood.

Gretchen put the finger in her mouth, and sucked on it.

Oa stared, openmouthed with surprise.

Gretchen took her finger out of her mouth and gave Oa a tight, empty smile. A crumb of bread was stuck to her chin. "You enjoy your breakfast now, honey," she said. A moment later, she was gone, striding swiftly and silently away across the white carpet.

For several moments, Oa lay where she was, waiting for her to come back. When the door didn't open again, and there were no sounds beyond it, Oa carefully inched back to the table. Her hunger was a hard, active thing, a twisting demand from her stomach. She knelt again beside the tray. In a rush of appetite, she ate all the bread and drank the juice. She sampled the white fruit, which had gone a little brown but was still sweet and chewy. There was a bowl of shelled nuts, too, white-meated and crunchy, vaguely reminiscent of the fruit of the nuchi. She ate these, thrusting handfuls into her mouth, until they were gone.

The tray was empty. Her stomach felt tight and swollen, and a burning began at the back of her throat. She sat back on her heels and stared at the spider machine in the corner. He would come again, she knew. Doctor would come, and the spider would crawl on her, end-lessly. Isabel had vanished, and with her, all hope.

All at once her overfull stomach rebelled. Oa raced to the little bathroom, and vomited the meal in one great rush that left her gasping for air. She lay on the cold tile floor, shaking with nausea, and with de-spair.

There seemed no reason to get up off the floor. She didn't want to open her eyes, or even to go on breathing. It seemed to Oa that she had been alone forever, and forever stretched ahead of her, with only pain to offer.

She struggled to her feet. She bent over the sink and rinsed her mouth with water. She splashed some on her face, not caring that it spattered the scalloped mirror and the wall, and then she looked at her-self in the glass. Her scratched cheek stung, but there was no more blood. There would be, though, if pale Gretchen wanted it. Why didn't Gretchen just take it all, take it from the spider machine, or straight from Oa's throat?

Oa examined her arm in the harsh light of the bathroom.

Under her dark skin, the vein on the inside of her elbow was a thread of indigo, pulsing gently with the beat of her heart. She knew what veins were. She had read about them in one of the books on Is-abel's computer. They carried her life in their red rivers, the same life the spider machine sucked and sucked at, but never finished. She would have to finish it herself.

She stood in the bathroom door, surveying the room until her eye fell on the piece of sunset glass. Her feet felt odd as she walked toward it, as if her legs, her ankles, already belonged in some other world. Would Raimu-ke turn away from her if she did it? The ancestors for-bade it for the people, of course, but the ancestors did not care about anchens. Their rules did not apply. Tursi had deliberately stranded her-self on the northern spit of the anchens' island, and when the tide came in, she had thrown herself into the water. And Ulan—she tried not to think about what Ulan had done. The anchens had let the birds pick his bones clean on the rocks before they buried him under the kburi.

Oa picked up the slender scarlet and yellow glass from its pedestal. She held it by the thinnest end, and lifted it above her head. When she brought it down, hard, on the pedestal, it shattered into glittering shards that spread over the white carpet. The piece left in her hand was perfect, long and sharp-edged. Already it had pierced the skin of her palm, leaving a thin line of blood like the blood Gretchen had drawn from her cheek.

She went to the window with the piece in her hand. She would do it here, she thought, where she could look out over the not-ocean, watch the not-canoes, and simply drift away. Would Micho be waiting for her? Or would it be darkness, like going to sleep, the same darkness Micho had gone into so suddenly . . . she didn't care, anyway. She wanted only to escape this well of hopelessness, this prison of loneliness.

The auto-cleaner whirred out of its little closet, and began bumbling about over the carpet, picking up the bits of broken glass. Oa glanced up at the amber light of the spy-camera. Its winking continued unchanged. Perhaps no one was watching. It didn't matter.

She crouched beside the sill. The sun shone, brightening the water to an opaque green. Frosty ripples spread across the bay. Oa watched one of the not-canoes float past the city docks, coming toward her. It was narrow and plain, with only a small round white canopy, like a bubble of seafoam on a bit of driftwood. There were people under the canopy.

She turned her left arm up, resting her elbow on the windowsill. She held the glass shard in her right hand, poised above her arm. She drew a deep breath, and prepared to make a strong slice, one that would go deep, that would make no mistakes. It was the way the anchens killed the fish they caught, slicing off their heads in a quick movement so there would be no thrashing, suffering, gasping fish to feel bad about.

Below her window she saw the boat bobbing past. The faces in the boat, four of them, turned up as they floated on to the next building, and the next. They reached the end of the bay, and the boat reversed its direction to slice back through the rippled water toward Oa. She lifted her right hand, and took a deep breath.

The sun reflected off the water, dazzling her eyes. She blinked back tears, and through the haze she saw . . . she thought she saw . . .

There were two dark heads, coming out now from beneath the canopy. She saw a head of pale red hair on a tall figure with broad shoulders. And she saw one bald head, exposed and shining in the sun. Isabel! It was Isabel!

She leaped up, dropping the shard of glass. She pressed her hands against the window, smearing the pane with the blood of her palm. Could they see her? Did they know she was here? She jumped up and down, once, twice, three times, and waved to Isabel.

The boat floated past, the heads all turned up. They were looking for her, weren't they? They must be! But the rising sun would be in their eyes, and the glass was so shiny . . . she had to think of something.

She had to get out to the little balcony, to get out where they could see her. She rattled the lock, but it didn't give. She banged at the glass door with her fist, and it shook and sang under her hand, but didn't break. She glanced frantically around her. What could she use? This glass was so much thicker than the slender red piece.

Frantically, she bounced on her toes as the boat floated away, on to the end of the dock. It made another slow circle, and turned back toward her.

She cast about her for something, anything she could use. Her eye fell on the uneven oblong of glass, the clear one with the yellow and blue forms suspended in it. She seized it by its base. It was cold and heavy in her hands, almost more than she could lift. She didn't stop to think, but swung it with all her might, as far back as her arms would stretch, then forward in a sweeping arc, letting go at the apex, willing it through the windowed door with every ounce of her energy.

Glass met glass with a great bang. The molded glass object, with its little yellow and blue not-fish, exploded into fragments. Oa ducked, and covered her face. Tiny shards struck the backs of her hands, caught in the wool of her sweater. When she straightened, and lowered her hands, she saw that a web of cracks had formed in the glass of the door, with a deep indentation where she had struck it. An alarm began to sound, a keening siren that pierced her ears. Heedless of the glass fragments covering the floor, she ran to the cracked door and pushed at it. It bent, but that was all. Below her she saw the boat coming closer, making another pass of the docks. She whimpered, and pushed again. The glass squeaked and seemed to stretch under the pressure of her hands, but it held.

The boat sliced neatly through the glittering water, away from her, back around the curve of the bay toward the city. The alarm wailed on as Oa watched the little boat slip in among the bigger boats, out of her sight.

She fell to her knees again in the rubble of glass, hardly knowing that her hands were bleeding and her socks were full of splinters. The alarm stopped ringing, leaving her ears echoing with the silence. The apartment door opened, and Doctor stormed in, shouting. Her chance was gone.

12

ISABEL WISHED THEY had not taken the boat trip. The blank, shining windows of the condo towers reproached her with the futility of her efforts. She wanted to call the police, the mayor, anyone. Simon spent an hour explaining to her that the best way to ensure her guardianship of Oa was to negotiate, which meant waiting for the board of regents to convene. Isabel thought she would go mad, waiting the full three days for them all to reach Seattle.

Now, at last, the moment was at hand. Somehow, the days had passed, days of anxious waiting. Isabel's stomach crawled with tension.

A car pulled up beneath the guest suites' awning to carry her and Simon to the meeting of the board. A false spring met them when they emerged, with a fresh breeze from the harbor that chilled Isabel's freshly depilated scalp. A cool sun shone from a pale blue sky. Yellow and purple crocuses nodded in the breeze, braving the February chill.

She touched her cross, wondering where Oa would be when Lent began. She slid onto the wide seat of the car, letting Simon instruct the driver. The car moved slowly through the confined streets of the

Multiplex and then more quickly up the steep Seattle hills toward the renovated hospital that was home to the North American branch of World Health and Welfare. Isabel rested her chin on her hand, staring blindly out the window. They turned a corner, coming upon a large gray brick building. Rectangular twin towers rose from its facade, stained with pollution and creeping mold. They were almost past the building when Isabel roused from her reverie, belatedly recognizing what it was.

"What church is that, Simon?"

He followed her pointing finger. "Cathedral of St. James, I think," he said. "I toured it once, a few years ago."

"I'm glad to see it's still there. So many of the old churches are gone."

"People like modern architecture, I suppose, at least in North America."

"Is the cathedral active, do you know?"

"There were people inside when I was there. I was told they have no resident priest."

She leaned back in her seat with a wordless sigh.

"Yes," Simon drawled. "Even ordaining women, there aren't enough to go around."

She cast him a look, and he chuckled. "Okay, okay, I won't tease you. But you can't blame me if your chosen institution is dying out."

"The institution may die out, Simon, but the idea is eternal."

He smiled at her. "People like you sustain it, Isabel."

She couldn't answer his smile. She turned away from his gentle gaze, letting her eyes roam over the drooping cedars and spiky firs that lined the streets. "No," she said softly. "Not like me. The church will truly be in trouble if it's dependent on such as me."

ISABEL TOOK HER seat in silence, watching Simon greet the regents already seated around the conference table. There were ten men and women, two of them physicians, the rest bureaucrats and politicians. Simon distributed flexcopies to each one. Isabel keyed her reader to the pages she would need, aware of the curious regard of the regents.

The room was windowless and bare, as austere as Gretchen Boreson's office was luxurious. Maps provided the only wall decoration, relieved by an occasional chart with numbers picked out in red and blue. Isabel had not been in this particular room before, but it varied little from other World Health conference rooms. She poured a glass of water from the pitcher near her elbow, and sat back in her chair, her hands linked in her lap.

Gretchen Boreson appeared a few minutes later, dressed in the silver suit, her lips painted a delicate mauve, amethyst earrings glinting beneath her perfect chignon. She tried to smile at the assembled men and women, but her left cheek jerked, tugging at her eyelid, and she pressed her lips together. Cole Markham walked beside her, and trailing them, a large reader folded under his arm, came Paolo Adetti.

Isabel felt heat rise in her face, and she looked away as they took their seats.

"Thank you all for coming," Simon said. "Dr. Martineau, Mr. Annan, Dr. Fujikawa." He went on, calling each name, ending with Isabel. "The issue at hand is the guardianship of the child from Virimund. Mother Isabel Burke was invited to the Multiplex by ExtraSolar Corporation to fulfil the requirements of an extraordinary empowerment provision." He paused, looking around the table. "Mother Burke is petitioning for permanent guardianship. And in my capacity as advisory physician for World Health, I question the right of ExtraSolar Corporation to continue building the Virimund power park, in light of the discovery that the planet is inhabited."

There was a little rustle in the room as the regents picked up their flexcopies, and shifted in their seats.

Simon turned to Isabel. "Mother Burke?"

Isabel's voice trembled at first. "It appears that the child—" She cleared her throat and began again. "This child has no other advocate than myself, and even now I know very little about her. I've collected as much information as I can, but the records are corrupted. We know Oa's ancestors were the Sikassa, a tribe in the African nation of Mali." She touched the keypad of her reader. "Drought and famine drove them out of their homeland, and the United Nations mounted a colony ship, the last one before the U.N. disbanded. The launch received little attention due to the world situation at the time. Monitoring stopped after six years, but they were already lost by then. The last record of

communication from the colony ship was three years after they left
Earth."

She glanced up. Adetti was frowning at one of the charts on the
wall opposite his chair. Gretchen Boreson sat with her fingers pressed to
her left cheek, her eyes on the manicured nails of her right hand.

Isabel went on. "We understand that ExtraSolar's hydrogen engi-
neers had no reason to think Virimund was inhabited until the Port
Forcemen noticed signs of activity on one of the islands. Then, upon
investigation, they found a small nontechnical indigenous population."

Adetti interrupted. "Excuse me, Mother Burke." His fingers on the
keys of his own reader were heavy, making angry clicks. "By definition,
indigenous implies native. The Sikassa were not native to Virimund,
but to Earth."

Isabel felt the tension in her stomach blossom and evaporate. It was
a relief to have the battle begin in earnest. She leaned forward to include the whole table in her answer. "The term 'indigenous' can be applied to 'any life form that has adapted and thrived in its new
environment.' I quote—" She glanced at her reader. "Auber and Fer-
rari, *Journal of Post-Expansion Anthropology,* Volume 112." She let a
beat pass. "Oa knows no other home than Virimund."

A flurry of discussion broke out. Isabel sat back, letting it swirl
around her.

A moment later, Simon broke in. "Excuse me, ladies and gentlemen.
I propose we table the question of the child's status as indigene until we
know more."

Adetti cried, "No—now wait a minute! You're playing with seman-
tics. If you're going to say that   "

Simon's level voice cut easily through the other physician's sputtering. "Would the regents agree this question can't be answered at this
time?"

Several heads nodded, and two or three bent together, conferring.
Adetti subsided, but his eyes narrowed and a pulse beat visibly in his
temple. Markham leaned toward Boreson to whisper in her ear.

Isabel resumed. "The hydro workers located the Sikassa's island by
flyer. There was a confrontation, in which two Sikassa and one Port

Forceman were injured." She swept the table with her glance. "The Sikassa were children. All of them. No adults have been found."

She felt the tension deepen in the room, as if the lights had dimmed. Gretchen Boreson's pale blue eyes came up to meet hers. Isabel pressed on. "The Port Forceman and one of the children died. Oa was treated for her injuries by Dr. Adetti at the power park, and survived." Isabel let her eyes rest on each of the people around the room. "For reasons that are not yet clear, ESC made the decision to bring her to Earth."

The Japanese representative, a diminutive man with a hesitant manner, said, "Pardon me, please. Why was this kept from the charter signatories? The rediscovery of a lost colony is a remarkable occurrence, is it not?"

Adetti opened his mouth, but Boreson shot him a glance, and he closed it again. Boreson said smoothly, "ExtraSolar thought it best to complete its investigation before revealing these events. I'm certain all the regents will agree there are far-reaching ramifications that needed to be explored first. Hiring Mother Burke was meant to be part of that exploration. ESC, of course, has the interests of the charter governments at heart." She folded her hands as if she were finished, and then added hastily, "And the child's, naturally."

Fujikawa shook his head. "Please pardon my slowness. Where is the colony?"

Boreson said, "There is no sign of them. That was the problem in the first place."

Adetti added sourly, "We've tried to ask the girl. She won't talk."

Isabel said as crisply as she could, "Oa's English is fragmentary. At first she could neither understand what was said to her, nor make herself understood. She began to learn English on the transport only thanks to the kind offices of one of the crew." She turned to fix Adetti with a hard gaze. "Dr. Adetti saw fit to keep the child awake the entire journey. Fourteen months in space. That offense is the first of my objections to ExtraSolar's custody of Oa."

She let a little silence fall. Adetti opened his mouth as if to deny the allegation, but evidently thought better of it. His face flushed.

Isabel went on. "My second objection is to countless examinations under the medicator on the transport and again here at the Multiplex, examinations that terrified and upset the child."

Adetti burst out, "There's no pain associated with those scans!"

"Oa dreads the medicator. That's perfectly clear. It was cruel."

"No one was cruel to the girl!" Adetti glared at Isabel. He moved in his chair, and his knee struck the table leg with an audible bump.

"My third objection is that three days ago, at a time when I was beginning to make progress with the child, she was removed from my care. In the middle of the night, and without my knowledge. I believe I was drugged, and so was Oa. I woke to find her gone." Her voice faltered. She took a sip of water, and Simon touched her elbow lightly with his fingers. "I haven't seen her since."

"Were drugs used?" This was from a startled-looking woman from Eastern Europe.

Adetti folded his arms. "There's absolutely no proof of such an allegation."

"I assume ExtraSolar believes Dr. Adetti's actions were justified?" It was the regent from Oceania, a man Isabel had met in Australia. She knew him to be hardheaded but fair.

"Of course they were justified!" Adetti erupted. "Listen, we brought in this—this Magdalene—as an anthropologist. She's not a physician, not even a medtech, yet she questioned my research and interfered with it. She broke quarantine, she destroyed equipment, and she obstructed communication with the subject!" He glared around the table. "We're replacing her as guardian."

Several heads were shaking. Boreson said icily, "You all understand how upset Dr. Adetti is by the interruption in his work."

"Where is the child now?" Fujikawa asked.

"We're going to explain about that," Adetti began.

Boreson interrupted him. "We deemed it necessary to place the girl out of the public eye." Her cheek twitched once, twice, three times. She pressed her hand to her face.

Isabel tapped her reader, and read from the screen. "I quote from the Offworld Port Force Terms of Employment: 'Interference in native affairs is forbidden to all Offworld Port Force employees. This includes, but is not limited to, dispensing unauthorized Earth materiel, interfering with native culture, engaging in violence against native citizens, and fraternization with native citizens.' " She lifted her eyes. "End quote."

Next to her Simon put his elbows on the table and set his fingertips together.

Isabel said firmly, "I count three violations of the Terms of Employment. In light of this, and my other objections, I request that the regents instate me as Oa's permanent guardian." She closed her reader with a click. "I am lodging a formal complaint with World Health over the violations of the human rights of this Sikassa child."

Adetti almost shouted, "She's not a child, dammit!"

His voice echoed in a sudden, embarrassing silence. Every face turned to him.

Simon made a small sound in his throat.

Fujikawa held up one hand. "Pardon, please. Forgive my slowness in understanding. We understood this was a young girl—" He glanced down at the flexcopy on the table before him. "One point thirty-seven meters of height, thirty-five point three-eight kilograms of weight, blood pressure and heart rate normal for a child of her size. There is nothing about her that is inconsistent with an age of ten years old." He scanned the sheet again. "No dwarfism, no other abnormality."

Gretchen Boreson said faintly, "We are delighted at this chance to explain . . ."

Isabel turned to Simon, her heartbeat thudding in her ears.

He gave her a small nod, a gesture meant to reassure. Everyone else stared at Adetti, some openmouthed, some frowning. Boreson's cheek wrinkled like paper where her fingers pressed against it.

Adetti coughed. "You're right, Dr. Fujikawa. The girl appears to be about ten years old. But in actuality, she is much older."

"How much older?" Fujikawa said.

Adetti said, "We're not sure yet."

Isabel stole another glance at Simon. He was gazing at his steepled fingers.

"Have you asked the child—the girl—herself?" Fujikawa pressed.

The ESC physician's lip curled. "Oh, yes. Repeatedly. She won't answer."

Isabel blazed across the table at Adetti, "Or can't answer. Or is afraid to answer."

The regent from the Middle East, an Iranian woman with a silk scarf wrapped around her thick graying hair, asked, "Why would she not answer? What would be the point in keeping her age a secret?" She looked to Isabel for a response.

Isabel took a deep breath. "I'm trying to sort that out, Madame Mahmoud. It could be a cultural issue. But I can't do it without her." She turned to Boreson one more time, and choked out, "What have you done with her? Where is Oa?"

OA HAD SPENT hours watching from the window as the not-canoes traced their aimless patterns back and forth across the bay. Her hands and one cheek were bandaged. Someone had used a heavy comb on her hair, tugging and tugging at her scalp to remove the splinters of glass. A guard now lounged just inside the door to the apartment, arms folded, yawning and bored. Oa ignored her.

A whole day passed, and then another. Pale Gretchen came. She ordered the guard outside, and then sat again on the couch, poised like a snake over Oa's food tray. Oa learned that she would leave sooner if Oa drank from a glass, or took a bite of some food and then set it down again. Gretchen would drink from the glass, or finish Oa's half-eaten fruit or bread, and abruptly depart. Once she clumsily replaced one of Oa's bandages, and carried the used and bloody one away. Doctor came once, making Oa lie down under the spider machine, but after that he, too, left her alone. Food trays appeared through a cupboard. The auto-cleaner whirred around the apartment. Towels and soap appeared while Oa slept. She saw no one else.

She knelt beside the tall window for hours, watching raindrops slither down the glass, or feeling the weak sunshine of this world on her cheeks, and she sifted through her memories.

Oa remembered the tatwaj on the island of the anchens. They knew it was time when the white smoke billowed up from the islands of the people, three steady columns far off, at the very edge of the blue horizon. They looked at each other, Micho and Usa and Ette and Bibi and the others, and then they ran to assemble the rough needles they made from the bones of birds, the ink they made by mixing water from Mother Ocean with a powder they ground from the gallnuts that grew on the nuchi trees. The anchens trudged together up the hill to the kburi, and built a fire. This fire they made very small. They didn't dare create the great white smoke columns of the people, or they would be punished for raising a false alarm.

Their tatwaj was a private thing. They knelt together around the tiny fire, in the presence of Raimu-ke, and they marked each other. Micho was the best at it, his designs almost as nice as their first ones. After his death, they took turns etching the four-pointed motif into their skin.

Once a man came to their island, his canoe blown off course by a storm. He was wrinkled and gray-haired. He was the man who used to be Ette's father. When he saw Ette, he seized her arm and sneered at the row of marks, the signs Micho and later Po had labored over. He shouted at all of them, saying how foolish they were to go on marking, to pretend that it mattered. Do you think, he snarled, that pretending to hold the tatwaj makes you people?

None of the anchens answered him. When he released Ette's arm, she fell in a heap at his feet, weeping soundlessly. He turned away from her, his face as tight and dark as a thundercloud.

He was right, of course. It was exactly what they thought. It was what they tried to believe. They knelt around the fire before the kburi and bore the prick of the needle and the sting of the ink, and they begged Raimu-ke to make them people.

Oa remembered the soft-skinned faces, the clear eyes, the tremulous lips of her fellow anchens. She remembered Micho's long, thin arms, Micho who had grown so tall he looked like a person, though a slender one. She remembered how Ette's little fingers curled around the inkpot, holding it for Micho, and in later ceremonies, for Po. She remembered that small Bibi cried out at the sticking of the needle, every time, every tatwaj. And she remembered how they would count, afterward, around the fire. The man who had been Ette's father had spoken truly. They were pretending. They were anchens, and pretending was all they had.

13

OA SPENT HER third day in the apartment alone with the sullen guard. Gretchen didn't come, nor did Doctor. Meal trays were slipped through the cupboard by invisible hands. The auto-cleaner whirred around the apartment, neatly dodging the guard's booted feet, circling Oa where she knelt by the windowsill.

Oa got up to go into the little bathroom. She looked in the scalloped mirror, and she saw that her bandaged cheek had gotten dirty, and her hair tangled again. She didn't do anything about it. She wandered back to the windows to watch for Isabel, but without much hope. Raimu-ke had tried, she thought, but it seemed the power of Earth was too great for her.

Darkness shrouded the white peaks of the western mountains, and shadows crept over the water while she knelt beside the windowsill. The white gulls cried to her from beyond the glass. She let her chin rest on her arm, nestled in the soft warmth of Isabel's black sweater, and she followed the circling birds with her eyes. When the darkness was complete, she could still see them, their white feathers glowing against the night sky.

She didn't realize she had fallen asleep until the click of the lock releasing woke her. She startled, and scrambled to her feet. The sudden light from the corridor dazzled her eyes, and she blinked, not knowing if it was night or day.

The guard spoke, and a man's voice answered, a voice she didn't recognize. She pressed her back to the window, the sweater pulled tightly round her, and she peered into the brightness.

Her eyes had not yet adjusted when she heard Isabel's voice. "Oa! Are you all right?"

Oa pushed away from the window, stumbling in her haste. Isabel! She tried to answer, but her voice squeaked and broke. She tried again, "Yes. Yes, Isabel! Oa is—all right." She ran across the expanse of white carpet.

Isabel met her halfway, looking just as Oa remembered, bare scalp gleaming above her white collar and black shirt and trousers. A man was with her, and some other people in the corridor. They came into the apartment cautiously, giving each other little glances, and then staring at Oa, but Oa cared only that Isabel was there, that she looked the same, that she had not changed. "Isabel is—all right?" Oa breathed. She wanted to throw her arms around her, but she felt too shy. She settled for standing as close as she dared.

Isabel's lamplight smile banished every shadow from the room. "Isabel is fine," she said, with a little laugh. "Isabel is fine now."

AT THE SIGHT of Oa, Isabel felt as if a weight had suddenly lifted from her soul, a weight she had not properly measured before that moment. The child wore white bandages on both hands, and on one cheek. No one had reported that the girl was injured, but Isabel's relief outweighed her anger. Her arms tingled with the urge to hug the girl. A rush of gratitude stole her breath.

She nodded to Simon, and included Dr. Fujikawa and Madame Mahmoud, the designated observers, in her glance. "This is Oa of Virimund," she said, her voice husky. "Could you say hello, Oa? This is my very good friend Simon. He and these other people wanted to meet you."

Oa needed a bath. Her hair needed brushing. Her bandaged cheek was smudged, and her nails were dirty, but she managed a smile at Isabel, and a shy glance at the others. "Hello," she said in a small voice. Her hand stole into Isabel's, and Isabel sighed and closed her fingers around it, feeling the stickiness of the bandage against her palm.

Simon said, "It's good to see you at last, Oa."

Oa turned her face up to Isabel. "Oa goes with Isabel now?"

"Yes, indeed," Isabel said. "Oa is coming with Isabel."

Oa's wide eyes flicked around the room. "Doctor?" she whispered.

Isabel followed her gaze to the medicator. "Not today, Oa," she said. "Not today."

Relief gave way all at once to a wave of fatigue, the aftermath of worry and of the hours of wrangling she had endured in the conference room. Adetti had fought Oa's removal from his control with every argument at his disposal. Without Simon, Isabel would have never won the battle. Simon had countered every assertion with facts. Since Isabel showed no infection, nor did the hydro workers, he convinced the regents that the child should be freed at last from her isolation. He failed to win revocation of the extraordinary empowerment provision, but he succeeded in securing Isabel's guardianship. As a concession, ExtraSolar was allowed to post a guard over both of them. But Oa was to be in Isabel's care until the next meeting.

They had a week until then, seven days. Isabel wished it were longer. It was hardly enough time, even with Simon's help, to solve the mystery that was Oa.

OA CLUNG TO the white rail that ringed the boat—ferry, Isabel had said, it was called a ferry—and laughed into the wind. Her hair, tied back with a wide red ribbon, lifted behind her head, and the cold air brought tears to her eyes. She felt intoxicated with freedom, with the joy of open spaces, moving air, birds wheeling above her. She glanced around to check that Isabel was still nearby.

She was. She had pulled a knit cap over her bare head, and wrapped herself in a black coat. Beside her stood the man, the doctor, called Si-mon. He was a little taller than Isabel, and a little older, with a thin face and clear brown eyes that seemed tired, and a bit sad. His brown hair blew in his eyes as the ferry chugged across the gray water. Behind Doctor Simon and Isabel was the guard, but Oa didn't mind this one. It was the ship lady. Matty Phipps.

She looked ahead once again, letting the wind blow into her open mouth, stealing her laughter even as it pealed into the misty sky. It hardly seemed possible that only yesterday she had wakened alone on Gretchen's hard gold couch. Now she had a bedroom right next to Isabel's, and a big bathroom with a tub to soak in. There was no spider machine. There were clothes, all warm and soft and new. There had been hot soup and fresh bread, and now there was what Doctor Simon called an "outing."

It wasn't easy to understand Doctor Simon. When Isabel spoke, her voice was clear and slow, each word precisely separated from the ones before and after. Doctor Simon spoke fast, and the words sounded different in his mouth. But Isabel liked Doctor Simon, Oa knew that. And if Isabel liked Doctor Simon, Oa would, too. She would listen very closely, and in a few days she would understand him as well as she did Isabel.

When Isabel explained that Simon was a doctor, too, Oa had asked anxiously, "Doctor?"

And Isabel understood immediately. "Yes. A very good, very smart doctor."

"Spider machine?"

Isabel had touched her hand. "Oa, I will not lie to you. Simon will be examining you. But if he needs to use the medicator, I will be right with you every moment. I promise."

Today, at least, there would be no spider machine. Today was their "outing." Ahead lay a green island where they would walk, Isabel had promised, and have a meal, and not come back to the city for hours. Oa bounced on her toes, and cried out her thanks. The wind snatched her words from her lips and hurled them away to sail up through the piled gray clouds, on through the emptiness of space, to fly past the stars to the island of the anchens, and the kburi, and the invisible ear of Raimu-ke.

*　*　*

SIMON CAME TO Isabel's suite very early the next morning, carrying a little sheaf of flexcopies and a wavephone in his hand. Isabel gave him a cup of excellent espresso, and he savored it, seated on the couch. Her window faced east, over the roofs of the Multiplex, all of them layered with solar panels.

"Do you suppose those are any help in this cloudy place?" he asked Isabel, gesturing to the panels.

"Doesn't seem likely, does it?" She stood by the window with her coffee cup in her hand. "I'll rouse Oa in a bit, Simon. I wanted to let her sleep. She was exhausted."

"That's fine. No hurry."

"Thank you for yesterday, by the way. We both needed it. A day off from worrying."

"It was a good day." His wavephone buzzed and he made a little gesture of apology as he picked it up. "This is Dr. Edwards."

"Simon?" The voice sounded even more fragile than usual.

"Anna."

Isabel turned from the window, her hand to her lips.

"Simon, I needed to know . . . I want to know what's happening. The news is saying . . ."

"Anna, I'm sorry. I should have called you. I—it's been a busy time."

Isabel averted her eyes as she circled the couch and disappeared into the tiny kitchen. Simon covered his eyes with his hand, and tried to think what to say to his wife. He could see her worried face in his mind's eye, the habitual lines of fatigue. He tried to muster some feeling of affection. Mostly he felt pity. And irritation. He hated himself for it. "I'm sorry if the news worried you, Anna. Tell me about it."

"It's about this meeting of the regents, and your name keeps coming up. Something to do with Virimund, and something about a child. What is it about Virimund that involves you, Simon? Who is this little girl?"

"I can't talk about it yet, Anna. But I was needed here. I'm still needed."

A little silence stretched between them, a little live silence, the r-waves erasing the miles as if Anna were only across the street, or across the hall. But the true distance between the two of them, Simon thought, could never be erased, even if they stood in the same room. It had nothing to do with miles.

"When are you coming home?"

"I'll call you when I know. There's another meeting in six days."

"Simon, is . . ." He heard her hesitate, and he knew what she wanted to ask. He dropped his hand, and stood up to walk to the window, struggling against a tide of impatience. Anna's voice was strained. "Is—is *she* there?"

He leaned against the windowframe, gazing out at the rain-spattered solar panels. "Yes, Anna. Isabel is here. ExtraSolar hired her."

"I thought so. Her picture was on the news."

"I'll tell you about it when I can, Anna. She's the child's guardian."

Another silence.

"Anna, I'm afraid I have to get to work. And you must be tired. Have you eaten?"

"I've only just gotten home, Simon. I was just . . ." Her voice trailed off.

"I know. But there's nothing to worry about." He took a deep breath. "I'll be in touch. I promise you."

When the call ended, Simon looked up. Isabel stood in the doorway, and he saw his own guilt mirrored in her face. "Is she all right?" Isabel said in a low tone.

"Not really."

"Is she angry?"

"I wish she were." He shrugged. "Part of me thinks it would be easier if she would shout at me, accuse me." He tucked the wavephone into his pocket.

Isabel leaned against the doorjamb, her gray eyes darkening. "She's hurt, of course."

"Yes." Simon turned back to the window. "We all are, Isabel."

"I know." Her voice was full of misery.

He gazed blindly out into the mist. "Don't you have some scripture that applies?"

She sighed. "It's the seventh commandment that troubles me."

"Oh. Right." He gave her a rueful smile. He went back to the table, and began to sort out the flexcopies he wanted to show her.

She sat down across from him. "I can't claim to know a thing about marriage, Simon."

He lifted his eyes to her face. "I'm not sure I do, either," he said slowly. "But Anna doesn't want to give up on ours."

"That takes courage, don't you think?"

"I suppose. Or stubbornness."

Her lips curved. "Sometimes those are the same, I think. Perhaps Anna is very brave."

He dropped his eyes, and stared down at his hands. "Isabel. People change . . . I've changed over the years."

"Hasn't Anna?"

He hesitated. In some obscure way, he thought Anna's inability to change was part of the problem. "She's changed in small ways. Superficial ways. She's devoted to her students, of course, and the school—she's intelligent, and hardworking. Kind, I think." And dull. But he wouldn't speak that disloyal thought aloud. He watched Isabel's face, and he suspected she understood.

"Perhaps, if you give it time, Simon . . ."

"Yes. Perhaps." He didn't want to have this conversation, and most especially not with Isabel. He tapped the stack before him. "I need to tell you about Oa."

Isabel nodded, accepting the change of subject. "Yes. You knew, didn't you?"

"I had an idea," he said. "But I needed the physical scans. The bone histology."

"And did you find it?"

"The complete file was waiting for me when we got back last night. I've been through everything," he said wearily. He had sat up half the night sifting through Adetti's confused records.

"She's all right, though, isn't she?" She bent to see the sheet in his hand.

"Yes, Oa's fine. But—" He pushed the flexcopy across the table, and pointed to an illustration. "I'd better start at the beginning." He traced the colored pattern with his forefinger. "This is a photomicrograph of a transverse section of cortical bone."

"Cortical?"

"The solid tissue of long bones. Bone is in a constant state of turnover, called remodeling, during which tissue is absorbed and transformed. The process creates particles called osteons. We can estimate age by counting osteons. A bit dicey without a representative population sample, but otherwise a dependable predictor of age, within a certain range of error."

"This came from one of Oa's scans, then."

"Yes." He picked up a second sheet. "This, too. Adetti did osteon counts from the ribs, the clavicle, the arms, the legs. It looks like he ran them a dozen or more times, and they didn't change substantially, even allowing for incoherence—that is, discrepancies in different bones from the same subject. And with a live subject—which is rather unusual, by the way—with a live subject we have reliable conclusions because we have all the bone measurements, not just fragments."

She took the second sheet, and put her coffee cup down. "What does it mean, Simon?"

He rubbed his eyes with his fingers. "Adetti's a terrible scientist, Isabel." He managed a sour chuckle. "He should have stuck with emergency medicine. But in this instance, he's not mistaken. Oa is a great deal older than she appears."

"I did ask her, once, Simon. I asked if she could tell me how old she was."

"And?"

"And she held up her arms. She has tattoos, dozens of them, running up and down her arms, over her shoulders, across the back of her neck."

"Yes, I know about the tattoos. Adetti called them tribal markings. Did you ask Oa what they were?"

"I did, but she got tears in her eyes, and she looked so—I don't know, ashamed, I think. I didn't have any idea why, and I didn't have the heart to press her."

"Her English isn't all that good, Isabel. Maybe she didn't understand the question."

"I'm afraid she did. All too well." Isabel sighed, and slid her palm across her naked scalp. She wore a black wool vest over her shirt, her white collar just showing above it. Rain began to patter against the window. "There's nothing in the records about tattoos in the Sikassa culture, other than as body adornment. But to Oa, clearly, they have great significance."

In the gray light Isabel looked very much as she must have when she first put on her priestly collar, her skin clear and smooth, the lines around her eyes and mouth almost unnoticeable. She leaned past Simon to pick up a third flexcopy, and he had to clench his hand to keep from stroking her cheek.

He said quietly, "Isabel, look at me."

She lifted her eyes to his.

"I know how shocking this must be. But according to the projections I ran last night, we can estimate Oa's age within a range of plus or minus twelve years."

"Twelve—*years*?" Isabel's voice scraped on the word.

"We can't be certain of accuracy beyond that window. Too many factors have to be taken into account, including accidents, toxicity, genetic variance, environmental effects." He saw, with clinical clarity, how her pupils expanded, her skin blanched.

"God help us, Simon! How old—" Her voice dried and she simply stared at him.

He couldn't hold her gaze. He looked away, out into the misty morning. There was no easy way to say this, no gentle way to reveal what he had learned. He blurted, "One hundred, Isabel. Oa is somewhere in the neighborhood of one hundred years old."

14

SIMON CAUGHT ISABEL just as her knees gave way, and she collapsed
in his arms with a little gasping breath. Her pupils swelled with shock,
and her face turned ashen. He lifted her, cradling her head on his shoulder, and laid her down as gently as he could on the couch. He tucked a
pillow beneath her ankles, and patted her cheek gently.

"Isabel?" Her eyelids fluttered, and she groaned. Her fingers reached
for her cross. "Isabel. It's all right. Take your time."

He knelt beside the couch, cursing himself for not finding a gentler
way to tell her. He chafed her wrist between his hands until she sighed,
and her eyes opened.

"Oh, Simon. Good lord. I fainted!"

He smiled at her. "Indeed, Mother Burke. You fainted."

She struggled to sit upright. "Good lord," she repeated. "I've never
fainted in my life!"

"Well, it's a shock. And I didn't say it very well."

She shook her head. "There's no good way to say such a thing. Did

I hear you right, Simon?" Her eyes on him were cloudy. "Did you say one hundred years old? Oh, my God. Poor Oa. Poor child."

Simon brought a glass of water from the little kitchen. He sat down beside her, watching to see that her color returned, that she drank the water, that her pupils contracted to their normal size. "Some would say she was lucky, Isabel. Eternal youth."

Her eyes widened again, but she was stable now. "Eternal? God forbid!"

He relaxed. She was herself again. "Why God forbid, Isabel? Doesn't everyone want to stay young?"

She shook her head. "Only the old, Simon. Children want more than anything to grow up. Can't you remember?"

He chuckled. "I'm very far from being a child now. And there are things about being young that I miss."

"But . . ." She paused, searching for words, touching her cross. "But it was so—satisfying—so right—to become a woman. And you, Simon. How could you do the work you do if you remained a child? You saw Oa, you saw how she is! It doesn't matter if she's lived a thousand years, she's still a child!"

"I agree with you. She has a child's body, and a child's mind."

Isabel pushed herself to her feet and moved unsteadily to the window, her slender shoulders bowed. "Do you know what they'll do to her? How they'll use her?" she choked.

"It's why Adetti brought her here, Isabel."

"And Boreson allowed it."

"I have an idea about that, too."

She turned. The soft light from the window haloed her bare head. "Her illness?"

He shrugged. "I hate to guess at diagnoses, but she obviously has some sort of chorea. If it's degenerative, then it's age-related."

"So Adetti wants—"

"What humans have wanted for eons. The fountain of youth."

"It's appalling."

"Why, Isabel? Not everyone has your faith."

"Simon, it's not about faith. It's about morality! Ethics! Who among us is entitled to live forever? The rich? The powerful?"

"I agree with you, of course, but I doubt the likes of Adetti would. Or even, I'm sorry to say, the regents."

Her voice was strained. "We have to do something. We have to protect Oa."

"It won't be easy. We have to start by finding out what is keeping her from aging. What keeps her a child." He rose, and walked to her side. "That's what Adetti's been looking for, of course. Why he kept running scans, though he isn't clever enough to work it out. I'm going to need to do a scan of my own."

"Oh, Simon, those other children." She pressed her palms to her eyes, and took a deep breath. "Those poor abandoned children. Are they all like Oa?"

"The deceased one was. And I'm concerned about the hydro workers at the power park."

"You think they're in danger of infection after all?"

He shook his head. "I just don't know. We know Oa's not a carrier, but we still need to discover the source of the virus. We don't know what its effects might be on a different population. We have to know what we're dealing with."

A sound came from the second bedroom, the creak of a bed, a sighing yawn as Oa woke. Simon watched in wonder as Isabel looked away, rearranged her face, prepared herself. This, he thought, is what it is to be a parent. The parent wears a mask, puts the child's needs before her own. She makes whatever sacrifices are necessary, for the child's sake.

Oa appeared in the doorway, sleepily rubbing her eyes, her mass of curling hair falling around her shoulders, and Isabel, somehow, smiled a peaceful and affectionate morning greeting.

Yes, Simon thought. Oh, yes. This is what it is to be a parent. Even if the child is a hundred years old.

"I WILL BE right beside you every moment," Isabel assured Oa. The girl's eyes were wide with anxiety, and she clung to Isabel's hand. The day before she had watched Isabel lie under the medicator as Simon ran a scan, but today her fear had returned. She had put it aside briefly as they rode up the outside elevator, exclaiming over the view of Seattle, lifting her teddy bear to see the scattered domes and spires glittering in late winter sunshine, windows of every shape and size glowing gold and silver. But now, as they passed the office doors in the medical building, she grew silent again, and her hand in Isabel's was cold. Isabel, glancing down at her, saw her reading the signs on the doors they passed, sounding out the names. Every one of them had "Doctor" before it.

Simon walked a little ahead, and the omnipresent guard, the pleasant Matty Phipps, came behind. Simon had located an old friend from medical school, and asked to borrow an exam room for an hour or two. Isabel had explained to Oa that Doctor Simon needed to do his own medicator scan. "But just once," she said firmly. "Only once. And I will be with you."

Oa had said she understood, but now the girl's fear radiated through her hand and into Isabel's. Isabel said, "Oa. Do you know what a machine is?"

"Ship," Oa said in a small voice. "Car. Es-presso maker."

"That's right. Those are all machines. They do only what we want them to do. And the medicator is a machine. Not a spider. A machine."

The girl's great black eyes lifted to Isabel's. "Doctor Simon needs to—"

"Yes. Doctor Simon needs to examine you."

"Ex-amine." Oa took a shallow breath. "Examine Oa."

"That means to study. Simon wants to understand you, to know things about you. Is that all right, Oa?"

"Permission?"

Isabel smiled at the quickness of Oa's mind, the alacrity of her memory. "That's exactly right. Permission. Will you give Simon permission?"

They had reached the correct office, and Simon opened the door and stood back for them to enter. Oa stepped cautiously through it into an elegant reception room. As she passed Simon, she looked up into his face and said gravely, "Oa gives Doctor Simon permission."

Simon nodded acknowledgment with the same gravity. "Thank you, Oa."

*   *   *

THE EXAM ROOM in this office was much warmer than the one on the ship, or even in the infirmary. Oa lay on the high bed, the paper sheet crinkled beneath her. An arrangement of miniature objects spun in the air above her head, a tiny girl in a scarlet dress, a four-legged beast with a silver horn, a bird with lavender feathers, a flat yellow fish with green eyes. They twirled in an intricate pattern, dodging each other, almost but not quite colliding. Oa decided they were some kind of toy she had not yet seen. She held tightly to Isabel's hand, her teddy bear in her other hand, and she concentrated on the dance of the little toys. When Doctor Simon bent over her, she flinched, and then forced herself to lie still. She must lie still. She had given Doctor Simon permission.

His hands were warm on her skin. Doctor's hands had been cold and dry, like the empty snakeskins the anchens found on the forest floor. Doctor—that other Doctor—had jostled her, pinched her, sometimes pulled her hair as he worked. He had treated her as if he understood exactly what she was.

Doctor Simon pressed the microneedles to her wrists with a motion so deft she had to glance down at her arm to see that they were really attached. When he fitted the syrinxes to her temples and to her ankles, he spoke to her. "Please tell me if there's any discomfort, Oa. Do you feel this, here at your ankle? No? Good. And now I'm going to patch these to your temples, just so. Is that all right? Good girl. You're a very good patient."

Oa didn't understand everything he said. When he moved her teddy bear to reach the inside of her arm, she gave Isabel an anxious glance.

Isabel murmured, "Here, Oa." She lifted her cross over her head, and laid it on Oa's breast. "We will share it."

It was the same spider machine, but it seemed different now. Isabel's cross lay on Oa's chest with a comforting weight, and the colorful creatures spun above her head. Isabel held her hand, and Doctor Simon chattered easily as he worked. The spider machine made its usual hissing and clicking noises, but Oa found if she listened to Doctor Simon's voice, even though she didn't understand most of what he said, the spider machine lost some of its power. She didn't shudder, or shiver.

And soon it was over, with Isabel helping Oa down from the high bed, Doctor Simon restoring her teddy bear to her arms and turning to take disks from the spider machine. They were leaving the office, Doctor Simon saying good-bye to his old friend, Matty Phipps rejoining them as they came out of the exam room. The four of them walked down the corridor, free again. Oa felt like dancing herself, spinning and twirling like the tiny girl in the scarlet dress.

As they floated down to the street in the transparent elevator, Oa admired the great city around her with new eyes, and she smiled at Isabel as they got into the car. "Oa is hungry."

Isabel laughed. "Oh, yes, Oa, Doctor Simon and Isabel are hungry, too." And when Matty Phipps grinned and nodded, Isabel said, "So is Matty, I think. Let's all have ice cream!"

And so they had another "outing," all of them, with a strange cold food that tickled Oa's tongue and made her head ache at first, but was so sweet and thick in her mouth that she had to eat it fast anyway. When she had finished hers, a pretty concoction of white and brown and red in a clear glass dish, she laid her spoon down with a clatter. "Oa likes it!" she cried.

Everyone laughed, Doctor Simon, Matty Phipps, and Isabel. Oa laughed, too, at first. But when she saw the affection in Isabel's wonderful eyes, the easy trust on Doctor Simon's face, her laugh died. She had to tell them the truth. It wasn't right to pretend. She stared down at the shiny table, seeing her own dark face looking back at her.

Oa remembered a tatwaj on the people's island. She remembered that a mother and father tried to hide their son, slip him away when it was time for the tatwaj so he could not be counted. There had been screaming and wailing. The elders sent the son to the anchens, and the mother and father were banished from the three islands. Oa's papi had been very angry, and had made a speech before the people. Oa was little then, but she remembered how Papi had thundered, and how the mother and father clung to their son as he was pulled away, how the mother screamed as the elders rowed him away in their canoe.

The memory slipped away, and Oa came back to herself. She looked up into Doctor Simon's lean, kind face, Matty Phipps's ruddy smile, Isabel's gentle eyes. They gazed back at her, trusting her, believing her to be something she was not.

Tears filled Oa's eyes, and the others fell silent. She knew they were wondering what was wrong. Even through the rich, sugary smell of the ice cream shop, she caught the change in Isabel's scent, the tinge of worry, of confusion.

She must tell her. And then what would Isabel do? Would she give her back to Doctor? Send her away? Perhaps she would feel she had no choice.

ISABEL LEFT SIMON to pore over the medicator scans. She persuaded Matty to let her take Oa for a walk, allowing her to follow at a distance, promising she wouldn't leave her sight. She wrapped Oa in the black sweater, and a thick coat that reached the girl's ankles. She had found boots to fit Oa's long-toed feet. She wore her own vest and coat, and they both wore knitted hats. They walked west from the guest suites, down a winding street toward the waterfront, leaving the cramped streets of the Multiplex to walk in the broader avenues of the city.

Oa had not spoken since the ice cream shop.

Isabel kept Oa's hand in hers as they walked, not hurrying, but keeping a steady pace down the hill, following the glimpses of Elliott Bay between the buildings. The waters of Puget Sound sparkled a cool blue in the fading light, a color that reminded Isabel of the ancient fishing villages in northern Italy, where a handful of people still lived in the old way, close to the land, shaped by it, dependent upon it. Oa's people must have lived that way, fishing, gathering, making clothes and implements from the materials the land gave them. She let her mind follow this thread, always ending up in the same place. The fisherpeople of northern Italy stayed bound to their homeland, all but inseparable from it. If the Sikassa followed that model, then where had they gone, and why? And how could they have left their children behind?

Isabel glanced down at Oa's hand. One of her tattoos, just a little jagged corner, showed beneath her coat sleeve. Oa's head drooped. Isabel felt the squeeze of pity in her heart, and she pressed her lips together, chastising herself. Pity would not help the child. Action would.

They came to a park, narrow tiers of winter-worn grass descending to a wide street below. There were foamcast benches facing the mountains and the water. Rhododendron bushes rose high enough on the southern edge to block the rising evening wind. "Come, Oa," Isabel said. "Let's sit down here. I want to talk to you."

Obediently, Oa sat down, and Isabel sat beside her. "Will you look at me, Oa?"

Oa's eyes came up to hers, as deep and empty as a dark sea.

"Oa, I know something is troubling you. I think you're afraid to say what it is."

Oa looked away. She whispered, "Yes. Oa is afraid."

"Sometimes I'm afraid, too."

The girl sighed, a tiny sound beneath the whine of the wind.

"Won't you tell me, Oa?"

The girl's whole body seemed to shrink, as if she had suddenly grown smaller. Or as if she had grown much, much older.

Isabel tried, "Is it the medicator? Something about the medicator?" There was no answer. Isabel waited, holding the girl's hand, wishing she could think of some way to ask, some better way. "Perhaps something happened, on the ship? Something you're afraid to talk about?" Again there was no answer, but Isabel felt the shiver in the child's fingers. She sensed Matty Phipps's presence at the top of the park, on the highest tier, watching them, but not close enough to hear.

When Oa spoke, her voice was so soft Isabel had to lean close to her, close enough to feel her breath on her cheek. "Isabel is afraid?" she murmured.

"Yes," Isabel said, not much louder. "I'm often afraid."

"But—" The child broke off. Isabel waited. "But," Oa began again, her eyes on her feet, "But you are a person."

"You are a person, too," Isabel said gently.

Oa lifted her head, and her great eyes were full of grief. "Not," Oa said. Her lips had gone pale. "Not. Oa is not a person."

Isabel's throat dried. "Oa, I don't think I understand. Why do you say that?"

"The tatwaj. Because of the tatwaj."

"What is that? What is a—a tatwaj?" The word was strange to Isabel, and did not come easily from her mouth.

Oa pulled her hand free, and wrapped her arms around herself. She looked over the water, where the early sunset gilded the distant mountain peaks with deep rose and pale gold. Tragedy spoke in every line of her face, in the slant of her body, in the timbre of her voice when she finally spoke. "Oa is not a person." She held herself tighter. "Oa—" she seemed to choke on the words, and Isabel saw her throat working until she blurted, "Oa is an anchen." She put her arms around her knees, and buried her head against them.

Isabel could see that Oa expected something to happen. She had made a revelation, and she expected to be punished for it. But Isabel still didn't understand.

OA DID IT for Isabel, because Isabel was so kind to her, had stood with her even though the cold legs of the spider machine brushed her arms and hands and even her bare, vulnerable scalp. Oa did it because in the ice cream shop she had heard the whisper of Raimu-ke in her ear, reminding her that she must tell Isabel, she must confess it all, and accept the consequences. But now, she thought in misery, now she had done it, and Isabel didn't know what it meant.

She felt Isabel's warm hand on her back, Isabel's arms around her. Isabel gathered her up as if she were a baby, and held her tightly for a long, long time. Bit by bit, Oa's spine relaxed. She released her stranglehold on her knees, and lifted her head. Darkness had fallen over the bay, but still Isabel kept her in the protective circle of her arms. A chill wind cooled Oa's cheeks. Isabel kept one arm around Oa's shoulders, and with the other hand, she pulled the collar of her coat higher against the cold.

Peacefully, Isabel said, "This is such a beautiful place. And here we are, just the two of us. Look up there, do you see the stars coming out?"

Oa followed her pointing finger. A few brave stars had twinkled to life, dodging gray wisps of cloud in a sky gone violet. A lighted ferry made its slow, majestic progress toward the city docks. Shadows hid the peaks to the west. The night sounds of the city were diminished by the wind. It did seem that they were alone, truly alone. Oa could almost imagine they were on the island of the anchens, on the great rock where the anchens sat together in the evenings, looking out over Mother Ocean, remembering.

Isabel said, "Oa, when I was a girl of about fifteen, I began to hear the call to priesthood in my heart. I tried not to, I tried to push it away, but it was still there. For a long time I kept it a secret, because I knew my parents wouldn't like it. I was eighteen when the Priestly Order of Mary Magdalene was established, and I wanted more than anything to join. I told my mother and father, and they were just as unhappy as I thought they would be. But I had to do it. I remember my father being angry, because he thought I would become something else, something he thought was more important. And my mother was sad, because she wanted me to have children. It was a very hard day, and it was hard for me to tell them.

"The difference was that my parents understood what I was saying. They understood about priesthood. And even though they were disappointed in my choice, they still loved me, and they said so."

Oa, listening to Isabel's calm voice, felt her eyelids droop. How easy it would be to allow her head to rest on Isabel's shoulder, to curl up against Isabel's slender body, safe, secure. How sweet it was to rest in the circle of Isabel's arm. She felt a yawn start in her throat, and she made herself blink and swallow it away.

"And now, Oa, you've tried to tell me something just as important to you as my priesthood was to me. I know how hard it was. I know you were being brave. But I didn't understand." She stroked Oa's cheek with her palm. "Important things are happening, Oa. I need to know what they are, to help you, to help the others. Could you be brave a little longer, sweetheart, and try to explain?"

Now she released Oa's shoulders. Oa sighed, relinquishing Isabel's warmth. She looked up into Isabel's eyes, like clear little lights beckoning in the dusk.

"Did you understand all that I said, Oa?"

Oa nodded, and looked toward the water again. The ferry had floated into its berth at the city docks. "Oa understands," she said. She felt Isabel waiting beside her, not tense like Doctor might have been, or quick like Doctor Simon, but simply still, open, ready.

It had been so hard to say the first time. And now she must do it again. She found a strand of her hair with her fingers and tugged on it.

ISABEL WATCHED OA struggling, knowing there was nothing more she could do to help her. She breathed deeply, letting her body be still. Oa's eyes flickered with reflected light, golden motes sparkling in their black depths. Her lips were moving. Isabel leaned toward her.

"Raimu-ke," Oa whispered into the night. "Raimu-ke."

If there was anything Isabel could recognize, it was a prayer. Oa was praying. But to whom? And for what? "Oa, who is Raimu-ke?"

Oa bit her lip, and one hand reached into the empty air, searching for a word. "Raimu-ke . . . Raimu-ke is . . . in kburi. Is an anchen."

"I don't think I understand."

Oa shook her head. "No. No." She tipped her head up, looking into the stars. "Oa," she said carefully, "is an anchen. An-chen, Isabel. Very—" She touched her trembling lips with her tongue. "Oa is very old. More old than Isabel. More old than Doctor Simon."

When her voice trailed away, Isabel nodded. "Yes," she said quietly. "Doctor Simon told me this, Oa."

Oa's eyes went wide, and she nodded vigorously. "Yes," she said. "Anchen."

"And is that what anchen means, Oa?" Isabel asked. "Does anchen mean very old?"

"Yes," Oa said again. She sighed, a sound so full of sadness that Isabel almost drew her into her embrace once again. "Oa is an anchen. Not—" Her voice caught, and she swallowed. "Not a person."

The girl's sorrow was as palpable as the foamcast beneath them. Isabel could bear it no longer. She took the child in her arms again, and laid her cheek against the soft curling black hair. "Oa," Isabel said softly. "Oa is a person. A person to love."

Oa leaned against her and began to weep, great deep sobs that shook her small body, the sobs of someone who has been holding back for a very long time. Isabel held her, and let her cry. Above her head she saw Matty Phipps watching them from the top of the tiered park. She lifted her free hand to her, and then pressed it again on Oa's back. For long minutes she held the weeping child, and she gazed out over the peaceful bay, her mind spinning. Not a person? What could it mean?

15

"IT'S NOT JUST a language barrier, Simon," Isabel said. She frowned, and her hand strayed to her scalp. "There's something cultural, too. Something I can't fathom." They sat together at the table in her suite. Oa was in bed, asleep almost before her head touched the pillow. They had come back very late from their walk. They had eaten a late dinner, though no one had much appetite after the ice cream feast of the afternoon. Simon had already shown Isabel the highlights of the medicator scan. A half-finished pot of espresso rested between them. Simon expected it to keep him awake too late, but he hadn't wanted to refuse Isabel's offer.

"Tell me what happened."

Isabel said, "It was as if she were confessing something shameful, Simon, something really awful. As if it could be her fault! Or as if she had been deliberately hiding it. She expected me to be angry, I'm certain of that. She was startled when I told her I already knew she was older than she seemed. The tattoos have something to do with it—I guess that's obvious. But I don't understand what it is that troubles her."

"She's picked up a good bit of English, though," Simon said.

Isabel nodded. "Well, she seems to understand everything I say. But these words she uses—anchen, and tatwaj—she can't translate them." She sipped from her cup, and set it down. "I'm no linguist, I'm afraid. The colony would probably have spoken Swahili, which became a sort of pan-African language in their time, I believe, but blended with Bambara and Old French. I tried these words in a translation program, but I didn't get any response. It could be idiosyncratic pronunciation, or it could be that the language mutated after the Sikassa emigrated. I can theorize that tatwaj has something to do with the tattoos. Oa was able to explain that anchen means very old, but not why that should be shameful. What written language the Sikassa had was obviously lost, which makes it the more remarkable that Oa was able to teach herself to read as much as she did with the books Matty gave her." She shrugged, and a fond smile curved her lips. "Children are so quick with languages."

Simon drew breath, but then he released it without comment. She needed no reminder. Isabel knew perfectly well what the issue was. And perhaps childhood should not be measured only by years of life. Perhaps the failure of Oa's body to mature meant that her mind, also, would not acquire the attributes of maturity. Along with the wisdom of age, after all, came a certain rigidity, a loss of receptivity. Old dogs and new tricks, he thought, smiling. Oa could never be called an old dog.

"Simon." He looked up, and found Isabel regarding him with her slender dark brows lifted. "What's amusing you?"

"I'm just thinking that we may have to reassess how we determine maturity," he said lightly. "Because Oa may be old, but she's still a child. An old child."

That brought on one of Isabel's glorious wide smiles, her eyes alight, the lines of her face smoothing. "That's it exactly, isn't it, Simon? That's it. Oa is an old child!"

ASH WEDNESDAY ARRIVED as they waited for the board of regents to reconvene. Isabel had called the cathedral on the hill above the Multiplex, the Cathedral of St. James, offering to say the Mass in the absence of a resident priest. She was informed in a chilly tone that the bishop was sending an itinerant priest from another city. The receptionist didn't say, A *real* priest, but the implication was clear. Isabel shook her head as she put down the wavephone. Marian would have been furious. Eighteen years . . . She thought of her sister priests, their discipline, their devotion, their self-denial. Centuries of tradition stood in the way of their full acceptance.

Isabel went to stand by the window, looking out over the roofs. Oa came out of her bedroom to stand beside her, letting her little hand creep into Isabel's as she often did now. The skin of her palm was delicate and warm. Isabel smiled down at her. "Good morning, Oa."

Oa nodded solemnly. "Good morning, Isabel."

"Did you sleep well?"

Another nod. "Oa sleeps well." And after a little pause, "And Isabel sleeps well?"

Isabel did not smile at the error. "Yes. I slept well, thank you."

And Oa said, "Thank you."

"It makes me happy, Oa, to hear you speak so well. I'm proud of you."

Oa flashed her white smile.

Their breakfast arrived, and as they sat down together, Isabel said, "Today is an important day for me, Oa. A day when I go to church to pray and to reflect on life, and death, and rebirth. It's called Ash Wednesday."

"Ash Wednesday."

"Yes. Would you like to go to church?"

"Oa goes with Isabel?"

"If you like."

"Yes. Oa likes to go to church. With Isabel."

THE CHURCH WAS different from anything Oa had yet seen on Earth. As they walked in through its tall doors, a bell was ringing with a deep, sweet tone that Oa felt in her bones. The floor was cold and hard, and the ceiling arched high, dim and smoke-stained and echoing. At first she thought there were people standing on shelves set into the walls, and then she realized they were not real, but carved figures wearing long robes and holding curious things in their hands. Little lights flickered below them like tiny lamps. Like the candle Isabel lit every morning for her prayers.

Oa followed the arch of the roof with her eyes, up and up and up, to a circular window set into the very center. Soft light came through the window to fall on an ancient, chipped table. Oa flared her nostrils, and they filled with the spicy fragrance of some burned herb, and the peaceful scent of an old, much-loved place.

She looked up at Isabel and whispered, "Oa likes it."

Isabel smiled. "I like it, too."

There were more people in the church than Oa had ever seen at one time, more even than at the tatwaj, when the people of the three islands all came together. She stared, openmouthed in wonder at the variety of them. She saw skin in every shade between Isabel's pale one and her own dark one, even one or two as dark as Oa, who wore their curling hair short, or wound into elaborate shapes. There were men, women, a few children, who looked at Oa and Isabel curiously. Oa peered shyly past the curtain of her hair, holding fast to Isabel's arm. Several people smiled and nodded at the two of them. Some glanced at Isabel's white collar and Magdalene cross, and they narrowed their eyes and turned away. One very young woman, with a baby on her hip, grinned at Isabel and said, "Hi, Mother." Isabel returned her greeting.

Isabel led Oa to a seat on a long bench facing the center of the church. Matty Phipps sat on the bench behind theirs. Isabel pointed to the white table. "That's the altar, Oa."

"Al-tar."

"Right. Altar. And you see, there beside the altar?" She pointed to the cross, with the suffering figure hanging on it.

"Raimu?"

Isabel shook her head. "I don't know, Oa. We call it a crucifix."

"Cru-ci-fix."

"That's right." Isabel knelt, and put her hands together, as she did in her morning prayers. Oa knelt beside her in imitation. Isabel smiled at her, and then closed her eyes and turned forward, toward the white table. And the crucifix. Some people in long robes, like those of the statues, moved here and there lighting candles, spreading a cloth on the table, setting silver cups on a sideboard. All of it together, Oa thought, made a kburi. She almost touched Isabel's arm to tell her so, but then she dropped her hand. She wasn't sure.

Isabel opened her eyes, and the two of them sat down. A moment later, a crash of sound made Oa jump. Isabel touched her hand, and Oa relaxed, but it took a few seconds for her ears to adjust to the volume of it, to understand that it was music. It seemed to fill her head right to the brim. The people in robes made a procession up one of the aisles to their places around the kburi—the altar—and Ash Wednesday began.

After a time Isabel left Oa with Matty and joined a long line of people making a slow progress around the altar. When she returned, she bore a smear of gray on her forehead, and she knelt again for a long time. There was singing, and a lot of incomprehensible words. Oa watched the people move back and forth, up to the altar, back to their seats, the robed ones weaving in and out with slow, sure steps. Everyone seemed to know just what to do and when to do it, as if they had performed the ritual many times, and always in the same way. Oa supposed that, as with the tatwaj, they had. The mark on Isabel's forehead reminded her of the tatwaj, too, although it couldn't mean the same thing. Of that she had no doubts at all.

They left the church together, with Matty following. One of the men in robes stood by the tall doors, shaking hands with the people who filed past him. He wore the same white collar as Isabel, and he put out his hand to her. "You're a Magdalene," he said.

"Yes." Isabel shook his hand. "I'm Isabel Burke."

He nodded. "I saw you on the news." He glanced down at Oa, past her to Matty, then back to Oa. He had kind eyes, she thought. Not brilliant ones, like Isabel's, but nice. "This is the girl, then?" he asked.

"This is Oa," Isabel said. "Oa of Virimund."

"Hello, Oa," the priest said.

Oa ducked her head. Isabel said, "Oa is rather shy, Father."

The priest chuckled. "I am, too, Oa. Don't worry about it." He released Isabel's hand, saying, "Mother Burke, the sacristan told me you called. It was generous of you, especially under the circumstances."

"I've missed saying Mass," Isabel said softly.

The other priest nodded, and bent closer to murmur, "Our bishop is old-fashioned."

"I understand," Isabel said. She turned to go down the broad stone steps.

The priest called after them, "Good luck, Mother Burke. I'll keep you in my prayers."

"Thank you, Father," Isabel said over her shoulder. As they descended the stairs to the street, Oa heard her say, under her breath, "We'll need them."

ISABEL GAZED OUT the car's window as they descended the hill to the Multiplex. Spring was in full swing, she decided, though the indifferent sunshine spoke of winter still. But daffodils and tulips had sprung up in window boxes and beds, and buds swelled slowly on the deciduous trees. The Tuscan hills would be turning green under the March sunshine. She thought with a pang of the Mother House, the quiet chatter of the novices clustered on the patio to study, the ringing of the bell for Mass in the ancient chapel. Marian in her office, waiting to hear of Isabel's success, of the bolstering of the Magdalenes' reputation.

"Isabel?"

She tore herself back to the present. "Yes, Oa."

Oa pointed to Isabel's forehead and whispered, a question, "Tatwaj?"

Isabel couldn't think for a moment what she meant. She put her hand to her forehead, and when it came away smeared with ash, she remembered. "Oh," she said. She turned her hand to show Oa the smudge. "This is ash, which is why we call it Ash Wednesday. Do you know the word 'ash'? Ash is what's left when you burn something. In this case, palm branches that is, fronds of the palm tree. The ashes remind us of our mortality."

Oa sighed and nodded. "Not-tatwaj," she said, with an unreadable expression on her face, something like relief, something like sadness.

SIMON WAS WAITING in their suite, and he stood up when they came in. "How was it?"

Isabel shrugged out of her coat. "It was traditional," she said. "The cathedral is a bit dilapidated, but it's a beautiful old building. Wonderful bronze doors, and an oculus." She turned and helped Oa with her coat and hat. "And a nice young priest to say Mass," she added, hoping she had kept the wryness from her tone.

"Ah." Simon smiled at her, and she allowed herself to enjoy the warmth that their mutual understanding always gave her. He said, "Do you want some lunch?"

"Not for me," Isabel said. "But Oa is probably hungry. Are you, Oa?"

Oa had settled herself on one of the chairs with her little reader. Matty Phipps had brought some new disks from the Multiplex library, and she was spending every spare minute with them. She spoke without glancing up. "Oa is hungry."

Matty laughed. "Oa is always hungry," she said cheerfully. "And so am I. How about if I take her down to the kitchens? Okay by you, Mother Burke?"

"Thank you, Matty. You're a great help."

"Nah." She grinned and turned to the door. "Come on, Oa. Food!"

With a glance at Isabel, Oa pushed away her reader and followed Matty.

"I'll see you soon, Oa."

Matty grinned and waved as they went out into the hall.

The moment the door closed, Simon said, "I want to show you something, Isabel."

The table was covered with piles of plastic-sleeved disks, a few scattered hardcopies, piles of flexcopies, and Simon's computer. He turned the screen to face Isabel. She sat down, and he pulled a chair close beside her. When his shoulder brushed hers, the warmth of flesh and solidity of bone radiated strength and confidence, made her want to lean into him. Sometimes, she thought, her little talent was more a curse than a blessing. She bit her lip to make herself concentrate.

"You see this," he said, pointing to a figure on the screen. "This is the hormone the medicator couldn't identify." He brought up a scanning image to overlay on the chart. "And this"—pointing again—"is a small anterior pituitary tumor. It was on the imaging scans, and Adetti didn't want you to see it. That's what's producing the hormone."

"What is the hormone, Simon? What is it doing?"

"Well," he said, sitting back in his chair. "As to what it is—give it whatever name fits, because we haven't seen it before. Adetti wants to call it delayed senescence factor. As to what it does—it's producing telomerase."

Isabel stared at the three-dimensional image, the tiny scarlet cloud Simon had touched with his fingertip. Her heart beat loudly in her ears. Even the word "tumor" was upsetting. "Benign tumor, Simon?"

"Yes, it's benign."

"And what's telomerase?"

"First you have to know what telomeres are." He leaned past her to bring up another screen. "Telomeres are the caps that stabilize the ends of chromosomes. Every time a cell divides, its telomeres get a little shorter, thereby dictating how many times a cell can divide before it shuts down." He pointed to an artist's rendering of a cell. "Telomerase is an enzyme that lengthens and strengthens telomeres, replacing the bits of DNA lost in ordinary cell division. Cancer cells have a lot of telomerase, for example. It stops malignant tumors from shedding telomeres, the natural process of cell decay and death, and helps make the tumors stronger than the healthy cells around them. Oa's little tumor is producing telomerase, and a lot of it. It's interacting with her own hormones in some way that will require more study. And it's stopping her from aging."

Isabel stared at the colorful diagram. Hardly knowing she did it, she took her cross in her fingers. "Simon . . . how long . . . I mean, theoretically . . ."

"Theoretically, Isabel, forever. Barring accidents. I suspect her immune system is almost impregnable. And she probably aged normally right to the point of puberty, and then stopped."

"And the others, then . . ." Isabel took a deep breath. "The other children must be the same. Old children."

"I think they must be," Simon said gently.

"And their parents? The adults?"

"I hope Oa can tell us something about that," Simon said. She turned to look at him. He was watching her intently, his expression sympathetic. "There has been no sign of other Sikassa on Virimund. Only the children on the island. I know you don't want to push Oa, Isabel.

But before anything else happens, to her or to the others, we need to understand. And we're going to be under a lot of pressure from ExtraSolar. They need that power park, to supply the long-range transports. And what they need, the charter nations want them to have. It's not just Adetti's ambition we're dealing with, but a necessity."

She nodded slowly. "Yes. I see that." She stood up, and moved to the window, which had the same view as her own, the flat rainwashed roofs of the Multiplex stretching away down the sloping landscape. "But what Adetti and Boreson care about is this hormone, this telomerase-producing substance."

"I presume so."

Isabel sighed. "He knew? Adetti?"

"He must have known about the tumor. Whether he was able to understand the function of the hormone, I don't know. I have more research experience in this area, of course, because I worked with reproductive problems in the Victoria Desert. And—" He laughed. "Frankly, I'm just a hell of a lot smarter than Adetti is."

"I know, Simon. I know." She twisted her fingers together. "He's so cold, though, he and Boreson both. I'm surprised he didn't just take out the tumor, squeeze it for all it's worth."

"Maybe he thought of the fable," Simon mused. "The goose that laid the golden egg."

"Yes, perhaps." She turned her back to the window, and folded her arms. "So this is a profit issue, for Adetti, and for Boreson."

"Sure. Fame and fortune. They think they've got their hands on an anti-aging miracle."

"Maybe they do, Simon."

He spread his hands. "If you believe in miracles," he said. "I'm all for science, myself."

She smiled a little, saying drily, "I believe I remember that, Dr. Edwards."

Simon stood up, and leaned on the table, his palms pressed flat against the wood. "Isabel. There's something else."

She raised her eyebrows, waiting.

"They threatened me. Us, I should say."

"Threatened us? How?"

He sighed, and she saw now how tired he was, the lines around his mouth deeply graven. "Somebody's been doing some digging, I'm afraid." He straightened, stretching his shoulders. "Probably happy to have anything they can use to discredit us. Somebody at the Victoria project told them."

Isabel's mouth went dry. "Oh, lord. Told them about you and me."

He nodded, his lips pursed. "Yes. I'm sorry, Isabel."

"But that's personal!" she exclaimed. She was surprised at how much it hurt, how fresh her shame still was. "That doesn't affect your professionalism . . . or even mine!"

"Question of character," he said shortly. He came around the table to stand beside her. She knew he meant to support her, to comfort her, but his nearness only sharpened her pain.

"You mean," she faltered, searching his face with her eyes. "My character. Because of Oa, and the guardianship."

"That's it."

He didn't touch her, but she felt the warmth of him, so close, and she longed to put her head on his shoulder, to let his capable arms take away the weight of responsibility. She shook her head sharply, and moved a step away.

"They don't know anything, though, Isabel. Not really."

"If they ask me . . ."

He gave a short, bitter laugh. "Oh, I know, Mother Burke. If they ask you, you'll tell them everything. But it's not you they threatened to ask. It's Anna."

Isabel put her hands over her eyes. "Oh, god, Simon. Anna."

"And if she tells them what they want to know, they'll use it against us."

"And will she?"

He nodded. "She's one of the most honest people I've ever known. I'm not sure she's capable of a direct lie. Or even a mild prevarication."

"Poor Anna," was all Isabel could say, wearily, sadly. "Poor Anna."

16

WHEN THEY WALKED into the boardroom at the Seattle World Health offices, Isabel felt tension grip the room, a heart-stopping cessation of sound and movement.

They had decided, she and Simon, that the board of regents should meet Oa.

Simon led the way, looking fresh and well-rested in a smoke-gray suit with pencil lapels and a cheerful green ribbon tie. Isabel wore a fresh clerical collar, and her Magdalene cross on its simple cord. With Jin-Li's help, they had shopped for Oa. The girl's slender arms and long, thin legs were exaggerated by the straight lines of her white neosilk jumpsuit, and her dark skin and hair were glorious against the pale fabric. Isabel had braided her hair into two long plaits that hung over her shoulders and across her flat chest, almost reaching her waist. Oa carried the plush teddy bear in her arms. Her eyes were wide with anxiety, and she touched her tongue to her lips, over and over. She clung tightly to Isabel's hand.

Simon had arranged for small readers to be set up at every chair for the tutorial on Oa's condition. Water carafes waited in the center of the table, and there was a flexcopy chart at each place. All the regents were present as well as Gretchen Boreson and Paolo Adetti. Cole Markham stood beside the door. Boreson held a silver pen in her right hand, and she tapped it incessantly into her left palm. She didn't look up when Oa came in, but everyone else in the room did.

Isabel and Simon and Oa sat together at one end of the long table.

Simon began. "Ladies and gentlemen, I think you will have guessed by now that this young lady is Oa of Virimund."

Isabel nodded to Oa, and Oa said, in an almost inaudible whisper, "Hello."

The Iranian regent smiled at her. "Hello, Oa."

Dr. Fujikawa stared at Oa, and then gave Adetti a deliberate frown. Simon let a silence stretch before he cleared his throat and began.

"Our purpose today," he said, "is to acquaint the board with the results of our work in the past week. Mother Burke and I will also explain why we think the installation of the Virimund power park should be postponed."

Boreson's eyes flashed, and her scarlet lips pursed. Adetti sat as if carved from stone.

Madame Mahmoud said, "I hope you know we're only here to help, Oa."

Oa leaned close to Isabel, her cheek almost touching her sleeve. Isabel said gently, "Do you understand Madame Mahmoud, Oa?"

Oa whispered, "Oa understands."

Isabel smiled at the Iranian woman. "Oa's English is improving every day. She understands almost everything, but she is often unable to express herself in detail."

Madame Mahmoud nodded. "Children are very quick in this way."

Adetti expelled a noisy breath, and shifted in his chair. Boreson shot him a cold look.

"Madame Mahmoud is right, of course," Isabel said. "And we understand, Dr. Edwards and I, that Dr. Adetti does not regard Oa as a child."

Beside her, Oa hung her head. Isabel went on. "Chronological age, as every medical practitioner knows, is not the same as biological age.

And in this unique circumstance, we must also take into consideration emotional and mental age. It's true that Oa has lived many years—" She squeezed the child's fingers to reassure her. She had already explained what she would be saying, and why, but Oa's unease radiated through her very bones, filling Isabel's hand with a prickly discomfort. "Oa is, by every other criterion, a child. A healthy, intelligent, and often charming child."

Simon gave Adetti his practiced cold smile. "Dr. Adetti does not agree with our assessment," he said. "But that's not the crux of our discussion today." He flicked on the small reader before him, and the regents followed his example. As he had with Isabel, he led them through the explanation about osteon counts in cortical bone. He spoke of the stability of Oa's hormone levels, and of the enzyme that the medicator had not been able to identify. He showed the scan of the small tumor on her pituitary gland, and described it.

As Simon moved on to his conclusions, Isabel watched Adetti across the table. She didn't need to touch him to feel his dismay and resentment. The regents gathered around the conference table were, without exception, quick-minded people. Although there was no hint of triumph or scorn in Simon's demeanor, the implication of Adetti's failure was unavoidable. And there was no time to waste on diplomacy.

"We need to discover what caused the tumor, to know if the hydrogen workers on Virimund are at risk," Simon said finally. "Oa is unable to tell us. Mother Burke has learned a lot from her, which she will share with you in a moment. But as World Health's advisory physician, I'm categorically opposed to kidnapping more 'subjects,' as Dr. Adetti and Administrator Boreson have proposed. What is needed is research on the planet itself, to discover the source of Oa's condition, and that, presumably, of any other surviving children."

Dr. Fujikawa leaned forward. "Dr. Edwards, we thank you for your presentation. Please clarify to me that there is still no sign of an adult population on Virimund?"

Beside Isabel, Oa drew a sharp breath. Isabel felt the fresh wave of fear that surged through her, but there was no time to wonder at it.

Simon glanced at Boreson. She said coolly, "Offworld Port Force on Virimund was instructed to cease any exploration, and they have of course complied. I spoke with the Port Administrator by r-wave yesterday, and he assured me this was the case."

Madame Mahmoud asked, "Do we know, yet, how old the girl actually is?"

And Isabel said, "We think we do."

OA COULDN'T LOOK at Doctor when she came into the big room behind Isabel and Doctor Simon. She saw him at the table next to Gretchen, but she averted her eyes. She clutched the fuzzy toy with one hand, and clung to Isabel with the other. She tried to keep her shoulders straight like Isabel's, but she trembled.

The room was cold. Oa was glad of her new clothes, the warm socks and shoes Jin-Li Chung had found for her. It was a strange place, with blank walls and no windows. The people sat around a long plain table, and their eyes burned her with their curiosity.

Doctor Simon talked a long time, and pictures flashed on the little reader set before Isabel. Oa watched the pictures, knowing they were about her, and she listened to Doctor Simon. It was hard to follow, but Isabel had explained it slowly to her the night before. Doctor Simon knew she was an anchen, and he was telling these strangers about her. And she knew what was coming when Isabel turned to her.

It wasn't as if she had a choice. She was, after all, an anchen, despite Isabel's kindness. She was still an anchen, even though Doctor Simon liked talking to her, and even though Jin-Li Chung brought her clothes that fit and shoes that were comfortable. She was still an anchen, though Matty Phipps didn't mind eating meals with her and standing by while she worked with Isabel. She could straighten her shoulders, and hold her head up like Isabel, but it didn't change anything. She was an anchen, but she would be a brave one. She had prayed to Raimu-ke, this morning, kneeling with Isabel before her crucifix, asking Raimu-ke to make her brave.

Oa remembered her last tatwaj. She had tried to pretend she didn't know what was coming. She felt like a person. She loved her papi and her mamah, she had fears and hopes and dreams. Surely, something would save her, she thought. She had prayed to the ancestors, along with every-one else, prayed for her menarche. But of course, if she had no soul, the ancestors would not hear her. Her prayers would mean nothing.

The roar of the bonfire filled her ears. Its heat burned her cheeks. Above her the stars twinkled menacingly, colder than she had ever seen them. Her menarche had not come. It was the tatwaj, and it had not come. She closed her eyes as the elder picked out her tattoo with the needle, as the ink stung her skin. When she opened her eyes, she saw her mother staring at her.

Why, Mamah? she wanted to cry. Why? You saw my tattoos, you counted them, one, two, three, you said them to yourself. Why are you shocked?

She turned to Papi. He had turned his face away, and would not look at her. The fire blazed, and the people chanted the old song, and one by one, the children went forward to be counted. One, two, three, four, and then the rising ululation, the celebratory wail. One, two three, four, five, six, another joyous cry. One, two, three, all the way to twelve, but still the acclamation. And then it was Oa's turn.

Oa stood to roll up the long sleeves of her jumpsuit. The fabric was soft and stretchy, and it folded easily up to her shoulders. She heard the little intake of breath around the table, and her fingers shook. Isabel stood with her, helping her, pulling her braids out of the way, pulling down her collar. The air chilled her exposed skin. At her shiver, Isabel touched her cheek with her fingers, just a quick caress, but it was calming. Oa looked up into Isabel's clear eyes, and then down at her own thin dark arms, covered with columns of tattoos.

She could see, without a mirror, the last one made by the elder of the people. It was inked into her right forearm, just above the elbow, a distinct ♦, four points to show the four seasons of the year, the seasons that rolled relentlessly by, leading from tatwaj to tatwaj. She had learned no word in English for the tatwaj. These people had no tatwaj. The children of this cold world did not have to fear the counting.

Isabel spoke in a clear voice, keeping a steady hand on Oa's shoulder. "As you can see, Oa bears ritual markings on her arms and shoulders." Gently, she turned Oa so that her neck, exposed by the braiding of her hair, would be visible to the observers. Just as gently, she turned her back to face them all. "There are two kinds of tattoos. These on Oa's shoulders—" She touched Oa's left shoulder with a finger. "These are neatly done, with a good deal of skill, even artistry." She lifted Oa's wrist. "You can see that the others are rougher, unevenly executed."

Isabel smiled down at her, as calm and assured as if they were alone. "Would you like to sit down, Oa?" she murmured. Isabel held out the chair for her, and waited until she was seated and had rolled down her sleeves again.

"The difference between the markings is important," Isabel said. "There are fourteen of the first type, the ones that seem to have been, shall we say, professionally done. Of the second type, there are eighty-eight."

Oa listened to Isabel saying the numbers. She had learned numbers on the ship, and could count in English all the way to a thousand. One number was missing. Surely all four seasons had passed since she left Virimund, and perhaps more. And before that? How long since the anchens had seen the white smoke, the sign of the tatwaj from the three islands? Oa squeezed the teddy bear anxiously.

"It was clear to me that these meant something essential to Oa. Before her English improved, she couldn't explain them to me, but in the past week, I think I have arrived at their meaning." Isabel's hand caressed Oa's hair. "Oa uses a word, tatwaj, for which there is apparently no English equivalent. The pronunciation makes it difficult to understand, and of course, she has no way to spell it. It doesn't mean the tattoos, I believe, but the ceremony when the markings are applied. The adults of her people are responsible for the first of Oa's tattoos, the fourteen."

Oa watched the reactions of these strange people to the revelation that was coming. Doctor Simon, on Isabel's left, had put his fingertips together and was gazing at them. Doctor, who Oa now understood was called Doctor Adetti, was glaring across the table. At first Oa thought he was glaring at her, and she wanted to look away, but then she realized his hard black gaze was fixed on Isabel.

"The other eighty-eight markings," Isabel went on, "were made by the other children. The anchens, Oa calls them, as she calls herself an anchen. Oa herself will try to explain the significance of these ritual markings to you."

A little stir rolled around the long table.

Isabel pulled out her chair and sat down. The room was utterly silent except for the mechanical sounds in the background, air moving, power humming. Oa touched her lips with her tongue. It was frightening, looking around at these strange faces, these curious eyes, pale Gretchen's hungry look, Doctor Adetti's fury. But she would be strong, for Isabel.

She had practiced the words, and Isabel had written them on her computer. It looked strange, seeing her own words spelled out like the words in books.

"Oa?" Isabel prompted softly. "Can you tell the regents about the tatwaj?"

"Yes," Oa said. She decided she would just talk to Isabel, and the others, the "regents," could listen. Doctor and Gretchen could listen, and Matty and Doctor Simon. But she would talk to Isabel. "Yes," she said again. "Oa is telling about the tatwaj."

Isabel gave her a private smile.

Oa anchored herself in Isabel's crystal gaze, and began.

"Tatwaj comes in dry time," she said. Her voice sounded thin in the big room, a thread of sound, easily torn. As she spoke, she could hear the breathing of those around her, the faint gurgle of someone's stomach. She swallowed, and tried to speak louder. "First comes singing time, when nuchi are ripe and fish are much coming. Then comes sleeping time, and comes much rain. The people stay in shahto. And forest spiders come in sleeping time." She stumbled over "forest spiders," remembering how hard she had searched for the words in English. Isabel had shown her many pictures before they found one that fit, but they had to put two different words together to make a word close enough.

Someone coughed, and Oa looked in his direction. Isabel said softly, "Continue when you're ready, Oa."

"After sleeping time comes time of—" She faltered, forgetting the word. Isabel's gaze was steady, patient. "Birth time," Oa remembered. "The people are fishing, are cleaning shahto and making mats. Babies are coming."

Across the table, Doctor Adetti shifted suddenly in his chair, making it squeak. Oa looked at him, and saw Gretchen lift a finger in his direction. Doctor's jaw clenched. No one else moved. Oa turned back to Isabel, trying to remember where she had been in her recitation.

"And after the birth time?" Isabel prompted.

"After birth time comes dry time," Oa said. "Dry time is last. Then is coming the tatwaj."

"And what is the tatwaj, Oa?" Isabel asked gently. She turned her face to sweep the room with her eyes.

Oa followed her gaze. "The tatwaj," she said, "is the counting."

The Iranian lady, Madame Mahmoud, was watching her with her lips parted, not a hungry look like Gretchen's, but one of wonder, and of waiting.

"And what is counted at the tatwaj?" Isabel pressed.

Oa's voice failed her the first time she tried to speak it. She swallowed, and tried again. "At the tatwaj, are counting the children. The . . . the marks. On the children." She held up her wrist to show hers.

"Can you explain why, Oa? Why do the people count the children's marks?"

Oa lowered her wrist to the table, and traced the ragged diamond shape with one finger. With her head down, she said miserably, "The people are counting the children. To know if they are anchens."

"What is an anchen, Oa?"

Oa's throat was dry, her voice growing smaller. "Not a person."

"And," Isabel persisted. "What do the people do when they find anchens?"

"They are sending them to the island," Oa whispered.

"The island of the anchens?"

"Yes."

"Who else lives on the island, Oa?"

"No one. Not people. Only anchens."

"Only children, then?"

"No. Anchens," Oa repeated. "Only anchens."

17

"THERE IS A tattoo for every year of age," Simon told the regents. "Virimund years. One hundred and two in all."

Though Isabel had braced herself, the gasps of the regents made her shudder. Oa, too, quivered. Isabel put an arm around her shoulders.

"I know this is shocking," Simon said. "But the bone histology, with a margin of error of plus or minus twelve years, supports this conclusion."

"I don't suppose . . ." The regent from India lifted his fingers from the table, and then laid his hand down again. "No, surely not."

"A hoax?" Simon asked. "I can't see how."

Madame Mahmoud leaned forward. "How is this possible? And are all the—" She hesitated over the word, and then, with a flicker of her eyelids, pressed on. "The children—are they all so—" She shook her head.

"We don't know if they're all as old as Oa," Simon said. "Some may be older."

"They should all be brought here," Adetti put in swiftly. "Although we will be content if our request for two more subjects is granted."

Isabel glared at him. "After what happened on Virimund?"

"What did happen?" asked Mahmoud.

"They call it an incident," Isabel said. "It was an outrage."

"And what does the girl say about it?"

Isabel took a deep breath. "Oa either can't remember it or can't speak of it. The hydros had hand weapons, shock guns. They fired them at the children."

"If they are children," Adetti said sourly.

"World Health categorically opposes ESC's request to force another Sikassa to emigrate," Simon said coolly. "Until we understand the situation fully, there must be no further interference with the population on Virimund."

Gretchen Boreson leaned forward, her hands linked before her on the table. Her nails were long and silver, making Isabel think of shards of ice. "Dr. Edwards," Boreson said smoothly. "This—child—" Her inflection was minimal, but pointed. "If she is unable or unwilling to answer our questions, what can we do but ask them of someone else?"

"We have no reason to think one of the other children will be more capable of putting things in perspective," Simon answered her. He looked around at the regents. Madame Mahmoud had a fire in her eye as she watched Boreson. Dr. Fujikawa frowned as he flicked screens on his reader. Simon went on, "There are a hundred unanswered questions. Even with the confidence Oa has developed in Mother Burke, there are cultural issues she cannot explain. It's not only language, but the lack of context. Mother Burke feels, and I agree, that the only way to solve the puzzle of the Sikassa colony is to go to Virimund, to interview the other—*children*—" He let the word hang in the air for a moment. "And to try to discover the source of the virus that caused Oa's tumor."

Adetti leaped to his feet. "Damn it!" he cried. Boreson lifted her hand, but she was too late to stop him. "This is *my* discovery!" he exclaimed. "You can parade your charts and scans all you want, Edwards, but that's no child sitting there, and DSF is going to be a priceless commodity!"

Simon let Adetti's outburst hang in the air for a moment before he said, looking around the table at the stunned faces, "By DSF, Dr. Adetti means 'delayed senescence factor.' He and Administrator Boreson have filed for a patent for the virus."

"Pardon, please, but this was not in our briefing." The furrows in Dr. Fujikawa's forehead grew deeper. "Would that not be a biological patent? I believe biological patents to be illegal since the genome scandals."

"Not," Adetti said triumphantly, "if the biological entity meets the criteria for function and application!"

Boreson put in, "We believe this virus does, since it—"

The regent from Oceania interrupted her, demanding of Adetti, "Delayed senescence? You're talking anti-aging, then. Longevity."

Adetti cried, "Exactly!"

Boreson gave the Oceania representative her chilly smile. "You can see that the benefit to humankind—"

Someone else called out a question, and someone else tried to answer it, and was interrupted. Voices rose. Gretchen Boreson's cheek began to twitch, and she pressed her fingers to it. Paolo Adetti, still standing, smiled across the table at Isabel and Oa. His eyes glittered in the cold light. Isabel dropped her eyes. Beside her, Simon sighed and closed his reader.

Isabel murmured, through the clamor, "That's all the progress we'll make today, I think."

Simon turned to look at her. His eyes shone with determination. "You know, Isabel," he said softly. "You're going to need me on Virimund."

"If they let us go," she said.

"Yes. If they let us go. But look at this bunch." He nodded to the regents, who were standing now in knots of two and three, arguing. "They're going to want answers."

"It's all about the virus, for them, isn't it, Simon? About long life. Not about the children. They're no better than . . ." Isabel let her sentence trail off. Paolo Adetti and Gretchen Boreson bent their heads together, talking.

"It's a great temptation, Isabel," Simon said. "Long life. Eternal youth."

Isabel closed her eyes against a deep wave of sadness, and breathed a prayer to her patroness for wisdom. Oa trembled beside her, a poor, frightened, ancient child.

JIN-LI AND MATTY Phipps hitched a ride on one of the Port Force trucks making early-morning deliveries in the city, jumping out when they reached the Old Space Needle. It was dwarfed by the spires and domes around it. Its old-fashioned supports were still visible, reinforced now from within, tubes of titanium alloy gleaming past painted steel. There had once been a restaurant at the top, now transformed into an observation deck for the spaceport. A nautilus slidewalk with translucent walls curled around the base and up to the Offworld Exhibit Gallery, just beneath the observation deck. To the east the Cascade range glimmered with snow, and to the west the Olympics lay shrouded in gray cloud.

The exhibit had only just opened for the day. They strolled past the yawning attendant, following a circular corridor to an arched portal leading to the first exhibit, Irustan. The holographic display shifted around them depending on where they stood.

The display was a simulated room with a white tile floor, a skyroof above their heads showing the constellations of an Irustani night sky. A wall niche held a met-olive, its gray-green leaves shining in the light. A mock rose grew from a planter, its vermilion blooms so true to life Jin-Li could almost smell their fragrance.

They moved to a new position, and found themselves looking out over a scene of an Irustani marketplace, where women in floating pastel veils were escorted by men in flat caps and soft shirts and trousers. In the distance they saw the rhodium mines, with the blazing star of Irustan turning everything to bronze. A recorded lecture on the uses of rhodium for r-wave communication began.

"Looks hot," Matty said.

"The star's very hot," Jin-Li said. "Earthers have to wear protective glasses and clothes. Even the Irustani do, and they've been there three hundred years."

"You liked it, Johnnie."

"It's a hard place, Matty. But colorful. Mysterious."

"Would you go back?"

"Can't." Jin-Li turned toward the portal to go to another exhibit.

"Why can't you?" Phipps asked, following. "If you liked the world, liked the work?"

Jin-Li stood gazing up at the skyroof. "I violated the Terms of Employment. Almost got booted out of Port Force and sent back to Hong Kong."

Phipps gave a low whistle. "You were taking a big chance, then, helping Mother Burke and the kid."

Jin-Li shrugged. "Sometimes you have to do what needs doing."

They moved down the circular corridor and stepped inside the next display. "Nuova Italia," Jin-Li said. "You've been there, Matty."

Matty grinned, looking around at the holographic images. "I'm seeing more of it right now than I saw when I was there," she said. "Never got off the transport."

It was a pastoral scene that might have come straight from an alpine meadow, had it not been for the odd, elongated beasts that cropped its short, yellowish grass. The recorded lecture described the vaccone, and the attempts of the research teams to make the meat edible to Earthers. It talked about the search for intelligent life, and the challenges of biotransforming the plant life of Nuova Italia. There was only one other display, a view from a hillside of the domed settlement Port Force had built for the scientific teams.

"Doesn't look like I missed much," Matty said.

Crescent was an ice world with soaring structures that the explorers had dubbed castles. No one as yet had any idea who or what had made them. It didn't look possible to Jin-Li that such shapes had grown naturally. Matty shivered, although the cold was only illusion.

Udacha was even more mysterious. Scattered monoliths rose from an empty plain, huge slabs of stone in some pattern that no one had yet discerned.

Virimund, though, was beautiful, a world of vivid blue sky, emerald green waters, white clouds, and pastel sand. They seemed to be standing on an island, looking out to sea. The sand glittered beneath their feet, and white-crested waves washed the beach. The lecture described hundreds of islands ringing the planet, mostly covered by rainforest. It spoke of the need for hydrogen, the abundant supply of water. No mention was made of the Sikassa.

"Beautiful," Phipps said. "If I weren't sick of space, I'd go there."

"Wish I could," Jin-Li said.

"Yeah? Haven't had enough?"

"I've always wanted to be an archivist," Jin-Li said, taking a last look at the view of Virimund. "I've always been curious, about people, about places. There's no archivist in the Virimund team. It was supposed to be uninhabited. Nothing to record."

"They'll need one now. You could ask for a promotion."

Jin-Li, with a low laugh, turned to the door. "I don't dare ask."

"Yeah. Sometimes best to lie low, huh?"

"Yes. Sometimes that's best."

AN ENORMOUS BOUQUET of spring flowers had appeared in Isabel's room, with a small card that read, FROM THE OFFICE OF THE GENERAL ADMINISTRATOR. Isabel raised her eyebrows at Simon, and he shrugged. "Oh, well," Isabel said. "It's not the flowers' fault." She left the arrangement where it was, in the center of the table.

Simon left early to attend another meeting of the regents. He thought it best that Isabel and Oa not come with him. They stayed behind, and sat over a leisurely breakfast. Isabel pointed out the different flowers to Oa, saying the names. "This is a tulip," she said.

"Tu-lip," Oa repeated.

"Yes. And this is a daffodil."

"Daff-o-dil."

"Baby's breath."

Oa's eyes widened. "Babies?"

Isabel laughed. "It sounds strange, Oa, but it's just a name. It doesn't have anything to do with babies. With a baby, I mean." She was learning to be careful about words. Oa took things literally. "Baby's breath is just a description."

"Baby's breath," Oa said slowly, tasting the alliteration. "Baby's breath."

"Tell me what flowers you have on Virimund."

Oa tugged on her braids, thinking. "Oa has nuchi flowers," she said. "And Oa has—" She frowned, struggling to find the words. "Water flowers? Flowers grow in Mar-Mar."

"You mean Mother Ocean," Isabel reminded her.

Oa flashed her white smile. "Yes. Mother Ocean."

"That's right." Isabel reached across the table and drew the pad and the colored pencils toward her. "Draw the flowers for me, Oa."

The girl selected a pink pencil, and sketched a flower that looked something like a sea anemone. Isabel watched her absently, wondering how Simon was faring with the regents. She had been relieved not to go again, to watch the curious faces staring at Oa as if she were on display in a zoo. She couldn't blame them, but it made her want to put herself between the child and—well, and the world. That, she feared, would not be possible.

"It's a beautiful flower," Isabel said. She was pleased by how quickly Oa had learned to use a pencil. She loved watching the deft, precise movements of her small fingers. "What is your word for it?"

"Marmala." Oa put a final touch on her drawing, and slid it toward Isabel. "Marmala grows in—in Mother Ocean—until the people are taking it. The people are eating the flower."

"Perhaps it's not truly a flower, then," Isabel said. "Perhaps it's a fruit, like the banana or the apple."

Oa frowned, tugging at her hair. "Not like banana. Not like apple. Marmala tastes like Mother Ocean. Like water of Mother Ocean."

"Ah," Isabel said, nodding. "Salty."

"Sal-ty."

Isabel smiled at her. "I don't know a flower like this one, Oa. Let's just use your word, the Sikassa word. We will call this marmala."

Oa smiled up at her. "Marmala is salty."

"Yes. Marmala is salty."

Oa chose another pencil, and Isabel gave her back the pad of paper. She rose and walked to the window to look out past the Multiplex to the city. Spring had brought color to Seattle. Shades of green layered the hills, lacy ferns, glossy rhododendrons beginning to bud, the feathery tops of evergreen trees bowing in the wind like dancers. Or, she thought, like priests reverencing the altar.

Marian Alexander had called the night before. Gretchen Boreson had been asking pointed questions about Isabel's relationship with Simon.

Marian said in a matter-of-fact way, "There's no question ESC has mistreated you, and the child as well."

Isabel bit her lip to stop herself protesting the understatement.

"You're in a political fight," Marian pointed out. "It's not your first. I know you can find a way to be diplomatic and still be effective."

"I don't think so, Marian," Isabel answered softly. "Not this time."

"They want you to step down. They're going to try to use your history to justify appointing someone else as guardian."

Isabel closed her eyes to picture Marian at her big desk, leaning back in her chair, the little r-wave transmitter glistening in her hand. She felt as far away from her home as if she were already on Virimund. "Oh lord," she breathed. "If Oa is hurt because of me . . . I can't bear it."

"Well, Isabel," Marian said lightly. "If they could make a case that your—shall we say, your relationship—reflected badly on your character as someone fit to have guardianship over a child, they may be able to remove you." There was a tiny pause, and then she added, "But my faith in you is unshaken, Isabel. The child is fortunate to have you as her advocate."

Isabel's throat had tightened. "Thank you, Mother," she whispered. "Thank you."

Her throat closed again, remembering. She took a slow breath, and turned back to Oa.

The child had laid down her pencil, and was gazing at a picture she had drawn, a sketch of a beach, the water vividly blue, big trees beyond in deep green, a column of gray smoke rising from somewhere among them.

"What is that, Oa?"

Oa didn't look up, but stared at her drawing. "Is the tatwaj," she said softly.

"It is? Because of the smoke?"

For a long moment, Oa didn't answer. Then she said, still staring at the paper, "Isabel? Are not finding the people?"

"I'm sorry—what do you mean, Oa?"

"The people," Oa whispered. "No sign . . ." She paused, and her fingers stretched over the paper as if the word she needed were there. "No sign . . . of adult pop—" The fingers curled, straightened. "Pop-u-la-tion."

"Oh." Isabel sank in the chair beside Oa once again. "You heard that at the meeting."

Oa pushed the drawing away from her. "Are not finding the people," she said.

Quietly, Isabel said, "Yes, Oa. That's right. The Port Forcemen on Virimund have not found your people."

"Are finding the anchens?" Oa asked, so softly Isabel almost couldn't hear her.

"Oa, the Port Forcemen are not allowed to go back to your island, not until I'm there, and Doctor Simon is there."

Oa reached for her teddy bear and held it close to her thin chest.

18

PAOLO ADETTI AND Simon Edwards glared at each other across Gretchen Boreson's office. The administrator sat with her hands on her desk, her linked fingers trembling even in repose.

"If you use this to hurt Isabel," Simon grated, "I will do everything in my power to discredit you."

Adetti glowered. "You're the one in trouble here, Doctor. Not me."

"Now, Paolo," Boreson said hastily. "Let's not talk that way. Surely, Dr. Edwards, we can reach some sort of understanding."

"Understanding? About your prying into my private life, and Isabel's?"

"Well," Boreson faltered. "Of course we only have the child's interests . . ."

"Rot," Simon said through stiff lips. "You may have beguiled the regents with talk of your 'delayed senescence factor,' but the media will be another question."

Boreson's pale cheeks grew even paler. "Please, Dr. Edwards,

Paolo. If all of this reaches the press, we'll have a circus on our hands."

"Exactly." Simon folded his arms, and leaned one shoulder against the wall, trying to let the tension out of his body. "Administrator, this entire incident was motivated by greed, pure and simple. You know it's true."

Adetti bristled. "You want Mother Burke's reputation ruined in the press?"

"You want your own ruined, Doctor? I can see that you lose your license."

"Wait, wait." Gretchen Boreson stood up. "Please, just a moment, Dr. Edwards. I have a compromise in mind."

He lifted one eyebrow.

"We—Paolo and I—we want to come with you. To Virimund. As observers."

Simon straightened. "Administrator, surely you're not well enough for a space voyage."

Her ice-blue eyes were bleak, and for the moment, the muscles of her face were still. "I won't get better staying here."

"But your physician must—"

Adetti interrupted. "We already have the clearance. We're going, Edwards."

"You're not," Simon said flatly. "I'll oppose it with the board."

"Dr. Edwards," Boreson began.

Adetti blurted, triumphantly, "I called your wife. We know all about it. The whole story."

Gretchen Boreson groaned, ever so slightly. Simon stared at Adetti, appalled and speechless. He thought of Anna, poor Anna, standing in the door of the house in Geneva, watching him drive away from her. None of this was her fault, not any part of it. How it must have hurt her to have this boorish man asking her personal, painful questions. Anna was as naive as she was honest. She would never have been able to deal with Paolo Adetti.

"Paolo," Boreson said. "Leave me alone with Dr. Edwards."

Adetti started to object, but the administrator gave him a frigid look, and he subsided. Simon watched, bemused by the power Boreson wielded, by the shallow stupidity that was Adetti's weakness. The ESC physician shot Simon an angry glance as he left. Simon would have laughed if he were not still reeling.

"I'm so sorry, Dr. Edwards," Boreson said. She sounded as if she meant it. "Please, come and sit down with me, and let's see if we can smooth things over."

"I want an apology," Simon said grimly. "From Adetti. And I want him to apologize to my wife as well."

"I'll see to it. You know, I didn't condone—"

"But you did," Simon said. Suddenly he felt weary beyond bearing. He crossed the room and took the offered chair, lowering himself into it slowly, as if his muscles hurt. "You condoned it by encouraging his greed."

Boreson met his gaze without flinching. "Well, yes. That may be true. We all want something, after all." She paused, and then added softly, "I expect what you want is to be with Isabel Burke."

SIMON HAD BEEN right. He so often was, Isabel reflected. It was all too easy to let him shoulder responsibility for making arrangements, filing reports. She watched him now, seated with his computer, a wavephone transmitter curling beneath his chin, his lean face intent. He had refused to discuss his meeting with Boreson and Adetti. As he reached to touch the computer screen, she thought how graceful his fingers were, deft and sensitive.

Her fingers tingled with the desire to touch his hand, to feel once again the rush of emotion that would surge from his skin to hers. That rush had been her undoing. Their first touch had been inadvertent and powerful. Irresistible.

Her cheeks burned at the memory. She forced herself to rise from the table, and go in search of Oa.

The regents had, at last, ordered ESC to lift the guard. Matty Phipps no longer shadowed them, nor did another guard stand outside the suite at night. They had three weeks of relative freedom before the transport departed for Virimund with Isabel, Simon, and Oa, an archivist, and a couple of Port Force technicians.

Oa's vocabulary and pronunciation improved rapidly with the books Isabel found for her. Isabel worried she was memorizing the pages of the books, but when she tested her on the computer or on flex-copies, Oa recognized the printed words. She had learned some simple math, a bit of Earth history, and what little was known of her people. But Oa was most interested in Isabel herself.

When Isabel knelt each morning before her traveling altar, Oa joined her, listening to the prayers, watching the ritual with her wide-eyed gaze. One morning, as Isabel bent to blow out the little candle, Oa asked diffidently, "Isabel? Mary Magdalene is an anchen?"

"Was," Isabel said automatically. "You mean to say, *was* Mary Magdalene an anchen?"

"Was." Oa repeated the correction. "Was Mary Magdalene an anchen?"

Isabel sat back on her heels, the crucifix still in her hand. "Oa, your word—anchen—it's a difficult one for me. I don't truly understand what it means."

The child looked up into Isabel's face with a trust that melted her heart. "Oa is an anchen." Only a week ago this very confession had caused the girl deep distress. Now she offered it almost eagerly.

"Yes," Isabel said gently, taking Oa's hand. "Yes, I understand that. But if you are an anchen—by which I think you mean a child who has lived many years—then Mary Magdalene was not. She lived to be very old, we think, but she was not a child."

"Mary Magdalene is—was—a person?" Oa's pronunciation charmed Isabel, the consonants slightly nasal, word endings lifting, almost vanishing.

"Yes, she was. As I am a person." Oa sighed. "As you are a person, Oa."

The child shook her head. "No." Her eyes were clear and dark, and Isabel imagined she could see the weight of years in their depths. "No," she repeated with an air of patience. "Oa is not a person, Isabel. Oa is an anchen. Raimu-ke is—was—an anchen. Not a person."

"Raimu-ke was an anchen?"

"Yes. Raimu-ke was—" The fingers of Oa's free hand grasped the air, searching for the word. "One," she finally said. "One—no, first. First anchen."

Sadness flowed through her small hand into Isabel's, an emotion as vast as space. Isabel tightened her grip on the slender fingers. "Oa. You know what a person is. Why can't an anchen be a person?"

The girl answered simply, "Because an anchen is an anchen. Oa is an anchen."

Isabel bit her lip. How was she ever to understand what the child meant? And how was she to help Oa, and the other old children, until she did?

ISABEL GREW WEARY of worrying, of wrestling with the mystery. She thought an afternoon away would give them both some relief. After consulting with Jin-Li, she took Oa to the waterfront to wander through the tourist shops, looking at the trinkets and souvenirs they sold. One store offered toys representing the expansion worlds. There were miniature replicas of the ice castles of Crescent, tiny robotic models of the long-boned, flop-eared vaccone of Nuova Italia, a row of veiled dolls from Irustan. Isabel turned one of the dolls over in her hand, its wisps of pastel silk falling over her fingers. Its base was printed with the circled star of ExtraSolar. She held the little veiled figure out to Oa. "Did you have toys on Virimund, Oa? A doll, perhaps?"

Oa looked at the Irustani doll for a moment, and then shook her head. She glanced around the cluttered shelves until she spied a wooden puppet, and pointed to it. "Wood. Wood of nuchi."

"A wooden doll, then." Isabel put her hand on Oa's shoulder to guide her closer to the puppet display. Oa took a step, and then stopped, her eye caught by an assortment of dull gray shapes of grainplastic. They were miniatures of the monoliths of Udacha. Oa stroked one with her fingertip and glanced up at Isabel. "Kburi?"

Isabel stood at her shoulder, looking at the little uneven thing. The molding had been poorly done. It looked like something made out of modeling clay by a rather clumsy child. "Is that what a kburi looks like?" she asked. "What is a kburi, Oa?"

She watched the child struggle for words. "Kburi is for Raimu-ke," she said after a moment. Isabel held her breath, not wanting to press her. "In kburi—no, under." She touched it again, reverently.

Isabel sighed. Somehow, she was not asking the right questions.

The next day, the Solemnity of St. Joseph, they hiked up the steep hill from the Multiplex to the old cathedral, guided by glimpses of its modest rectangular towers holding their ground among the soaring geometric shapes of more recent architecture. They had to make a complete circuit of the building before they found an unlocked entrance that led into a small chapel. It was chilly inside, but Isabel, used to the marble floors of old churches, had brought coats. She helped Oa to put one on, and she pulled hers over her shoulders as they went down the steps to the main sanctuary.

Cool sunlight fell through the oculus, the circular window high in the center of the roof, to glow on the cracked white stone of the altar. The north and south transepts were shadowed, the apses illumined only by red and blue tones of light filtered through stained glass. The cathedral was empty except for two people kneeling separately in the east apse, heads bent over their folded hands. Isabel knelt near the altar, with Oa beside her. She looked around at the ancient figures of the saints, of the Virgin, of a graceful Christ with supplicating hands. The sculptor had made those hands slender and long-fingered. They reminded Isabel of Simon.

She closed her eyes, and tried to imagine how it all must seem to Oa. She doubted her ability to explain the Roman Catholic Church to the child of Virimund, to help her grasp the essence of it, the centuries of tradition and fable and fact and faith all woven together in a grand tapestry that spanned two and a half millennia.

And if Oa could not understand her world, how would she comprehend Oa's?

She tried to pray, but instead she found herself returning again and again to the questions that plagued her. Anchens who could not be persons. A child who had lived an entire century, and yet was still, beyond any doubt, a child. She pressed her hands to her face, trying to concentrate, asking her patroness for guidance, for patience, for a safe journey, for wisdom. She couldn't clear her mind, and she found no peace.

She opened her eyes, and nodded to Oa. "I'm ready to go," she whispered. Oa, patiently waiting beside her, stood up. Isabel restored the kneeler to its position and straightened.

The two other worshippers were waiting in a side aisle, standing at angles to each other in the awkward way of strangers. One was a middle-aged man, tall and stooped. The other, a woman with gray hair, leaned on a cane. When Isabel and Oa stepped out of the pew, the two moved forward to intercept them.

"We don't mean to intrude, Mother," the man said hesitantly.

"You are a priest, aren't you?" the woman asked more boldly. "A Magdalene?"

"Yes," Isabel said. She put out her hand. "I'm Isabel Burke."

The woman shook her hand. "We want to ask you something."

"Is that all right?" the man said anxiously. "We don't want to be a bother."

Isabel smiled. "Of course it's no bother. What can I do for you?"

The woman said, "We saw your collar. I thought you must be the one on the news. Would you say Mass for us, Mother Burke? We only have a priest every few weeks, and none since Lent began."

Isabel's smile faded. "Oh," she said. "I'm sorry. Of course I would say Mass, except the cathedral doesn't want me to. I couldn't go against the bishop's wishes, I'm afraid. Not everyone accepts us—the Magdalenes. Not yet," she added.

"But we have another church," the man said. "St. Teresa's. It's across the Sound, a ferry ride of about half an hour. Please, Mother Burke. You just don't know what it would mean to our congregation."

"Are you sure the others in your church would be amenable?"

The man said, "Yes, I'm sure. I'm positive."

Oa moved under Isabel's hand, stepping closer, as if to encourage her. Isabel stroked her hair. Grace often came from unexpected directions. Her smile returned. "I'll be delighted to say Mass," she said. "How about this coming Sunday?"

"Oh, Mother Burke," the tall man said with enthusiasm. "That's wonderful. Here—" He handed her a printed card. "That's my wave-phone number. If you'll call me tonight, we'll make arrangements to meet your boat." He gave one to the white-haired woman as well, and both of them bid Isabel a respectful farewell.

"Come, Oa," Isabel said softly, pleased and touched. "Let's walk around the church, and try to see everything."

OA GAZED WITH wonder at the multitude of images above her head, some set in colored glass, some carved of white stone. They made a circuit of the church, following the smoke-stained walls. She followed Isabel into an alcove that was as dark and narrow as a cave. Its walls had once been gold, but were now dingy and cracked. At its innermost end stood a painted statue of a woman holding a chubby baby. Oa tipped her head back to look up into the woman's delicate face.

"This is the Blessed Mother," Isabel said. "Holding the Christ child."

Christ child. Child. Was this an anchen?

"What is your word for mother, Oa?"

"Mamah."

"Mamah. Yes. It's almost universal, that word," Isabel said.

Oa turned to her. "The child . . . ?"

"The Christ child?"

"The Christ child . . . is an anchen?" She held her breath, awaiting the answer.

Isabel touched Oa's hair again. Oa's mamah had touched her hair like that, before she knew. "No," Isabel said gently. "No, Oa, the Christ child was not an anchen. He grew to be a man, though he didn't live long. Not as long as you, not even as long as I."

"Why?"

Isabel's eyes were bright in the dimness of the alcove. "Christ died young. He died for His people."

Oa looked back at the figures. The Mother cradled the Child securely in her arm, and the Child looked down on Oa with eyes that seemed to know everything. The toes of the Mother were worn away, as if many hands had touched them. The foot of the kburi was the same, its rough base of piled stones rubbed smooth from the stroking of the anchens.

"It's a beautiful statue, isn't it?" Isabel asked. "And very old, I think."

"Toes are gone," Oa said.

"Yes. It happens a lot. People touch the statues, or the icons, and they rub away the paint, sometimes brass or even marble, if they touch it enough times." She turned in a circle, taking in the pattern of stars set into the ceiling, the empty candle sconces. "Once, there might have been a hundred candles burning here. I suppose there is no one to take care of them now, to take away the burned ones and put fresh ones out."

"Is not kburi?" Oa said.

"No, I don't think so."

"But, Isabel . . ." Oa struggled for words. "People pray to the Ma—the Mother?"

"Yes, in a way."

"And the Child?"

"Yes." Isabel looked back at the statue, and her face softened. "Many of us are moved by images of the Blessed Mother and the Child. It's a perfect model of love. It helps us to focus on God."

Child. Oa frowned, staring at the statue, struggling with the ideas.

"What is it, Oa? What are you thinking of?"

Oa bit her lip. "The child—Christ child. People are praying to Christ child."

"Yes."

"Is not kburi, but is like kburi."

"Is it, Oa?"

Oa nodded. "Anchens pray to Raimu ke. People pray to Christ child."

"I don't know how to say Raimu-ke in English, Oa."

Oa tugged on the ends of her hair. "Raimu-ke was an anchen."

"Yes—a child, then."

"Raimu-ke is like Christ child. Raimu-ke died . . . for anchens."

Isabel took Oa's hand in a warm grip. "Ah. You see, Oa. Anchens and people are not so different. People pray. Anchens pray. And we love. The capacity to love makes us very like each other."

Oa wanted to protest, to assure Isabel it wasn't true. She had tried to make her understand, but she didn't know enough words. Isabel didn't comprehend the crime it was to be an anchen, the offense to the ancestors. When she reached Virimund, when she met the others, would she understand then? It was tempting to let her think they were truly alike. To let Isabel think Oa was a person. To let Isabel love Oa.

Isabel put her arms around Oa, and Oa let her cheek rest against Isabel's shoulder. She wished the moment could last forever. She wished she could believe it were all true.

JIN-LI WATCHED THE little group emerge beneath the awning of the guest suites, Oa skipping at Isabel's side, Isabel carrying a large black case. Simon, with an armful of coats, walked slightly behind. Jin-Li held the door of the car for them, and then climbed in to sit beside Simon, facing Isabel and Oa. The car backed and turned, heading to the western exit of the Multiplex, and out onto the throughway that led to the ferry terminal.

Oa gazed at Jin-Li from under lowered eyelids. Jin-Li smiled at her. "Hello, Oa. It's good to see you again."

"Hello." The girl tugged at the ends of her long braids.

"How are you?" Jin-Li asked.

"Oa is fine, thank you." It was curious, Jin-Li thought. Even after all these weeks, and Oa's much improved English, the girl spoke of herself in the third person.

"We're looking forward to the ferry ride, aren't we, Oa?" Isabel asked.

Oa nodded. "Yes, Oa likes the ferry," she said. Her white smile flashed at Jin-Li. "Oa sees a whale!"

Jin-Li laughed. They were lovely together, the dark-skinned child, the slender bald woman. Jin-Li turned to include Simon Edwards in the moment, and the laugh died.

He was gazing at Isabel with a look of such longing that Jin-Li felt guilty to have seen it.

Jin-Li had welcomed Isabel's invitation, had looked forward to the day trip, the congenial company, to the fresh salt air and the new experience of a Catholic religious service. The discovery that Simon Edwards was in love with Isabel Burke was a surprise.

THE TOWERING PINES and full-branched spruces of Bainbridge Island almost swallowed the tiny Church of St. Teresa of Calcutta. The church itself was only a foambrick square with a cross painted in white above its doorway. A few homely icons hung on the interior walls. In place of pews, a dozen rows of plastic chairs ranged around the altar, which was a simple table draped in white cloth, set on a little raised dais.

Jin-Li followed Isabel and Oa and Simon into the church. A tall man with bent shoulders took Isabel's case from her hands and led her off to the back of the building, leaving Simon, Oa, and Jin-Li standing uncertainly in the austere space. Oa looked longingly after Isabel.

"It's all right," Simon told her. "She'll be back soon."

"Isabel says Mass now?" Oa asked.

"Soon." Simon glanced over the girl's head at Jin-Li. "Are you a Catholic, Longshoreman Chung?"

"Please, Dr. Edwards, call me Jin-Li. And no, I'm not. I don't practice any religion."

"No," he said thoughtfully, his eyes straying over the simple adornments of the church. "No, I don't either. But for Isabel . . ."

"Isabel is a priest," Oa told them firmly, in her lilting accent. "Isabel is a priest of Saint Mary Magdalene." Her great dark eyes sought Jin-Li's. "Mary Magdalene was a person."

Jin-Li nodded gravely. "Yes. I know something about her."

Oa spread her small hand in a gesture to take in the room, the plastic chairs, the plain altar, the icons. "Not Mary Magdalene's church," she said. "Te-re-sa's church."

"That's right."

Oa tugged on her braids and grinned up at Jin-Li. Jin-Li grinned back, charmed by her.

People began to appear, coming into the church in little groups of three and four. Jin-Li was startled to see, after fifteen minutes or so, that the church was full. At least seventy-five people had gathered, sitting quietly, standing against the walls, some chatting, some with their heads

bowed and eyes closed. Simon watched the door at the far end of the
room, waiting, like the others, for Isabel.

When she appeared at last, someone rang a small bell, and everyone
came to their feet. Isabel's bare head gleamed above a white linen robe. A
gold-embroidered alb draped her slender shoulders. Her wooden cross
hung on her breast, as always, and she held a covered dish in one hand, a
stoppered bottle in the other. She radiated power, a quiet and benevolent
strength. The tall man walked behind her with two candlesticks.

"My friends," Isabel said in a clear, carrying voice. "It's good to see
you, and very good for us to be here together on this lovely morning."
She stepped up to the altar, including every corner of the room in the
radiance of her smile, and she lifted her hand in the old, old cruciform
gesture. "I greet you all in the name of the Father, and of the Son, and
of the Holy Spirit."

Jin-Li saw the hands moving in the sign of the cross, saw tears glisten in more than one eye, and understood that this was a moment of
profound importance to these people. Even without understanding the
ritual, the faith and hope and intensity of the worshippers was impres-
sive to see.

Spring sunshine poured in through the windows. The ceremony
went forward, Isabel chanting the words of the old rite, the assembly re-
sponding, kneeling, standing, singing hymn verses from memory. Before
the communion procession began, Isabel quoted, "I leave you my peace.
My peace I give you." People turned to each other to shake hands, some
to embrace.

Jin-Li watched Isabel's eyes meet Simon's over the simple altar, and
understood that Isabel Burke loved Simon Edwards as much as he
loved her.

"Peace be with you," said a voice on Jin-Li's right. Jin-Li turned to
shake the proferred hand, and then another. Isabel and Simon broke
their contact, and the Mass continued.

Later, when farewells had been said, thanks offered and accepted,
and Isabel had stowed her things back in her case, they all strolled
down to the ferry dock in cool afternoon sunshine. Jin-Li noticed the
distance Isabel and Simon kept between them. By the time they boarded
the ferry, a chill breeze had sprung up, and to Oa's disappointment,

they abandoned the open deck to sit inside, sheltered from the wind. She had not seen the hoped-for whale.

Simon took her off to be consoled with a sweet. Isabel, pulling the collar of her long black coat high around her chin, shivered a little. "Cold," she murmured. "I forgot my hat."

"You're tired, I think," Jin-Li said. "Wouldn't you like something hot to drink?"

"Thank you, Jin-Li. Maybe a little later."

"It was a lovely service, Isabel," Jin-Li murmured.

"Did you think so?" Isabel smiled, but there was sadness in it, and regret.

"Didn't you like saying Mass?" Jin-Li ventured.

"I did," Isabel answered slowly. "I do. It's just that . . ." Her voice trailed off. Jin-Li waited in silence. Isabel glanced up, and met Jin-Li's eyes. She laughed a little. "You're a very good listener, Jin-Li Chung. You would have made a wonderful priest."

"Except that I have no faith," Jin-Li said lightly.

Isabel's eyes darkened, and she turned them back to the view of the gray waters of Puget Sound, choppy now in the rising wind. Jin-Li waited, but when Isabel spoke again, it was on a new subject.

"I've never been to space," she said. "Another world. I find I'm a little anxious about it."

"I was on Irustan," Jin-Li offered. "Of course, I spent the journey in twilight sleep, but I loved being offworld. When I was young, all I wanted was to travel, to go everywhere, see everything. I longed to be an archivist."

"So you became a longshoreman."

"It was the only way I could find out of Hong Kong."

Isabel's unusual eyes seemed alight from within. "And what did you think of Irustan?"

"It was wonderful. And terrible." Jin-Li gave the priest a rueful smile. "I could have stayed forever."

19

ISABEL SAID A sunrise Easter Mass at St. Teresa of Calcutta in early April. They were to leave for Virimund on the Octave of Easter. Isabel's gear was packed, a dozen cartons, valises, and padded equipment carriers. Simon's portable lab was assembled and ready to stow. Isabel had catalogued and recorded all the information she had on the Sikassa, with files waiting for the archivist who would be assigned to them. She and Oa grew restless, waiting.

Three days before their departure, a hydro worker at the Virimund power plant became ill. Simon hurried to the World Health offices, but the Port Forceman had already expired by the time he reached the r-wave center and contacted the power park. The medicator had been ineffective, and the medtech on Virimund was baffled. Simon spent an entire day sending instructions and receiving information, struggling to identify the cause of the worker's illness.

With Simon occupied, Isabel cast about for a way to fill the time, and to quell her rising anxiety about the journey. When Jin-Li offered to take her and Oa to the expansion worlds exhibit, she accepted with gratitude. The weather had grown cooler after Easter, and a light rain showered the cityscape. The driver dropped them off directly in front of the Old Space Needle, but Isabel's scalp was wet by the time they reached the entrance and bought their tickets.

Oa loved the nautilus slidewalk, prancing from one side to the other as it bore them up to the gallery level. Isabel and Jin-Li smiled at each other above her dark head.

"Happy," Jin-Li said quietly.

"She lives in the moment," Isabel murmured. "I suppose we all should do the same."

"Try, anyway," the longshoreman said.

"Indeed."

On the gallery level a thin stream of people strolled around the external corridor, a few admiring the mist-shrouded view, others sampling the exhibits. Jin-Li led the way, stopping before one of the entrances and extending a hand with a slight smile. "Welcome to Irustan."

Isabel, with Oa beside her, stepped through the portal and into another world, a holographic projection so convincing that even the air felt different. An indoor scene shimmered into existence around her, a large bright room with a tiled floor, white walls, and a windowed sky-roof. Just like an oculus dei, Isabel thought. Except that in this case, the eye of God looked down from an alien heaven.

Jin-Li pointed to a free-form sculpture. "That's a classic example of Irustani nonrepresentational art. Notice the flow of the stone. It's meant to lift the eye, or the hand, upward to the Maker."

"The Maker?"

"The Maker, or the One. From the Book of the Second Prophet. And that tree is a met-olive, a biotransform of a Cretan variety. Thrives on Irustan. The shrub with the floppy flowers they call a mock rose. Also a biotransform. Untransformed Earth plants only live a couple of seasons on Irustan. Interesting, too—Port Forcemen can't digest the fish, at least not for the first couple of years, but the Irustani do. So adaptation has taken place."

A recorded lecture droned in one corner. "Would you like to hear that?" Jin-Li asked.

"No," Isabel said with a smile. "I prefer your version."

They moved, and found themselves on a hill with a view of the rhodium mines. Huge machines rolled over distant red-brown hills, and masked miners walked in the foreground. Jin-Li said, "The miners wear masks to protect them from the unstable isotope of the rhodium dust."

When they took another step, the scene shifted again. People in colorful clothes strolled past vending booths shaded by striped canopies. "This is the Medah," Jin-Li said. "They sell fish, cloth, jewelry . . . wonderful things."

"And the women are veiled."

"Yes. They're not allowed outside of their homes unveiled." Jin-Li spoke of the religious life of Irustan, the economic structure, the social strata, the interaction with offworlders. By the time they left the exhibit, Isabel knew that Jin-Li Chung should probably have been an anthropologist. And at the very least, would make an excellent archivist.

They moved on to the other exhibits, gazing in wonder at the soaring ice structures of Crescent, the mountain meadows of Nuova Italia. They goggled at a life-size model of an Udachan monolith, listening to the recorded lecture. Oa tugged at her braids and frowned.

"Do you still think these are like the kburi?" Isabel asked.

Oa shook her head. "No," she said flatly. "Not kburi. Too high." She stretched her arms as far as they would go, not more than a third the height of the monolith. "Anchens not high."

As they approached the last door, Jin-Li touched Isabel's arm, murmuring, "That's Virimund. It's not much, but . . . do you think it might upset her?"

Oa had already read the sign that flashed across the entrance. She tugged at Isabel's hand, whispering, "Isabel! Isabel! Oa sees Virimund!"

Isabel, with a little flutter of nervousness in her stomach, followed Oa through the portal.

They stood on a beach looking out over waters of vivid emerald. The sand beneath their feet sparkled with subtle color, pink and violet and beige and ocher. Behind them was dense rainforest, heavy-trunked trees buttressed with vertical roots, a canopy hung with vines. A few birds flew here and there, splashes of scarlet and blue and gold, and the waves rippled, but otherwise it was as static a display as Udacha or Crescent. Oa looked up, and around, turning in a circle, tugging on her braids.

"Is it like Virimund, Oa?" Jin-Li asked.

The girl released her braids and stood still, staring into the image of sea and sky. "Not," she said in a small voice.

"Not even Mother Ocean?" Isabel said.

"Yes, Isabel. Mother Ocean. But no shahto. No people. No . . ." Her voice trailed off, so that Isabel could only just hear, "No anchens."

Isabel put a hand on her shoulder. "Oa," she said softly. The girl turned her face up, her eyes liquid and vulnerable. "When this exhibit was made, Port Force didn't know anyone lived on your planet."

"Are not finding the people."

"Is that what's worrying you?"

Oa turned her back on the vista of water. "People are—" She made a sad, small gesture with her hand. "People are being losed."

"Lost."

"Lost. People are being lost, and Oa is—worrying—that anchens are being lost."

Isabel put her arm around Oa, and drew her a little closer. She pressed her cheek to her hair, feeling its soft texture against her skin, breathing its fragrance. "Oa, sweetheart. We will be there as soon as possible, and we will look for the anchens."

As they left the exhibit, Oa stumbled, as if her feet had grown suddenly heavier. Isabel supported her with her arm, her heart aching for the lonely child. What a terrible burden she bore on her thin shoulders. How awful to fear you might be alone in the universe, the last of your kind. Isabel prayed it wasn't so.

ISABEL STARED AT Simon over the table, unbelieving. "They're *coming*?" she demanded. The roast salmon, garnished with bright spring vegetables, lay untouched before her. "How could the regents agree to that?"

"Try to enjoy your dinner, Isabel." She didn't move. He said, gesturing helplessly with his fork, "The regents have a vested interest in the power park. Adetti and Boreson convinced them they needed to be there to ensure the charter provisions are observed."

"But they were the ones to violate them in the first place!" Isabel exclaimed. She felt Oa's anxious gaze on her, and she sat back, striving for calm. "Simon, I need to be alone with the children to get to know them, to understand them. We don't want to frighten them. Oa will translate, of course, and you will support the two of us. It will be like it was in the Victoria project. It's more than enough!"

"Isabel, we'll need somone to help with the equipment. And the provisions require an archivist as well."

"Two more, plus Boreson and Adetti?" She twisted her fingers in her lap. "It's too many, Simon. Can't we oppose this?"

He pleated his napkin with his fingers. "I'm afraid not," he said, not meeting her eyes.

A chill crept over her scalp. He was keeping something from her. "Simon—what is it?"

He cleared his throat. "Never mind. They obtained clearance, and I couldn't stop them."

"Good lord. It's outrageous!"

"We're stuck with it."

Isabel looked across the table, where Oa sat watching and listening, not touching her meal. Isabel forced a smile. "Come on, Oa, let's eat this lovely fish before it gets cold." Still the girl wouldn't pick up her fork until Isabel did. The salmon was moist and rich, fresh from Puget Sound. To Isabel, it may as well have been grass for all that she could taste it, but she forced herself to eat so that Oa would, and her brain churned.

After dinner, when Oa had settled herself with a book and the dinner things had been picked up, Isabel sat again at the table next to Simon. He had his wavephone transmitter on, but he wasn't speaking at the moment. He was going over a list of supplies and checking them off.

"Simon," Isabel said quietly. "I have an idea." He raised his eyebrows, waiting. "Let's take our own Port Forceman with us to Virimund. Our own choice. I know someone who can serve double duty, and reduce the number of people by one at least. They owe us that much."

"It's short notice."

"It's one less person on the shuttle, one less on the transport. They should like that."

"Who do you have in mind, Isabel?"

"Jin-Li Chung." At Simon's raised eyebrows, Isabel hastened to say, "It's a perfect choice, Simon, truly. Jin-Li is strong, and honest, and observant. We all know each other. And it will be good to have an objective view."

"I suppose I could request it. But be certain, first, that Jin-Li wants to go. Ask."

Isabel folded her arms, sure of her ground. "I will ask, of course, but I already know the answer. I'm positive."

"Because of your little talent, you mean?"

Isabel laughed. "No, not that, Simon. Because we talked. And I'm absolutely certain.'

He gave her a tired smile. "Yes. I'll bet you are, Mother Burke."

SIMON, ONCE AGAIN, handled the change of archivists with apparent ease. When the day came, the sun rising in a clear sky on the Octave of Easter, Jin-Li Chung was an official member of the mission to Virimund.

Isabel's jittery nerves, now that the day was at hand, had calmed. The night before, a call had come from a representative of St. Teresa of Calcutta, promising the prayers of the congregation for Mother Burke and her mission to Virimund. Marian Alexander had called as well, and offered the blessing for pilgrims via r-wave. Isabel had gratefully accepted all these good wishes, and now that the day of departure was at hand, she was eager to be off, to go in search of the answers they all needed, and to take Oa home.

Every detail of the day seemed carved in light. The car that carried them to the port gleamed in the sunshine, and the fuselage of the shuttle itself shone white. The open passenger door seemed an invitation to adventure. Isabel helped Oa with her seat restraints, and put on her own. Jin-Li, passing on the way to a rear seat, stopped briefly beside them.

"Isabel, this is an opportunity I never hoped for. I hardly know how to thank you."

Isabel smiled up at the brand-new archivist, dressed for the first time in the cream-colored syncel tunic of a ranking Port Force officer. "It's one you deserve, Jin-Li," she said warmly. "And I'm so glad you'll be with us."

Cole Markham helped Gretchen Boreson to her seat, fussing a little, returning twice to bring her something she thought she needed for the flight. On his way out, he, too, stopped to speak to Isabel.

"Good luck, Mother Burke," he said, and put out his hand. "I hope it all goes well."

She shook his hand, and thanked him. His gaze rested briefly on Oa, and then shifted back up the aisle to Boreson. Isabel thought he gave a slight shake of his head, but she couldn't be sure. Paolo Adetti pushed past him in the narrow aisle, and Markham, with a last nod to Isabel, went down the little stairway to the tarmac.

Simon grinned at Isabel from across the aisle. "Okay over there, Mother Burke?"

She chuckled. "I'm fine, Dr. Edwards."

He gestured at the sleek aircraft furnishings. "Not exactly like the cruiser to Australia."

"No."

He sobered, holding her eyes with his. "I'm glad to be going with you, Isabel," he said softly under the rising whine of the engines. "Very glad."

She let her head fall back against the padded seat as the shuttle began its long taxi, keeping her face turned to him as the engine noise grew louder. "I couldn't have managed without you," she said.

THE SHUTTLE TRIP to the transport passed in a rush of sensation for Oa. She lay in the padded seat, the webbing securely around her, her head cradled in a cushion that felt like a cloud. With Isabel beside her, the roar of the engines no longer terrified her. As they shot upward, the sky grew pale and gray, and then dissolved into a starry blackness, as if someone had put a giant finger into a cloudy pool and stirred until it cleared. Soon the transport swelled to fill her window. Its flanks sparkled with reflected light, and its great drive housing made the shuttle seem tiny. Its bridge canopy glittered as if it were embedded with jewels.

It wouldn't matter, this time, that the journey was long. Isabel had explained the twilight sleep that had been denied Oa on the trip to Earth. Doctor and Gretchen would be on the transport, but Oa didn't care. She and Isabel would sleep side by side in their suspension cradles, watched over by the crew, rousing once in a while for mild exercise, then sleeping again. Her first space voyage had been an endless round of wakings and sleepings, an eon of solitude and tedium punctuated only by visits from Doctor in his quarantine suit, and sessions under the spider machine. Those memories were dark ones, and she didn't want to relive them.

Her first glimpse of the cradles shook her, but Isabel's steady hand was on her shoulder.

"It's not a medicator," Isabel said. "Come and look, Oa. It's more like a bed."

Doctor Simon was with them. He led Oa to the cradle that was to be hers, and showed her the pillowed headrest, the sheath of material that looked metallic but was quilted and soft. Slender silver wires ran through it, to keep the sleeper warm.

Doctor Simon explained all of that, and then pointed to the syrinxes that hung at the head of the cradle. "These will give you the medicine that will help you sleep, Oa. And they will monitor all the parts of your body, so that when you wake, not long before our arrival, you will be as strong and healthy as you are now."

Oa touched one of the tubes. It was not frightening, not when Doctor Simon explained it. She curled her fingers around it, and it folded in her hand. A machine. It was only a machine.

A technician came to help Oa into her cradle, to adjust the sheath around her, to patch the syrinxes to her wrists and elbows. Doctor Simon and Isabel stood by, watching, and Oa wasn't afraid. It wasn't like the spider machine at all. When the technician stepped back, and nodded to Isabel, Doctor Simon said, "I guess it's time."

"I'll see you soon, Simon," Isabel said softly.

Oa couldn't see him, but she heard his step as he left their cubicle. Doctor Simon and Jin-Li Chung had their own cubicles. All of them would sleep, kept warm by the sheaths, protected by the cradles. Isabel came into Oa's view again, bending to press a kiss on her forehead. Her lips were smooth and cool. She murmured, "Sleep well, Oa."

Oa repeated, "Sleep well, Isabel."

Isabel smiled down at her. "I will." She turned away to her own cradle, and the technician went to help her.

Around them the ship was alive with muted noise. The great drives sang a deep, bone-vibrating pitch. The many toned hum of machines melded into one bland noise, a quiet roar like the eternal song of Mother Ocean. Oa's eyelids grew heavy. Her feet and hands felt distant somehow, as if they belonged to someone else.

Oa turned her cheek into the soft fabric of the headrest, sweetly drowsy, warm, relaxed. Something tickled beneath her chin, and she reached a hand up, surprised. It was her toy, her fuzzy toy. Her teddy bear. The technician had found it in her bag, and tucked it under the sheath.

Oa buried her fingers in the soft fur. She tried to mumble her thanks to the technician, but she was asleep before her lips could form the words.

She began a long dream of Virimund, Mother Ocean, and the island of the anchens. In her dream the anchens were waiting for her on the southern shore of the island, gathered on the sand, waving and calling her name. Calling her home. She waved back to them from her cradle. She was on her way.

20

JIN-LI WOKE TWO weeks before the others to complete the studies barely begun on Earth. It was deeply satisfying to wear the cream-colored tunic and trousers of an officer, to access the transport's library with only name and Port Force number, to be referred to as the archivist and treated with deference. There were long days of relative solitude to spend with the status reports from the power park, to walk the deserted corridors of the ship, to meet with the crew at meals before retiring again to the library. When the planet first became visible, Jin-Li joined the crew on the bridge to watch Virimund grow in the spacewindow.

They were too far out to see the ring of equatorial islands, but the brilliant colors of the ocean world were stunning, even from space. The polar caps glimmered with ice, and the vast seas were deeply, vibrantly green. Jin-Li stood beside a crewman, gazing in wonder at the planet.

"Bit different from Irustan, isn't it?" the crewman said.

Jin-Li nodded. "As different as it could possibly be." The first view of Irustan had been like looking at an old bronze coin, a yellow disk against the blackness of space, its star blazing beyond it. This was a world of abundant water, clean atmosphere, an old and temperate star. It lacked land, but ExtraSolar didn't want land. The expansionist movement needed power, and Virimund had the resources to produce a great deal of it.

"You know what it's like down there?" the crewman asked.

"I've read the reports. It's rainforest, essentially. Moderate climate, lots of birds and insects and a few reptiles. No mammals, apparently. Not much landmass."

"Well, you'll be planetside before you know it. Two more days, and we wake up your group. The doctor's waking up now, though."

"Which one? Dr. Edwards? Waking early?"

"That's the schedule."

"Why?"

The crewman raised his eyebrows. "Don't ask me what the suits are up to, Johnnie. You're the archivist."

"I am now, in any case."

The crewman smiled. "I thought your tunic looked new. Not always an officer, then?"

"No. Longshoreman." Jin-Li turned back to the spacewindow. "I got a break."

The crewman folded his arms, and came to stand beside Jin-Li at the window. "More power to you," he said. "Not easy to move up in Port Force."

"No."

"Your doctor seems like a nice guy. He was awake for two weeks into the voyage, but we didn't mind. You know how the suits can be, but this one was easy. No care and feeding."

"I suppose you don't know why he stayed awake?"

"Nope. But the r-waves were sure busy. Messages back and forth every day between the power park administrator and your doctor. And he called Geneva a few times."

"You never heard what that was about?"

The crewman looked grave. "Nope. But we know one of our guys died out there."

"Dr. Edwards was probably trying to figure out why."

"That's my guess. You know anything about it?"

"Only what you do."

"None of us thought it was too smart to leave the power park without a physician."

"But they have medicators. And medtechs."

"A medtech's not the same as a doctor."

"No. I suppose not."

"Anyway, your Dr. Edwards went into twilight sleep twelve days into the voyage. He's just coming out now."

SIMON EDWARDS LOOKED pale when they met in the mess hall at the next meal. Jin-Li carried a tray to his table and, with a raising of eyebrows for permission, sat across from him.

"Jin-Li," he said, his voice rasping slightly. "When do you start to feel human again?"

Jin-Li chuckled. "It takes a day or so. Do the exercises, drink a lot of water."

Simon reached for a glass. "I'll do that."

"The techs tell me you stayed awake for two weeks of the voyage."

Simon drained the glass of water. "Yes. Jacob Boyer sent me the postmortem on the hydro worker who died. I was trying to find out what happened."

"And did you?"

Simon tried to clear his throat, unsuccessfully. Jin-Li poured him another glass of water and he lifted it in salute before drinking it down. "Thank you. No, I don't have an answer yet. I'm working on it." He hesitated, swirling the glass on the table, making concentric rings of condensation. "There's an odd coincidence, though, between the postmortem scans and Oa's."

Jin-Li paused, holding the teacup. "Oa's?"

Simon nodded, his lips twisting slightly. "Yes. Not a welcome discovery, is it?"

"Isabel won't like it."

"No, and I don't either. But I don't know what it means yet."

"If you want to give me a copy of the readouts, I'll put them into the file."

"Oh, yes," Simon said. "I should have thought of that. I'm not used to working with an archivist, you know. In the Victoria Desert, we kept our own records."

Jin-Li smiled. "Not Port Force."

Simon chuckled wearily. "Most definitely not Port Force."

Jin-Li waited a moment, and then asked delicately, "And so— Dr. Edwards. You'll be there when Isabel wakes up?"

His eyes slid away, up to the blank wall of the mess. "Yes. I planned on it."

"She'll be glad of that."

Simon's brows drew together and he glared at the empty wall. When he spoke, his voice was hard. "She may be, Jin-Li. I don't know. Things are . . . Things are difficult between us."

Jin-Li said nothing, letting a long pause stretch between them. The mess was empty except for the two of them, and the sound of the ventilation system swelled in the silence. Jin-Li stared at the table, wondering whether Simon wanted to talk, or be left alone.

"I'm not a religious man," he said at last. "And I don't really understand what drives Isabel to . . . to be what she is. I understand the work, her dedication to studying people, trying to understand the societies that shape them. But her calling mystifies me."

Jin-Li supposed he was referring to the Magdalenes' vow of celibacy. Perhaps he couldn't bring himself to speak openly of something so close to his heart.

"I knew someone on Irustan," Jin-Li ventured. "Someone extraordinary, rather like Isabel. Someone who felt a responsibility I could not understand."

Simon drank more water, and waited.

With one finger, Jin-Li traced a crack in the plastic of the table. "It was something about honor. Duty."

Simon said, "I'm not sure I would want to change Isabel, even if I could."

Jin-Li refilled the glass. Simon sipped automatically, and then stared into the clear water. "I'm not half so honorable as she is," he murmured. "I've acted in my own interest, and people have been hurt by it."

Jin-Li waited, watching the doctor's lean, sensitive face.

"I have so much to atone for," Simon said, and pushed himself away from the table. "And right now, I should . . ." There was an undertone in his words, a tinge of regret, and of shame. "I should call my wife."

SIMON FOUND THE r-wave center deserted. He routed his call after checking the chronometer for Geneva, and used the speaker. He leaned back in his chair, glad there was no video feed from this far out. It was clear enough by the sound of her voice that she was tense and unhappy.

"Simon? Are you there?"

"I'm here, Anna. How are you?"

"I'm all right." She paused. "Thank you for having Hilda check with me now and then. It's good to see someone who's not from school."

"Are things okay at school?"

"Yes. But very busy. Our head count is twelve over maximum."

"Did you tell Hilda?"

"She's making a request at World Health for more staff."

"Good, that's good. Weather?"

He heard Anna's sigh, cut off as if she had made up her mind to be cheerful. "It's summer here, Simon."

"I know. I guess that means it's hot."

"Unbearably."

"You should get away, Anna, go up to the mountains for a weekend."

She paused, and he could imagine her straightening, rubbing her face, determined to be pleasant. "Good idea," she said, although he knew perfectly well she would never do it. "You've been sleeping all this time, then," she said.

"I just woke up a few hours ago," he answered. "We're almost to Virimund."

"What happens next?"

"The rest of the team wakes up, gets adjusted. And then we make planetfall." He heard a noise in the corridor outside, and he shifted in his chair. "Anna, I'll have to go now."

"But, Simon—I haven't spoken to you in more than a year! Can't we—when will you call again?"

He hesitated, not certain what was the right thing to do. "Anna—I don't know what we'll find when we land, what the facilities are. It may be hard."

She paused again, and when she spoke, her voice, even over the vast reaches of empty space, had an edge to it. "I'll just wish you good luck, then, Simon."

"Thank you, Anna. I'll call again as soon as I can."

"Simon—" Her voice faltered, and steadied. "I miss you."

"Take care, Anna. Take care of yourself."

When the call was over, Simon sat on for a few moments, listening to the hum of the ship's machinery around him. He tried, for a few moments, to remember the young woman he had married, the shy, smiling girl whose quick mind and quiet ways had appealed to the young, preoccupied physician he had been then. He could hardly retrieve the memories. They seemed beyond his reach, as distant as Earth from Virimund, and he could see no way to recover them.

ISABEL HAD SPECIFIED that she wanted to be fully awake and recovered from twilight sleep before Oa roused. Simon watched her sleeping face as the tech spoke to the medicator. Her closed eyelids and slightly parted lips were pale, her brows smooth. Her hair had grown in, fine straight dark strands that stirred in the gentle breeze from the circulation fans. Simon touched her hair with one finger to feel its texture. He knew it would be gone within an hour of her waking.

"Doctor?" the tech said. "She'll be awake in a moment. There's nothing more for me to do, as long as you're going to stay here. You can buzz if you need me." He pointed to a button on the wall beside Isabel's cradle.

"That's fine," Simon said. "I'll be right here."

The tech nodded, gathered up a few bits of equipment, and left them. In the cradle opposite Isabel's, the child still slept, the brown teddy bear tucked under one thin dark hand. Simon pulled a stool close to Isabel and sat down.

Her breast rose and fell, and then again, her breath coming quicker as she swam up from oblivion. Her eyelids fluttered, opened, closed again. Her fingers, twined together over her midriff, opened and stretched, and she drew an audible breath. She muttered something Simon didn't catch, and he bent close to her.

"Isabel," he said gently. "Time to wake up now."

She breathed, "Time?"

"Yes," he said. "Time. It's Simon, Isabel."

"Simon?" Her hand groped, reaching out.

"Yes." He took her hand in his, lightly. "Yes, Isabel, it's Simon. I'm right here."

Her lips curved. "Simon. Simon. I thought I was dreaming . . ."

He had one eye on the medicator readout, the other on her eyelids struggling to open. He chuckled softly. "You may have been dreaming, Isabel, but I'm here. It's time to wake up. Do you feel all right?"

Her eyelids lifted slowly, reluctantly. Her eyes were blurry with sleep. "Simon," she breathed again, smiling. "Darling Simon." She put her hands on the sides of the cradle, trying to pull herself up. He reached to help her, his hands under her shoulders, sliding down her back as she rose to a sitting position. He glanced back at the readout, checking that her blood pressure was stabilizing, her temperature coming up, her heart rate and respiration reaching normal levels.

Startled, he felt her hand on the back of his neck, her cheek against his arm. She drew herself to him, and her slender warmth, the very aliveness of her fine-boned body, was irresistible. He put his face against her hair, and held her close.

"Where have you . . ." she began, still hoarse with sleep.

"Isabel," he murmured. "We're on the transport, remember? Almost to Virimund."

He felt the stiffening of her shoulders, the slight intake of her breath. Over her shoulder, he saw the numbers on the readout screen spike, and then settle. She didn't move, but he felt, very distinctly, how she shrank within herself. She was still in the circle of his arms, but she had, definitely and unmistakably, withdrawn.

He released her abruptly. "Isabel . . . you reached for me . . . but I didn't mean to . . ."

She put her hands to her face and rubbed her eyes. "No, Simon, don't. I know. I know."

He stood, and stepped back from the cradle. "I just wanted to be here when you woke."

A long, painful moment passed before she took her hands from her eyes, and turned her face up to him. In her habitual gesture, her palms went to her scalp. "Oh," she said in surprise.

He managed a grin. "Oh, yes," he said. "Mother Burke has hair."

Her answering smile was tremulous. "Not for long."

"I thought not."

She looked past him, to the sleeping Oa. "Is she all right?"

He glanced at Oa's readout, and then back to Isabel's. "Yes, she is, and so are you. Give yourself a couple of hours, do a few exercises, and you'll be ready to wake her."

Isabel drew a deep, shaky breath. "Okay. Okay. Help me out of here, will you, Simon?"

He stepped back to her cradle, and extended his hand to her, keeping his grip on her hand and elbow as impersonal as he could. She swung her legs over the edge of the cradle, put her feet gingerly on the floor, grimacing.

"What is it?" he asked.

"Pins and needles," she said briefly. She tried to stand, but had to lean on his arm. "Sorry."

"It's okay, Isabel," he said. He knew his tone sounded flat, even a little angry. He tried to lighten it. "I felt the same," he added. "Take your time."

Her eyes were beginning to regain their usual clarity, that lighted-from-within quality that had turned his head from the instant of their first meeting. "I'm sorry about . . . about what happened just now. I wasn't fully awake."

He patted her hand where it rested on his forearm. "I know. Vulnerable moment," he said. "Forget it."

She took another deep breath, steadier this time. "All my moments with you are vulnerable, I'm afraid."

He averted his eyes to hide his rush of emotion. His chest ached with wanting to hold her. "I can't help it, Isabel," he said softly. "Nothing has changed for me."

*   *   *

COMPUNCTION MADE ISABEL'S heart thud painfully in her chest. For that brief time, those seconds of first awakening, being in Simon's arms had felt like coming home. It was the dream that had betrayed her, a dream in which she wasn't Mother Burke but Isabel, without commitments, without duty, without her vow to honor. In her dream her body ruled, and Simon was there. Waking, with his hands lifting her, his familiar voice assuring her, the transition had been seamless, and all too easy. And now, knowing she had hurt him, she wished it had not happened.

At least, she thought, part of her wished it; the other part of her, the betraying part, wanted to step back in time, to savor those few seconds once again.

She saw how he dropped his eyes, disguising his feelings. She wanted to reach out to him, to draw him back to her, to comfort him, but it was not her prerogative. She had made her choice long before.

She turned away from him, and went to bend over Oa's cradle.

"We can wake her whenever you're ready," Simon said. He stayed where he was as he spoke.

Isabel glanced over her shoulder. "I want to take an hour or two first," she said. "So that I'm really . . ." She lifted one shoulder, searching for the word.

"Back in the world?" Simon said.

She managed a smile. "That's it. Back in the world." She touched her ragged, half-grown hair. "And oh, my lord, get rid of this."

"It's not so bad, you know," he told her, laughing. He seemed to be recovered.

Isabel groaned. "I'm sure I look an absolute horror! And Oa would be frightened to death at the change."

"You could never look an absolute horror," Simon said. "But go on, there's time. Get rid of your hair. Get some exercise and have a shower. Then we can wake her."

Isabel gathered her things and turned to the door, then turned back. "Simon," she said expectantly. "Have you seen it? Virimund?"

He nodded. "It's beautiful. Shades of green I've never seen before.

Go on and get yourself together. When you're ready, we can go to the bridge. There's an observation bay."

Isabel moved carefully, feeling a little shaky on her feet. Surely, she thought, it was the aftereffect of twilight sleep, or it was anxiety about what was to come. It was not the memory of her dream, or the waking sensation of Simon's arms around her, that made her tremble. It couldn't be. She would not allow it.

THE OBSERVATION BAY was kept purposely dim so as not to fade the view beyond the long, curving space window. Jin-Li watched the Magdalene, her newly depilated head shining under the amber lights, lead Oa into the bay to look down on the planet beneath. Isabel kept a protective arm around the child's shoulders. Simon Edwards followed, the lines of his face sharpened by the lighting, his eyes shadowed. Jin-Li observed them all from beneath lowered eyelids, thinking they looked something like an unusual family, cobbled together of disparate parts that didn't quite fit.

Oa's eyes took in everything, their whites glowing in the dimness, their irises dark as space itself. Though she had been awake only an hour, she seemed to have thrown off the aftereffects of twilight sleep without difficulty. She moved to the window, and rested her small hands on the molded sill as she gazed down at the world of emerald waters. Her home. Isabel stood beside her, pointing, murmuring something. Simon stood apart. Once, Isabel looked back at him, and a moment of silent communication flashed between the two of them.

They were close enough now to see the scattered islands ringing Virimund's equator. Fly-overs had counted six hundred fifty-eight of them, most little more than atolls. Tides were minimal, with no moon to stir them. Only in the western hemisphere were the islands large enough to support any settlement, and there were no more than a dozen of those. ExtraSolar had chosen the most level island it could find. Port Force had almost completely deforested it before beginning construction of the power park.

The island where the children were found was seventy-eight

kilometers southwest of the power park. There were only three other islands of any size.

"Jin-Li?" It was Isabel, brows raised as if she had spoken more than once.

"Oh! Excuse me," Jin-Li said. "I was thinking."

Isabel's eyes flickered with reflected green from Virimund's oceans. "Indeed," she said easily. "There's a lot to think about just now, isn't there? I only wondered if you had learned anything new."

"Assuming you mean about the Sikassa, no."

"But the anchens—the other children—are still there?"

"Something is there. The scanners show heat signatures, but they can't say how many . . . and they can't say that they're people, either."

"No," Isabel said. She turned her eyes back to the planet. "No, I suppose that's up to us."

Oa was staring through the thick glass. "Oa does not see the people."

"I think we're still too far out to see anything," Isabel said.

Jin-Li stepped up to the window and traced the globe with one finger. "Your island is about there, Oa. As far as I can tell."

Oa glanced up at her. "Jin-Li goes to the island?"

"Yes. I'm the archivist now."

Oa tried the word, carefully. "Ar-chi-vist."

Jin-Li smiled down at her. "Right. Observer and recorder. Historian."

"Ar-chi-vist." Oa looked back at the rippling green and white of Virimund. "Jin-Li sees the anchens."

"Hope so."

"Oa, too. Oa hopes."

21

THE SHUTTLE FLIGHT from Earth had not troubled Isabel, but the descent to Virimund left her headachy and slightly nauseated, the roar of the thrust engines vibrating in her very bones. She supposed it to be the aftereffects of twilight sleep. She had always felt slightly disoriented when she slept through a transcontinental flight and waked in a different hemisphere and completely different time zone, but she knew no word for the depth of the disorientation she felt now. It made her muscles feel strange, and her mind cloudy. The chronograph on her portable told her it was the memorial day of the humble St. Anthony of Padua, patron of those whose lives take unexpected turns. It was appropriate, she thought wryly. When the cabin door opened at last, and the rich, salty fragrance of the ocean world swept in, she took a deep, slow breath. The air felt thick in her lungs, and heavy with moisture after the dry air of the ship. It smelled of salt and some pungent, utterly alien spice.

Oa pattered down the metal stairs ahead of her, but Isabel stepped gingerly down to the gray-black bitumen of the runway, clutching the handrail. She looked across the expanse of the airfield to an assortment of blunt, rectangular buildings shaded by a few thick-trunked trees. Oa's nuchi trees. In the distance, hundreds of solar panels angled into the sky, and between the collectors the ocean flashed its vibrant, other-worldly green.

Two longshoremen were already climbing up into the cargo bay by the time Isabel had reached the end of the stairs and was standing un-certainly in the brilliant afternoon light. A tall, stooped man, in the cream-colored syncel of a Port Force official, emerged from the shadow of the delta wing. He greeted Paolo Adetti by his first name, and stuck his hand out to Gretchen Boreson, paler than ever under a wide-brimmed hat. She touched the proferred hand with the tips of her fin-gers. Simon stepped forward to shake the official's hand, and then turned to Isabel.

"This is Mother Isabel Burke. Isabel, this is the power park admin-istrator, Jacob Boyer. And this is our archivist, Jin-Li Chung."

Isabel, shading her eyes with her left hand, extended her right to Boyer. He took it, and murmured some courtesy, but his eyes had al-ready strayed past her to Oa.

"This can't be—" Boyer began, and then stopped. He looked back at Adetti. "Paolo? You're telling me this is the same girl?"

The note of triumph in Adetti's voice intensified Isabel's discomfort. "Oh, yes," he grated. "She's the same, all right."

Boyer had a long, rather morose face, and his eyes were round now with amazement. "But—it's been two years! She hasn't—she can't—"

Simon stepped forward. "Administrator. If you could have some-one show Mother Burke and Oa to their rooms, and Ms. Boreson? I'd like to go to the medical facility as soon as possible. Dr. Adetti and I need to review the postmortem on the man you lost."

Isabel cast Simon a grateful look. Boyer said, "You don't want to rest first, Dr. Edwards?"

Simon smiled. "Thanks. I've been asleep for the better part of four-teen months as it is."

Boyer nodded gloomily, saying, "True, true. Okay, then." He called someone's name, and a man came around the nose of the shuttle, squinting in the glare from the particle shields. Isabel and Gretchen

Boreson and Oa followed him away, leaving Simon and Adetti and Jin-Li with Boyer. Boyer watched them go, and Isabel saw Oa cast an anxious glance over her shoulder. Her back must be burning under Boyer's wondering gaze. Isabel slowed her steps to let the child go ahead, putting herself between Oa and that hot curiosity. Boreson stumbled once, and Isabel thought she must feel as odd as she herself did.

JIN-LI FOUND JACOB Boyer to be as straightforward as Gretchen Boreson was complex. And the Virimund Power Park, three years into its existence, was almost raw in its simplicity. The foambrick of new construction had not yet weathered to a natural color. No one had bothered with flower beds or landscaping. The natural vegetation crept up walls and over paths. The roads were loosely surfaced with pale sand that flew in sparkling sprays from the wide tires of Port Force carts. Long, narrow barracks ranged behind the terminal. Longshoremen came out to the airfield, beginning the labor of offloading the shuttle's cargo, replacing it with the tanks and cubes waiting to be shipped out.

"They don't waste any time," Jin-Li said to Boyer, nodding in the direction of the longshoremen.

"Job has to be done quickly," Boyer said. "Those are cryogenic containers, but even superinsulated storage units admit a small amount of heat. Have to keep hydrogen at minus four hundred twenty-two Fahrenheit to keep it liquid." He pointed to a thick-walled structure where several men labored in an open-sided room. "Vacuum-insulated hoses move the hydrogen from the power park to the storage facility. We've cut our time from production to storage by six and a half percent."

Jin-Li murmured appreciation of the achievement.

Admin, the r-wave center, and the infirmary all shared the Port Force Terminal. The installation would grow, Jin-Li assumed, if the power park was allowed to expand. The infirmary consisted of three rooms and a tiny reception area with a wavephone, a narrow standing desk, and two chairs. There were two surgeries, each with its medicator and CA cabinet. The data room held readers, computers, data stacks, boxes of rewritable flexcopies. Adetti and Simon and the medtech crowded into the data room, and Jin-Li stood in the doorway with Boyer, watching. For once the two physicians were in accord, discussing details, asking questions of the medtech, checking the deceased's medical history.

Boyer's long face was dour. "We're not set up to store bodies," he muttered. "Had to put the poor sod in a body bag and stick it in the storage facility. Not very respectful."

Jin-Li nodded acknowledgment. "Did the best you could, Administrator."

"My guys don't like seeing it there. And they want a funeral."

"Expect so. But Dr. Edwards will want to look at the body."

Simon glanced up. "Yes," he said. "I will. Can you have the cadaver brought here?"

Boyer winced, and shot Jin-Li an unhappy glance. Jin-Li nodded sympathy, and Boyer sighed and went to give the order.

Simon said, "Jin-Li, you don't need to wait. If you're not used to autopsies . . ."

"I promise I wouldn't faint," Jin-Li said, winning a grin from Simon. "But I might be more useful getting the hang of the place. Meeting some of the people."

"Good idea."

"Be sure to make archival copies, or give them to me to do."

"Right, Jin-Li. I'll see to it afterward. Remind me if I forget." Simon waved an absentminded hand, his attention already turned to the task at hand.

Jin-Li nodded, and set off to circle the terminal. The Virimund Power Park followed the general pattern of other Port Force installations, with most of the space taken up by the airfield and storage facilities. Where the forest had been bulldozed, the ground was still hillocky and uneven. Behind the terminal, a scattering of trees had been spared to shade the barracks. The trees were beautiful, old and densely canopied, supported by flaring root buttresses.

Birds twittered somewhere, and Jin-Li looked up into the forest canopy, hoping for a glimpse. The biologist, when not working on biotransforms, had already recorded a dozen species of long-feathered, colorful birds. The biologist had created a name for the trees, too, but to Jin-Li, as to Isabel, they were the nuchi trees, Oa's name. Jin-Li si-dled through the thicket of their roots to try to catch sight of the singing bird, and was rewarded with a flash of scarlet.

Voices sounded through an open window in the barracks.

Jin-Li turned toward the sound, lifting one foot to take a step.

"Look out there, bud!"

Jin-Li froze in place, staring at the ground.

A big-shouldered, cheerful-looking man leaned out of the window to call out, "Gotta be careful. Those damned things bite!"

"Whoa." Jin-Li let out a breath, and replaced the foot.

"You from the shuttle?"

"Right."

"Welcome to Virimund," the man said with a laugh. "Crawlies and all. Most of 'em were wiped out when we took down the trees, but we still see 'em once in a while."

Jin-Li gave a nervous laugh. "Thanks for the warning."

"Officers' quarters are on the other side of the terminal, you know."

Jin-Li touched the collar of the cream uniform self-consciously. "Well, I prefer the barracks, actually. I was a longshoreman. Kind of new as an archivist."

"Not quite a suit, then, huh? Come on in, buddy. Give you a cup of something, and you can tell me about it."

"Thanks. I'll do that." But Jin-Li didn't move until the enormous long-legged black spider minced its way across the path and disap-peared into the jungle of roots.

"BOYER'S OKAY," LEO said. His big hands were deft with the teapot as he measured tea leaves and poured boiling water. The barracks were communal, rows of bunks, shower rooms at one end, common room at the other, all empty at the moment except for Leo, who had explained he was on evening shift this rotation. "Yeah, Boyer tries to watch out for the guys. Couldn't stop Adetti from leaving with the kid, though. We figure Adetti had a friend with some power."

"He does. She's here now."

Leo's thick eyebrows shot up. He was heavyset and balding, with a day's growth of beard stubbling his chin. "Who is it, Johnnie?"

"Administrator of Earth Multiplex."

Leo whistled. "So who's she answer to?"

Jin-Li accepted a teacup with a nod of thanks. "Only the other administrators. And the regents of the charter governments."

"But why come all this way?"

Jin-Li sipped the tea. "Good question, Leo. Can't give you a good answer."

Within an hour, Jin-Li knew Leo was a cryotech, knew where he was from and why he had emigrated, learned which cooks were best in the cafeteria, which barracks threw the best parties, what biotransformed vegetables were flourishing in the nursery, and all about the two hydros who had died. One had been buried in the fledgling cemetery on a hill west of the power park, next to a small grave marked UNKNOWN CHILD. The other hydro had been waiting more than a year for his burial services. There was general condemnation of ExtraSolar for leaving an Offworld Port Force installation without a physician, and an equal amount of ill feeling against the "savages" on their island. Loyalty to Boyer and the constraints of the Terms of Employment kept the hydros from going back to the island, despite feverish curiosity. They had been impatiently awaiting the contingent from Earth. Jin-Li fielded Leo's questions about the Magdalene, about the physician, about Oa.

Leo directed Jin-Li to the barracks where he thought Isabel and Oa and Gretchen Boreson must have been installed. "Dinner will be on soon," he said cheerfully. "Come back sometime, Johnnie. Meet the rest of the guys."

"Thanks, Leo. I will." Jin-Li waved, and headed out, keeping a close eye on the path for crawlies.

22

"NO NECROPSY TABLE, I suppose?" Simon asked.

"No. Guess it wasn't considered necessary." Adetti looked uneasy. The body, sealed in its vacuum bag, lay on a collapsible table he had found in a closet, a swath of paper sheeting beneath it. They had pushed the medicator to one side of the room, but kept its screen extended for imaging. The stillness of the shape in the bag, the air it had of waiting, of ageless patience, made all of them speak quietly. Even Simon, a veteran of such procedures, felt the tension.

"I brought a mobile t-unit with me," he said. "But I need some way to suspend it." He glanced around the cramped surgery. "I guess I could borrow the medicator's scanning arm. The problem is putting the wiring back together afterward. It's tricky."

Boyer stood in the doorway, having dispatched the medtechs to other jobs. It seemed the less people present at the autopsy, the better, and no one had objected. "Show me the piece," Boyer said. "I'll find something that will work."

Simon bent to his stack of equipment and brought out the imaging ring, unfolding it from its pillow of soft plastic, and held it up for Boyer to assess.

"What did you call it? A t-unit?"

"Well, more properly, tomography unit."

Boyer stroked his long chin with one finger, frowning. "How stable does it have to be?"

"Fairly. It has its own power source, though, as long as it has a frame to ride on."

For a few minutes they discussed tolerances, and then Boyer went off in search of something that could be used as a framing device. Simon saw that Adetti was setting out the other bits of his equipment, still avoiding the corpse itself. He felt a stir of sympathy.

"Paolo. It's been a while since you assisted at an autopsy, I'm afraid."

Adetti nodded without looking up. "Always hated them."

"I can understand that. Not the easiest part of medicine." Simon opened another carton with masks and gloves, and connected the t-unit to the medicator readout screen. He checked to be certain the wavebox was empty, ready to deal with their contaminated materials. Boyer came back with a rack pirated from the meal hall that had a smooth horizontal rod. In moments, Simon had rigged the t-unit to slide down it, from the head to the toe of their subject. He used a sterile tray from a cupboard to lay out the remote samplers. Adetti pulled on mask and gloves, and set the tissue cubes next to the needles.

Simon stood with his hand poised over the body bag. The height of the table was too low. His back would ache by the time he was finished, but there was no help for that. "Ready," he said. "Administrator, you'd better put on a mask. Paolo, all set?"

"Guess so." Adetti's eyes above his mask were grim

Simon said. "Let's begin, then. Start the recorder, will you, please, Dr. Adetti?"

"Recording."

Simon touched the suction tab at the head of the body bag. The vacuum released with a hiss, and the bag unsealed itself to reveal the white, still form of the deceased Port Forceman.

*   *   *

THREE HOURS LATER, Simon straightened, stripping his gloves from his hands. He dropped them into the wavebox. The cubes were filled with specific tissue samples, and the cadaver was sealed in a fresh vacuum bag, ready for burial. The medicator's disk held both the audio record and the imaging data. Adetti and Boyer looked as weary as Simon felt. He gestured to the wavebox, and they both dropped their protective gear into it. The needles and the single scalpel he had used were already inside. He pushed the button to start the cycle that would reduce everything to sterile ash.

"Administrator," he said softly. "I think we need some coffee."

"I certainly do," Boyer said with fervor.

"I do, too," Adetti said. He gave Simon a look of respect. "That was good work, Edwards. I couldn't have done it."

Simon, scrubbing his hands, nodded thanks. "Well. It's always been part of my job," he said. He gave way at the sink to Adetti, and wiped his hands on a towel. "And I'm always glad when it's finished."

They sat together at a long table in the cafeteria. The room was empty except for the cooks just beginning dinner preparations behind the steam tables.

"You can tell your people one thing, Administrator," Simon said. He rested his elbows on the table, and traced the rim of his coffee cup with his fingers. "Even if I'd been here, or Dr. Adetti—we couldn't have saved your man. It went too fast."

"My people will be glad to know that," Boyer said gloomily. "And they'll be glad they can finally hold a funeral."

"I know." Simon sat back in his chair, wincing at the pinch of strained muscles. "You could ask Mother Burke to help with that."

Adetti's flat black eyes were on Simon. "He had the virus," he said. "Yes."

"Virus?" Boyer asked.

"That's right." Simon twisted his shoulders, trying to stretch the small of his back. "I think I can put an antiviral together, and everyone at the power park should be immunized. Sooner the better."

Boyer's long face creased. "You're saying he died of a virus?"

"More specifically, he died of the side effects of the virus," Simon said. "I'll write a full report in the morning, but you might as well know the gist now." He paused, glancing at Adetti, finding himself reluctant to put it all into words.

Adetti didn't hesitate. "I told you, Jacob, that there was something strange going on with that girl—the one who survived the skirmish."

"Yes?" Boyer looked wary.

"You saw her," Adetti said with a gleam of satisfaction in his eyes. "Two and a half years, and she hasn't changed. You saw for yourself!"

Boyer turned to Simon. "Can you explain this, Dr. Edwards?"

"Not yet," Simon said. "Not fully. But it's true, she hasn't changed. And she had the same virus as your hydro worker."

"But it didn't make her sick!"

"No. But it did cause her to develop a tiny tumor on her pituitary gland, a benign tumor. And your deceased worker has the same tumor."

"Benign? But then why . . ."

Simon steepled his fingers and stared at them. "I have a theory, only. I need to compare Oa's scans with the dead man's to draw a final conclusion."

Adetti made an impatient noise in his throat. "Come on, Edwards," he said. "You're hedging. You know what it is."

Simon let his eyes slide to Adetti. "A theory," he repeated.

A few people started to wander into the cafeteria. The cooks were settling big pots of things into the receptacles on the steam tables, and stocking the tables with condiments. Boyer said quietly, "Tell me your theory, at least, Dr. Edwards. How worried should I be about my people?"

Simon dropped his hands to the table. "Both Oa and the dead man have elevated levels of an enzyme called telomerase," he said bluntly. "In Oa's case, it retarded the aging process."

"Delayed senescence!" Adetti exclaimed. "Exactly!"

Simon shot him another glance, and then looked back at Boyer. "In your worker's case, the flood of telomerase was fatal."

"But—where did the virus come from?"

"That's what I need to find out," Simon said slowly. "And no one should leave the power park until I do."

*   *   *

ISABEL THOUGHT SHE had never seen such a utilitarian place as the Virimund Power Park. The barracks were only an oblong of foambrick, with low ceilings and unadorned walls, a common area with a table and a big reader. The administrator's secretary showed them to a room that reminded Isabel of a nun's cell she had once seen in an archeological project near Assisi.

Isabel set her valise down. Sheets and blankets had been laid ready, but the beds weren't made up. The secretary went to show Gretchen Boreson to her room as Isabel began to shake out the sheets.

Oa stood uncertainly in the middle of the little room, tugging on a lock of her hair. "Oa likes to go to the island."

Isabel stopped, a half-unfolded sheet in her hand. "I know, sweetheart. I want to go to the island, too. But we have to wait until Doctor Simon says it's all right. And I need to interview someone—" She hesitated, and then decided she must be straightforward. "I have to speak with the man who brought you here."

Oa looked at her feet, and Isabel saw that her eyes reddened and her lips trembled. She dropped the sheet onto the bed. "What is it, Oa?"

The girl gave a shuddering sigh. "Oa is afraid."

"You don't have to be afraid of him, Oa. You don't have to see him."

"No, Isabel. Oa is not afraid of the man." Oa's nose began to run.

Isabel put her hand under Oa's chin and lifted her face. "Then tell me, sweetheart. Tell me why you're afraid."

Oa sniffled. Isabel fumbled in her pocket for a handkerchief and gave it to her, then led her to the bed, where they sat together on the bare mattress. She waited until Oa's tears had subsided, and then repeated her question. "Why are you afraid?"

Oa leaned against her shoulder, and Isabel pressed her cheek against the soft black hair. "The anchens. Oa is afraid there are no more anchens."

"Ah. Yes, I see. That is a frightening thought." Isabel stroked her hair, and felt her trembling. Oa sniffed again. "Blow, sweetheart," Isabel said, lifting the handkerchief to the girl's face. Obediently, Oa blew her nose. Isabel patted her shoulder. "We have to be patient a little longer, I'm afraid."

"Be patients?" Oa asked, distracted, frowning.

"Oh, no, not patients. Not as if we were sick. We have to be patient . . . let's see, that means calm, I guess. Waiting without being upset. Not because we like to wait, but because in this situation we don't have a choice."

Oa put the handkerchief down. "Patient. Oa is patient."

"Good. That's good, sweetheart."

Oa turned her reddened eyes up to Isabel. "Oa does not like to be patient."

Isabel hugged her. "No, I can see that. Sometimes we just have to." She stood up, and pulled the girl to her feet. "Let's go for a walk, shall we? We can make the beds up later. Let's see if we can find our way past all that equipment, and you can show me Mother Ocean."

When they left the barracks, Isabel hesitated on the sandy path, trying to get her bearings, but Oa turned unerringly toward the sea, tugging Isabel after her. The pastel sand was resilient under their feet, and the fading daylight left the air soft and sweet. Invisible birds sang somewhere, twittering their evening greetings.

"Jin-Li!" Oa called. Isabel looked up to see that the archivist had emerged from one of the other barracks and was waiting for them at the turning of the path.

"Hello, Oa. Isabel." Jin-Li lifted a hand. "How's your room?"

"It's fine," Isabel said. Oa danced ahead to meet Jin-Li. Isabel walked slowly, still feeling uneasy on her feet.

"Are you all right?" Jin-Li asked when she had caught up with them.

"I feel odd," Isabel said with a shrug. "As if the gravity were off, or something."

Jin-Li nodded. "It is, a little, but I don't think it's the gravity. I felt the same when I first made planetfall on Irustan, and some of the others did, too. I suspect there's no logical explanation. It's just—alien."

"Yes. A good word for it. It feels alien, to my feet, my eyes, even my lungs."

That made Jin-Li's narrow lips curve. "Better air than home."

"I know. But different." Isabel glanced down at Oa. "Did you feel strange when you first came to Earth, Oa?"

Oa considered for a moment. "Oa feels strange on Earth," she said. Her eyes flicked around at the scene, the dull buildings, the bristling ranks of solar collectors. She added, quietly, "Oa feels strange on Virimund."

Jin-Li and Isabel looked at each other. "Tough on her," Jin-Li said.

"Yes. In every way."

The girl looked up at both of them. "Oa is . . . a-li-en. Alien."

Isabel caught her hand, and held it between hers. "No. No, sweetheart. Not alien."

"That's right, Oa," Jin-Li said. "You belong to both Earth and Virimund. You're a child of two worlds."

Isabel looked into Jin-Li's long dark eyes. They were hard to read, and yet full of intelligence and honesty. "Beautifully said, Jin-Li."

The archivist laughed a little, and looked away.

Oa tugged at Isabel's hand again. "Isabel. Oa sees Mar-Mar now. Mother Ocean!"

"Yes, Oa, I'm coming. We'll find our way to Mother Ocean. Jin-Li?"

"Sure."

Isabel laughed. "Not that we can't see Mother Ocean all around us! But Oa and I want to find the beach."

"Sounds good."

The three of them trooped along the path that ran behind the terminal. It bypassed the cafeteria, and the curious eyes of the Port Forcemen and women, and led through banks of solar collectors to a narrow slice of beach curling around a tiny inlet. It was empty, but it looked as if it must be a popular spot. A couple of collapsible chairs rested in the sand, and someone had left a folded blanket, with a pair of sandals on top.

Oa kicked off her shoes and raced ahead, the pink soles of her feet leaving brief sparkling footprints. She held out her arms as if to embrace the sea as she splashed into the water. The gentle, almost imperceptible surf swirled around her ankles, and then her knees, but though she walked a good distance, it grew no deeper. Isabel picked up Oa's shoes and carried them in her hand as she and Jin-Li walked down onto the beach. She bent to unbuckle her own shoes and turned up her trouser legs.

"Are you going to wade, Jin-Li?" she smiled.

"I'll watch from here."

The foamy shallow water was cool on Isabel's skin. The breeze from the ocean caressed her bare scalp, and tickled her nostrils with its scents of salt and fish and that unfamiliar scent, something pungent and sweet. She wondered what leaf or herb gave off that unique odor.

She waded out to Oa, digging her toes into the resilient sand, taking deep, refreshing breaths of salt-scented air. Her mind could hardly take in that there was actually another world beneath her feet, a different gravity, a slightly different atmosphere, a world with its own plants and creatures and constellations. She laughed at the immensity of it, and began to feel better.

Oa, seeing, flashed her white smile. "Mother Ocean is beautiful," she said.

"Very," Isabel agreed. "Is it good to be home, Oa?"

Oa pulled her hair ribbon off to let the long locks of her hair float in the wind. "Home is good!" She stamped, splashing the salty cool water over Isabel's trousers, and her own, and she, too, laughed up into the darkening sky.

As they watched Virimund's mild star settle past the horizon, their feet grew cold. Stars began to shine on the eastern horizon, and the sky turned to violet, shading to purple in the distance. They waded out of the water, and rubbed the wet sand from their feet. They put their shoes on, feeling the grit of sand inside, and turned to walk back up the path. Jin-Li led the way, and Oa and Isabel followed.

"Isabel," Oa said softly.

"Yes, Oa."

"Oa . . ." She paused, and her small hand searched the air for the words. "Oa likes to see the anchens. But Oa is home with Isabel."

"Ah." Isabel drew Oa's hand under her arm and patted it. "Do you mean that home is where I am?"

Oa's eyes flashed white in the dusk, and she nodded. "Home is where Isabel is."

Isabel offered a prayer that she would never, ever disappoint this mysterious creature, this ancient child. This child of two worlds. She couldn't bear to fail in the face of such trust.

23

SIMON CARRIED HIS computer to his room in the barracks, where he sat poring over the data until his eyes burned and his head ached, and he judged there was no more he could do until he rested. Isabel had taken Oa to their room right after dinner, away from the intense scrutiny of the hydro workers in the cafeteria. Jin-Li, after asking if he needed any help, had gone to bed, too. Gretchen Boreson had not made an appearance at dinner, and Adetti had gone to check on her before seeking his own bed. It had been a long, arduous, and worrisome day. Simon knew he should find the r-wave center and send a message to Anna, to keep his promise to call when they made planetfall. It was hard to believe they had only arrived today, and he had seen nothing of Virimund past the airfield and Port Force terminal. He was exhausted. He told himself he would take care of it first thing in the morning. With a mental apology to Anna, and a wish for her not to be unhappy, he fell into bed, and was asleep in moments.

He woke early to the sounds of the power park gearing up for the first rays of light to touch the solar collectors. Cart motors hummed on the road, and in the other rooms, all as small and plain as the one he had been given, he heard the thump of boots, the yawns and other noises of people rising for work. At one end of the barracks, showers splashed, and at the other, the door banged open and shut. By the time Simon had gathered his toiletries and found the shower, most of the hydros were up and gone, leaving their doors ajar. Only one or two, night workers perhaps, were still in their rooms, the doors closed. Simon showered, brushed his teeth, applied a depilatory, and went in search of the r-wave center.

The tech on duty smiled when she saw Simon. "You're Dr. Edwards, aren't you? Jacob—Administrator Boyer, that is—said to expect you." She rose, and pushed her own chair forward. "Here you go. Would you like some coffee? We ran out last week, but your transport brought a whole new supply, thank goodness."

"Coffee would be wonderful." Simon accepted the chair, and fitted the transmission wand into the receptor. He spoke the numbers and letters to route the call to Geneva, and sat back, yawning, to wait for the connection.

The tech brought an enormous mug and set it before him. "Got everything, Doc? Call me if you need something else." She vanished into another room. He took a grateful sip of strong black coffee.

"Simon? Is that you? I can't hear you. Simon?"

He leaned forward, pushing the cup to one side. "Yes, yes, I'm here, Anna. I'm here. There's a slight delay. You have to allow for it." He had explained it to her before, that the r-waves were almost, but not quite, instant. He rubbed his forehead, willing himself to be patient.

"Are you all right? Are you finally on Virimund?" Even over the reaches bridged by r-waves, her voice sounded thin and tired.

"Yes, Anna. I'm—we've reached Virimund. Right on schedule. I'm fine. And you? How are things going?" He drank more coffee while he waited for her answer.

"I'm all right," she said. Her voice grew a little stronger. "Our funding came through, with Hilda's help. We're going to be able to add two classrooms, and hire two more teachers."

Simon closed his eyes. He imagined her sitting at their kitchen table, the wavephone in her hand, leaning on her elbows. Though he had seen her in that posture a hundred times, it felt like looking at a stranger. It seemed impossible they were a couple, that the two of them had once decided to live together, to be married. What Simon had that been, to marry someone like Anna, someone as predictable as the passing of days into weeks, months into years? When had he begun to change? He couldn't think now if Anna had always been—dull, was the disloyal word that came to mind. Or maybe she wasn't. Maybe it was only that they were dull together.

She prompted him gently. "What's it like there? Is it hot?"

He glanced out the small window of the r-wave center at the patch of jungle left by the bulldozers. "Not hot. It's rather like Hawaii," he said. "Only more—more vivid."

"What did you say? Vivid?"

"Yes. Vivid."

He could feel her puzzlement over the romantic word. It was not a way they usually spoke of things. "What does that mean?"

"Oh, I don't know, exactly." He lifted one hand, rather like Oa, searching for a way to explain his thought. "The colors seem more intense. The sea, the trees, the sky . . . The air is so clean, and it smells spicy."

"I wish I could see it," she said sadly.

"Yes." He dropped his hand. "I wish you could, too."

"I miss you," Anna said.

Simon bit his lip. Whatever was between them, he and Anna, they never lied to each other. He couldn't do it now, either. "It's exciting being here, Anna," he finally said. "The most exciting thing I've ever done."

She hesitated for a long moment. "I understand," she said. "I can certainly understand that."

"I need to get to work now."

"Yes, of course." But she didn't ask about it, didn't ask about the girl, or the research. Or Isabel. It was remarkable, he thought, that he could sense her misery even over the immense distance that separated them. "Well. Call when you can."

"I will."

It was a relief to turn the r-wave tech's desk back over to her, and take up the computer and reader and disks, to bury himself once again in work.

THE MORNING, LIKE the evening before, was warm, the air soft with humidity that promised to be muggy by noon. Isabel stepped outside the barracks with Oa, to make their way to the meal hall for breakfast. Gretchen Boreson stood on the path, shading her eyes as she looked out toward the ocean. Oa shrank back when she saw her, and Isabel put an arm around her.

"Good morning, Ms. Boreson," Isabel said.

Boreson turned toward her abruptly, almost staggering, as if she had lost her balance. She pulled a pair of wide dark glasses out of a breast pocket and put them on with a visibly trembling hand. Her silver hair was ruffled, and she had forgone her cosmetics. "Mother Burke," she said hoarsely. "When are we going?"

"Excuse me?"

"Do you know when we're going? To the island?"

Oa stood stiffly, eyes cast down. Isabel said gently, "Simon thinks we should wait. Until he knows exactly what happened to the Port Forceman who died."

"But I want to go now. Today." Boreson's voice rose, and she lifted a shaking hand to her mouth.

"I'm sure Simon's doing the best he can," Isabel said. "And apparently he and Dr. Adetti are in agreement about . . ." She watched in alarm as Boreson swayed, a strange involuntary movement, like a marionette on invisible strings. "Administrator—" Isabel began. She put out her hand, and Boreson seized it with her own, the polished silver claws glinting in the morning light. Isabel gasped aloud.

Her "little talent," as Simon called it, could be a painful thing. The desperate need that blazed through Gretchen Boreson's white hand into Isabel's sensitive fingers felt like the lick of an open flame. She wanted to pull away, but Boreson's grip, though her arm shook with palsy, was like a vise.

"Where's Paolo?" Boreson hissed through pale lips. "He knows I want to go today."

"Gretchen," Isabel said. She made herself put her other hand over Boreson's thin fingers, trying to soften their death grip into a handclasp. "No one can go yet, Gretchen. They don't want to put more people at risk. It's the virus, remember?"

Boreson wavered on her feet, swaying like a sapling in a wind.

"Come now, Gretchen. You and I will go to breakfast, with Oa, and you'll see Paolo and Simon there, and they can explain everything. And look, here's Jin-Li. Come now. Everything will be all right."

Jin-Li approached. Boreson's grip eased, and a moment later the administrator seemed to pull herself together, smoothing her hair, folding her arms around herself. Isabel made a small gesture, and Jin-Li and Oa started down the path ahead of them.

"Are you ready, Gretchen?" Isabel said quietly.

Boreson cleared her throat. "Yes," she said. "Yes. Breakfast. It's just that . . . we've come so far. Waited so long."

"We certainly have," Isabel said mildly as they started after Oa and Jin-Li. "A great distance. Another day or two won't hurt, surely."

She stayed close to the older woman, worried she might fall. Boreson, her hands tight on her elbows, walked carefully, as if the pastel sand were made of broken glass, or as if she didn't trust her feet. She didn't answer.

"DR. EDWARDS?" JIN-LI knocked briefly on the open door of the data room. "Isabel sent me to remind you to eat lunch."

Simon looked up, frowning, then rubbing his brow with his hand. "Oh, Jin-Li. Good morning. Where is Isabel?"

"In Administrator Boyer's office. She's meeting with the cryotech who brought Oa from the island."

"She didn't need you there? Or me?"

"She said not. Nothing medical. The administrator will be present, and his secretary."

"Okay." Simon turned back to his computer. "Look at this." Jin-Li saw a three-dimensional figure rotating slowly on the screen, a human figure. A pattern of scarlet dots radiated across the figure, lighter at the head, growing darker in the torso, almost solid in the left leg. "It's the pattern of the viral infection, and the computer is tracing it down to its source." He spoke a command, and the figure rotated again, and the leg, the ankle, the foot enlarged. The dots converged into a patch of solid scarlet at the heel. Simon spoke again, and it froze. "There's the initial site of infection. The red dots show the dispersal pattern of the virus through the body—pretty generalized, probably travels right through the cell walls. Bet it moved fast. He could have stepped on something, I suppose. Or been bitten."

"There's a spider here," Jin-Li said. "A long-legged black one. One of the Port Forceman told me it bites."

Simon looked up. "It does? Others have been bitten?"

"Guess so. He said it hurts."

Simon leaned back, rubbing his reddened eyes. "Okay. We need to look at those spiders, then. What else?"

"There are several varieties of snake, but mostly a lot of birds. Long feathers, long beaks. The biologist hasn't had time to catalog everything. She's been pretty busy with the biotransforms, and getting hydroponics up and running."

"Can you ask her what samples she has so far? I know a lot of this isn't in your job description, but we're shorthanded all around."

"Happy to do it." Jin-Li hesitated in the doorway.

Simon looked up, brow creased again. "Something else?"

"Yes. Isabel—"

At her name, Simon's face brightened. "Oh, lord. Right. Lunch." He laughed. "I'm going, Jin-Li. Promise. I don't want Isabel to worry."

Simon's grin dropped years from his lean face. Jin-Li thought of Simon and Isabel, isolated in the Victoria Desert, spending hours together every day, eating their meals together every evening, falling in love under the blistering Australian sky. Surely it had been inevitable, if complicated. And where did it leave them now?

Simon hurried off toward the meal hall, and Jin-Li turned to go into the terminal, to ask at the comm center for the biologist. Above the drab buildings the sky was a vault of clear blue, punctuated by fluffs of white cloud. Grains of pastel sand glittered on every surface, and wherever the eye turned, the emerald waters stretched to the horizon. Jin-Li paused for a long moment, savoring it, breathing the spicy air, wondering what dark secret marred the perfect beauty of the planet.

THE CRYOTECH CALLED Ice was small, with thinning hair that had once been blond, but had faded to a yellowish-white. His sunburned scalp showed through in ragged patches. He perched on the edge of a chair in Jacob Boyer's office, his red-knuckled hands resting uneasily on his knees. He spoke with an accent Isabel recognized.

"You're from Australia," she said with a smile. "I worked there two years ago, in the Victoria Desert."

"Other side," he said in a reedy tenor. "I'm from Adelaide."

Isabel nodded. She pointed to her reader, set up on Boyer's desk. "I thought you might be more comfortable with fewer people present, so I told our archivist I'd record everything, if it's all right with you, Mr. Foster."

"Yeah, it's okay," he said. "But call me Ice." He managed a wan grin. "I don't answer to much else these days."

Isabel put out her hand, and he took it diffidently, giving it a tentative shake. "Ice." The touch of his fingers gave her a faint feeling of sadness, as of long-suppressed grief.

"Yeah." His smile faded, and he crossed his legs, then uncrossed them. "Listen, Mother Burke. It all happened a long time ago, and I've kinda tried to forget it. I told Mr. Boyer, here, everything at the time."

"I know you did, and I read the report. But it would help me to hear it for myself. You understand how important it is, not only to the children on the island, but to your colleagues."

The look that crossed the man's weathered face had only one meaning. Without thinking, she breathed, "You blame yourself."

He nodded, mutely.

She watched him trying to disguise his emotion. "You couldn't have known."

"Should have."

"Mr. Foster. I mean, Ice," she said gently. "Let's work together.

Perhaps we can prevent more deaths. Sometimes a tragedy can be turned into something positive."

"Won't bring my buddy back." His voice was strained.

"No." She shook her head. It may have been, as he said, a long time, but she suspected it was as fresh to Ice as if it had happened yesterday. As fresh as it was to Oa. Oa had difficulty talking about it, but at least Ice could express himself. She leaned forward and tapped her reader to begin recording.

"Ice, tell me why you landed on the island."

"Well. No need for cryo that early in construction. No product yet, you know? So we were checking out the other islands. Not looking for anything, just . . . looking. New planet, lots of islands . . . Other guys were doing it, going in different directions."

"And when you reached this particular island?"

"Well, we picked that one because we thought we saw smoke. Just a little, a thin stream . . . could have been from one of the old volcanoes, or even a grass fire. But then we saw this monument kind of thing. Square on top, wider at the bottom, piled-up stones. It didn't look natural." He dropped his eyes to his work-roughened hands. "We were just curious," he muttered. "We never meant—" His eyes came up to hers, slid to Boyer, came back to Isabel. "We never meant for anyone to be hurt. They came at us!"

Jacob Boyer sat stiffly behind his desk. Isabel sensed his effort to be silent, to let her conduct her interview. She turned to him. "Mr. Boyer, you can add whatever you like. This isn't official. I just want to understand what happened before I go to meet the other children."

Boyer opened his mouth, but Ice broke in. "Mother Burke, I don't think they're children. They may look like children, but they carry knives and they throw stones the size of baseballs. If you're going to that island, and they're still there, you better go armed."

Isabel touched her cross. There was danger in this moment. Jacob Boyer was nodding slightly. The man called Ice was watching her with absolute sincerity in his weathered face. She wanted to remind them both that violence begets more violence, that it had already done so in this case. But there was more she needed to know.

*　*　*

SIMON FOUND ISABEL and Oa in the meal hall. Oa huddled beside Isabel, shrinking from the regard of the Port Forcemen and women. Jacob Boyer sat across from them. "Where are Adetti and Boreson?" he murmured to Isabel.

"Gretchen's not feeling well," Isabel told him. "She couldn't eat anything."

Simon nodded, frowning. "Twilight sleep didn't help, I imagine," he said.

A server came to the table with a plate of food, and set it before Simon. It appeared to be some kind of pink fruit, and there was a creamy wedge of something he couldn't identify.

"Eat, Simon," Isabel urged, pointing to the wedge. "It's delicious."

He sliced a bit of it with his fork. "Biotransforms?" he asked Boyer.

"Not that. There's a kind of nut here," Boyer said. "High protein content, easily digestible. The cooks found a way to make this sort of cake with it."

Simon tasted it. "It's good," he said. "What do you call it?"

"The cooks decided to call it coconut. Everyone seems to like it, and we can all eat it. It's the one thing we haven't had to transform."

Across the table, Oa was whispering in Isabel's ear. Isabel nodded. "Nuchi," she said. "That's Oa's word for it." She smiled. "It's nice to put something real to one of the words we haven't been able to translate." Oa ducked her head again under Boyer's stare.

He looked back at Simon. "It's just unbelievable," he said bluntly.

"I know."

Oa slumped lower.

A server came to refill coffee cups and pick up their empty plates. The meal hall was beginning to clear, the hydros talking and laughing together as they went off to work.

"How did the interview go, Isabel?"

"I didn't learn much that's new." She glanced down at Oa, hiding behind her curtain of hair. "He thinks he saw about a dozen children, maybe more. They wore rags, and carried crude weapons. Ice—the cryotech—says they burst out of the forest, throwing stones and knives.

He and the other man carried shock guns . . ." She looked at Boyer. "Why were they armed, Jacob?"

Boyer looked uncomfortable. "I've explained this," he said sadly. "New world, maybe new animals . . . we didn't know. Men have to protect themselves."

Isabel made her voice deliberately mild. "The children had to protect themselves, too, didn't they? That's the problem with carrying weapons. They get used."

Oa moved at her side, and pushed back her fall of hair. She whispered to Isabel, so softly Simon could hardly hear her, "Anchens protect Raimu-ke. Not anchens. Raimu-ke."

Isabel sighed. "I've explained to Oa that Ice tried to save her. That he brought her here so the doctor could treat her."

"Oa, did you understand what Isabel said to you?"

Oa's eyes looked ancient in her childish face. "Oa understands," she whispered. "Anchens are frightened. Men are—" She lifted a hand, making a claw of the fingers. "Men are touching kburi. Taking stones."

"The kburi is sacred to the anchens," Isabel said. "Ice and his buddy were curious about it, but the anchens thought they were stealing it, or trying to."

"Ice isn't the only one who doesn't think they're children," Boyer said bluntly. "Twice I've had to intervene, stop a few rowdies bent on revenge."

"It's good you did," Simon said. "Come to the infirmary with me, and I'll show you what we've found. It's best you see for yourself."

ISABEL WANTED TO go with Simon, and Oa didn't want to leave Isabel. She trailed behind as they all walked to the infirmary. She understood what the tall, sad-looking man had said, that his people suspected the anchens were not children. They seemed to know what Isabel would not believe. They frightened Oa with their hard eyes, their stiff necks when they looked at her.

Only the scent of the breeze from Mother Ocean spoke of Virimund to Oa. What she had said to Jin-Li and Isabel was true. She was as alien here, at the power park, as she had been on Earth. She yearned to go to the island, to know that Ette and Bibi and the others were still there. She longed to take Isabel to Raimu-ke.

The sad-faced man opened the door to the infirmary and stood back to let everyone enter. Oa followed Isabel inside, her eyes on her feet. Doctor Simon started into the data room, but a sound from the small surgery distracted him, and he stopped. The others stopped, too, crowded into the too-small reception area.

Doctor Simon stood before the closed door. "Someone's in there."

Oa recognized the noise. It was the hiss and click of the spider machine doing its work. She remembered that room too well.

They had landed on the top of the island, that man and the other one, the one Nwa stuck with his digging knife. They had come down in their noisy flyer that was like the fables of the ancestors, passed down in songs and stories. Their flyer had been so close to the kburi that it seemed its strange whirling wings might bring it tumbling down. The anchens had been digging for pishi on the beach, and at the noise, despite their fear, they ran up the mountain to the kburi, their digging knives still in their hands. And the men, those strange big men in their odd clothes, had been taking the kburi apart, tearing at the stones the anchens had painstakingly carried and placed and revered. The anchens thought the men wanted Raimu-ke.

Oa had been utterly confused when she came to at the power park the first time. Even the concept of a door, a hard thing that closed and locked, had been beyond her understanding. Still stunned by the death of Nwa, her leg gushing blood, she had been forced onto the table of the spider machine in the small surgery. Its cold legs trailed over her, testing her wrists and ankles and temples, searching for her soul, hissing its fury that it wasn't there. She had thought she was dead, that she should be dead, but surely, death meant no more fear, no more suffering! Yet she lay on the table, trembling, more afraid than ever.

The man had brought her back in his flyer, thrown her in beside Nah-nah's still small body, and the bloodstained, lifeless body of the other man. The man shouted, and he smelled utterly different from anyone she had ever encountered. He smelled of fear and anger and of his sunburned white skin and thinning yellow hair, and other things she couldn't identify. He had carried her as if she were a rolled-up mat, and

he and Doctor tied her onto the table. They let the spider machine at-
tack her with its terrifying shining eyes and long, long legs. She didn't
understand, then, that it was a machine. She didn't know what a screen
was, or a reader, or a computer. She didn't know that a Doctor could be
like Doctor Simon, kind and helpful and warm-handed. In this very
place, in that very room, she had lain sick with fear and grief and pain,
and her new ordeal had begun.

Doctor Simon went into the small surgery. As the door opened, Oa caught a glimpse of bare white feet twitching against the paper sheet, silver hair beneath the master syrinx of the medicator. The door closed again.

Boyer said awkwardly to Isabel, "The Administrator—she's pressing to go to the island, to see the other . . ." He broke off, his eyes sliding to Oa, past her.

"The other children, Mr. Boyer? Is that what you mean?"

Boyer cleared his throat, and nodded, looking mournful. "If they are children."

"Oh, they are." Isabel's arm was warm and steady around Oa.

But Oa saw the disbelief in Boyer's face, the way he avoided looking at her. He knew. They all knew. Except Isabel.

24

SIMON CLOSED THE surgery door and joined Adetti beside the medicator. "Anything I can do?" he asked. Gretchen Boreson's closed eyelids
twitched, and her legs jerked with spasms.

Adetti glanced up at him. "She'll sleep through the treatment." He
looked back at Boreson's face, his dark features drawn with fatigue.
"Gretchen has Crosgrove's chorea."

"I guessed as much. She takes dimenasphin, I assume?"

"Yes, but she's developed a tolerance. Relief from the tremors is
lasting a shorter and shorter interval after each treatment." Adetti
straightened, keeping his eye on the readout screen. The medicator
clicked softly, the master syrinx vibrating slightly at the passage of the
medicine through the tube.

"You must have brought a supply," Simon said. "Or did you make
it up here?"

"She included it in her own weight allowance."

Boreson's twitching seemed to ease slightly as Simon watched her.

"Twilight sleep won't have helped," he mused. "Exacerbates neuro-logical problems."

"She knew that. She was determined."

Simon tapped the screen once to slow the scrolling. "What is it she wants here?"

Adetti folded his arms. "What we all want," he said flatly. "De-layed senescence factor. If it works, it will reverse her illness."

"But we're ages away from understanding it," Simon said.

"Are we? It seems fairly simple to me. We know there's a virus. We can see its effect on Oa. We need to see what's happening to the others, the ones like her. What are we waiting for, Edwards?"

The clicking of the medicator stopped, and Boreson, on the table, gave a slight sigh, beginning to wake. As Adettti turned to begin re-moving the patches, Simon said, "It's bad science, my friend. Rush-ing things. We have one death already."

Adetti's eyes came up to meet his. "Would you care about that? If you knew you were dying anyway, by inches?"

Obscurely, Simon thought of Anna and her fading youth, her hair graying too early, her body thickening. He shook his head. "We don't know enough yet," he said. "She'll have to wait." He turned to the door, and then looked back over his shoulder at the other physician. "You will, too," he said.

Adetti's flat black eyes flickered, and shifted away. A moment later, Gretchen Boreson opened her eyes, and Adetti helped her to sit upright. Her hands, Simon saw, had steadied, and when she stood, her back was straight and her eyes flashed with their old authority. She was a remarkable woman, really. A determined woman, rather like Anna in her own way. Although Anna, Simon knew perfectly well, would never apply her energies to her own ambitions.

When they all emerged from the surgery, they found only Jin-Li and Boyer waiting for them. Isabel had taken Oa to the barracks to go to bed. Simon led Jacob Boyer into the data room. "Jin-Li, did you find the biologist?"

"I did, Dr. Edwards. She has a few specimens you can examine. No spiders, though. She's working on it. Couple of hydros volunteered to help."

"Good. Okay." Simon tapped his reader, and the autopsy report appeared. "Here, Administrator, I'll show you what we found."

AN HOUR LATER, Simon walked slowly toward his own barracks with Jin-Li. The sky was bright with stars, the wind from the ocean soft, perfumed with Virimund's unique fragrance. The resilient sand of the paths made him feel like taking his shoes off.

"In the Victoria Desert," he said, "the sand was too hot to touch. The natives there walked barefoot where I couldn't even put my hand."

Jin-Li nodded. "Irustan was hot, too. And dry."

"But this . . ." Simon gestured up into the star-strewn sky. "This is paradise."

"Except for the crawlies," Jin-Li said, and then laughed at Simon's startled look. "That's what the hydros call the spiders. Crawlies."

Simon grinned. "Paradise with crawlies, then." They reached the first barracks, where Isabel and Jin-Li both had their rooms. Light still streamed from several windows. The night shift in the storage facility had begun hours ago, he knew, because they had watched four cryotechs cross the airfield. "Looks like everybody's up," he said.

Jin-Li pointed to a darkened window. "That's Isabel's room."

A twinge of disappointment marred Simon's mood. "She probably went to bed," he said. "Well. See you in the morning, then."

When Jin-Li opened the door, Simon saw several people, Port Forcemen and women, seated around a table in the common room, cards spread out between them. They weren't playing, though. He caught a glimpse of Isabel's bare head, bent forward as she listened to someone. Every face was turned to her. She was being a priest, he supposed, hearing confidences, sharing concerns. He imagined the sparkle of her eyes, the intensity of her fine features as she listened. She always listened with perfect focus, as if nothing existed for her at that moment but the speaker. It was one of the things that had first drawn him to her, that quality of listening, of opening herself.

If only Anna . . . But he pushed away the thought. Anna couldn't help what she was. Nor could Isabel. Nor, for that matter, could he.

IN GAY SUNSHINE, Isabel stood before a simple casket fashioned of scavenged materials. It was her first visit to the nascent cemetery of the Virimund Power Park. Its two graves were already carpeted with the native yellow grass. Someone had carefully trimmed it to show the flat foamcast headstones, one inscribed with the name of GARCIA, the Port Forceman who had died on the island of the anchens. The other read simply UNKNOWN CHILD. Isabel's heart ached at the thought that it might have been Oa who lay beneath the grass and sand. She had to tell someone the child's name, find a helpful soul to reinscribe the stone, to record Nwa's passing.

She had worked with the men and women in her barracks the night before to create a short liturgy. One of the women had suggested a poem from *The Prophet*, another a passage from *The Rubaiyat*. No one objected when Isabel offered the text of "In Paradisum," and she recited it as the casket was lowered into the freshly dug grave.

MAY THE ANGELS ESCORT THEE TO PARADISE,
MAY THE MARTYRS RECEIVE THEE AT THY COMING,
AND BRING THEE INTO THE HOLY CITY.
MAY THE CHOIRS OF ANGELS RECEIVE THEE,
AND MAYST THOU HAVE ETERNAL REST.

Everyone who could be spared from the work of the power park was present. They had gathered first in the meal hall, where several who had been close friends of the deceased offered memories. The hydros already had their own ceremonies of greeting and farewell, and when it was time to form a procession, they shouldered their tools, long-handled diggers, a kind of spatula-shaped tool for cleaning solar collectors, coils of connecting cable. They began a song that had developed here, on Virimund, and they walked in ragged single file to the cemetery on its gentle hill overlooking the ocean. The incoming shuttles would sweep above it, their passage stirring the leaves of the low-lying shrubbery.

Isabel was moved by the simplicity of the place, the sincerity of the Port Forcemen and women sharing their feelings through the ceremony. Human beings throughout the centuries, she reflected, had marked their comings and goings just so. The trappings differed from age to age, the details changed, but the essence remained the same, on Earth or off world, human beings struggling to see past the veil to what lay beyond.

The graveside ritual ended, and the man's friends sprinkled farewell gifts into his grave before it was filled in, dropping flower petals, scraps of paper scrawled with handwriting. One laid a small book gently on the casket lid. Isabel stood with her head bowed, praying for the soul of the departed, for the safety of the survivors, for her own guidance.

She meant every word, every thought. She yearned toward the divine, her heart longing for the wellspring of inspiration, of comfort. She failed to find it except in memory.

The mourners began to wander back to the power park, walking in twos and threes, on to the feast they had felt it was appropriate to have. Only Oa and Isabel remained. Isabel turned her face up into the pale blue Virimund heaven, murmuring, "Sometimes I feel soulless."

"Isabel doesn't feel well?" Oa asked.

Isabel startled, hardly aware she had spoken aloud. She gave a humorless laugh. "Oh, no, that wasn't what I meant, Oa." She made a helpless gesture. "I don't know how to explain it to you. It was silly, anyway. I meant that sometimes I feel as if I have lost my soul."

Oa gave her a quizzical look. "What is soul?"

Isabel took Oa's hand, and they started after the others. "Soul," she said. "Let's see. Soul is spirit, the spirit that each person has. It's our consciousness, our sense of self—but more than that. It's what makes us human, not like a rock, or a machine, but a living, feeling being."

Oa's fingers went cold in hers, flooding her hand with a strange sensation, a feeling of shock, almost of horror. "Soul," Oa breathed slowly.

"Yes, Oa. Everyone has a soul . . . I didn't mean it, really, it was foolish . . ."

But Oa's expression was bleak. "Soul," she repeated. "Oa is not having a soul. Anchens are not having a soul." She glanced back over her shoulder. Two men were shoveling dirt into the grave. "The man's soul is gone."

Isabel felt she had done something terribly wrong and yet . . . was this what the child had been trying to tell her all along? "Oa, the man's soul has left his body. It's not gone. It's what the 'In Paradisum' is about, asking for God to accept his soul into paradise."

"Anchens," Oa said, and her bitterness flowed through her fingers and made Isabel's hand ache as if she had plunged it into ice. "Anchens are having a body. Are not having a soul."

ISABEL SAT BESIDE Oa's cot until she slept, and then she sat in the darkness, gazing at her. Her long lashes lay like birds' wings against her dark cheeks, stirring now and again as she began to dream. Isabel touched her forehead and whispered a blessing. Silently, she apologized for being slow to understand, for the lack of inspiration that left her blind. Oa needed someone unencumbered, who could make the intuitive leap that would bring it all clear. What good would she be, on the island of the anchens, if she couldn't understand this one precious old child?

Loneliness overwhelmed her. She went to the door and looked out into the corridor. Jin-Li's door was closed, the light off. The Port Forcemen and women had feasted, mourned, and now slept. The barracks were dark, with only one covered light left burning in the common room, enough to find the way down the corridor to the bathroom, or the other way, out into the compound. Quietly, Isabel slipped out of her room and pulled the door closed. She wouldn't go far, she thought. Just out to see the stars, to breathe the night air, to search for something to soothe her troubled soul.

Soul. That word again.

The sand glowed beneath her feet, slightly phosphorescent in the starlight. Around her the barracks were quiet, and the power park itself stretched in somnolent darkness to the east and west. She knew the night shift was working in the storage facility, across the airfield, but she couldn't see past the terminal. The terminal building, too, was dark, even the r-wave center left unattended on this ceremonial night. It was as if she were alone on the island.

Her feet led her unerringly to the beach, the same path she and Jin-Li and Oa had found on their first day. Later she was to think that it was not her feet that led her, but her heart. Her heart betrayed her while her spirit lay dormant, as still and dark as the buildings she passed. She found herself standing on the crescent of sand, watching the waves of Mother Ocean wash the little beach with gentle strokes. The water glimmered with reflected stars.

To her right a slender figure stood at the edge of the water, a dark silhouette framed by the starlight. Isabel knew without asking that it was Simon. She couldn't distinguish the pulsing of the surf from the beat of her own heart.

"Isabel." She didn't know if he had come to her, or she to him. They stood at the edge of the night-dark ocean, the unfamiliar constellations stretching above their heads, the pale sand glittering at their feet. The touch of his hand on hers was as intimate as the deepest lovemaking.

They didn't kiss, or touch beyond that clasping of hands. She looked up into his familiar, ordinary face, and she knew that this was the moment of decision, a moment she had postponed by fleeing the Victoria Desert without a word.

"I've missed you so damned much," he said in a low tone.

"I've missed you, too."

"Why did you leave Victoria the way you did, Isabel? With no word, no warning."

"I was a coward," she said simply. "I was afraid, if I faced you . . . I wouldn't go."

"I didn't want you to go." His hand tightened on hers.

Her throat ached with remorse and longing. "Simon. We're not free, either of us."

"We could be."

"Do you really think so?" Her voice caught, and she turned her head to gaze out on the glassy starlit water.

"You're thinking of Anna."

"Not just Anna, Simon, although, yes, of course I think of her, and your promise to her. But the Order, as well. My vow."

"People change, Isabel. It's part of being alive." He took a half-step closer, and the temptation to step back, to feel his lean body against hers, almost overwhelmed her. He said, "Even if you won't come to me, I can't go back to Anna. It could never be the same."

"Because of me," she said sadly.

"Because I've changed. Because I'm not the man she married. And Anna—" He hesitated. She knew, by the sensation in her hand, that he was loath to speak disloyally of Anna. "Anna doesn't change. She can't change. It's not in her character."

"It doesn't matter." She made herself turn her body away from him, though her flesh protested. "Before I met you, Simon, the vow of celibacy was a pale sacrifice for me. It cost me nothing. And then, when faced with a real challenge to my commitment . . . I failed."

She felt his anger through his fingers, prickling in her hand like rose thorns. His voice was rough when he spoke again. "Why should you consider loving me to be a failure, Isabel? How does it help your order to deny your feelings?"

"How can I love you, Simon," she said slowly, "if I fail in my love for God?"

"Does your God require you to reject me? Wouldn't He be just as pleased with you if you joined a noncelibate order?"

Isabel didn't answer at first. Simon understood, she knew, that there was only one Order for her. And that the Magdalenes, with everything to prove, had decided as a community to make the absolute commitment that so many orders no longer made. How far away her community seemed now! She thought of the Mother House, the sprawling castello, its lights beckoning from the hilltop, the ancient chapel bell calling the Magdalenes to prayer.

And she thought of Simon, in his stifling tent in the Victoria Desert, the two of them utterly alone in the vast empty night. She remembered with an aching clarity the touch of his lips, the smoothness of his body, the cooling fire that blazed between them. For a long moment she couldn't speak at all. Only one small step, a shifting of her feet, and she could feel it again, that ecstatic, forgetful, exhilarating sensation . . .

She stiffened her back, and closed her eyes, lifting her face into the breeze to let it cool her cheeks and eyelids. "It's not God's requirement,

Simon." The words hurt her throat, brought a swell of longing into her chest. "It's my own, and my Order's. It's a discipline we chose." She took a deep breath, and turned to face him. "What good are promises, Simon, if they're not kept? What kind of people are we, any of us, if we can't honor our vows?"

He lifted his free hand to her cheek, and traced it lightly with his fingers. His sensitive fingers were warm on her skin. "I love you, Isabel Burke," he said softly. "Everything about you. Including your damnable honor."

She tried to smile, but her lips trembled. "I love you, too. You know that."

"But you won't be with me."

"No." She stepped back, away from his beguiling touch. It was like a renewal of her vow, a recommitment to her purpose. She felt God's eye looking down on her from the field of stars, gazing up at her from the expanse of Mother Ocean. Her body felt suddenly light, set free from the dragging weight of guilt and regret. "No, my darling Simon. It's not a question of being faithless to you. It's a matter of being true to myself. I won't be with you. But I will love you just the same."

"I won't go back to Anna," he said.

"Then I am terribly sorry for Anna," Isabel said. "Because I know what it is to love you."

25

JIN-LI WOKE EARLY to the clatter of a flyer lifting off from the airfield. The sky was just paling beyond the small window. It was still early, too early for the shift change. Jin-Li lay still for a moment, wondering. Leo had said the flyers were grounded, had been sitting idle in the hangar ever since the order came from Earth Multiplex. Jin-Li pushed back the covers and sat up. Sleep was gone.

A few hardy stars still flickered on the western horizon. The terminal blocked the view of the airfield, but the flyer's passage was audible as it banked above the island and veered to the southwest. Jin-Li frowned. Where was it headed?

In sleep shorts and shirt, Jin-Li went to the door and opened it. Across the hall a woman stood blinking sleepily. "What's on?" she asked. "I heard something."

"Flyer took off," Jin-Li answered.

The woman yawned, and turned back to her bed. "Multiplex must have lifted the restriction."

But Jin-Li didn't think so.

*   *   *

SIMON HAD RETURNED to the infirmary after leaving Isabel at her barracks, and had worked late over the specimens the biologist had supplied. He still had no spider as large as the one Jin-Li had described, but he had several small ones, two snakes, a dozen birds, and an assortment of water and sand creatures. The biologist had helped him set up a sampling program, and he worked until almost dawn, without success. He overslept, missing breakfast in the meal hall, startling awake at a knock on the door of his room. The window was closed, and the light streaming in made the room hot and close. He staggered to his feet, heavy with sleep.

He found Isabel and Adetti waiting for him in the common room. He fell into a chair opposite them, rubbing his eyes, knowing he must look like hell. "Something wrong?" he asked thickly. "Where's Oa?"

"With Jin-Li," Isabel said tersely. "Simon. She's gone. Gretchen is gone. She took a flyer out this morning, and she hasn't come back. Jacob didn't know until he heard the flyer."

"Who's the pilot?"

Adetti said grimly, "She is. Gretchen keeps a house in the San Juan Islands. She flies up there all the time."

"Bloody hell," Simon said. "This is a direct violation of the agreement with the regents."

"I know," Adetti said with evident misery. "I told her not to go. I never thought she'd go alone. She's half out of her mind wanting to get that virus."

"She's all the way out of her mind," Simon snapped. "We don't know the vector yet."

"That's what I told her."

"And she's put all of our efforts at risk. The power park could be decommissioned."

"We can deal with that later." Isabel leaned forward, her whole body a picture of tension. "Simon, I have to go after her. I'm so worried about the children. She might do anything!"

"Good god," Simon muttered.

"She won't be able to talk to them, Simon. They won't understand who she is, what she wants . . . I have to go after her! I have to go now, with Oa. Oa can translate for me."

Her eyes were dark with worry. He wished he could reassure her, but a sense of foreboding dragged at him. "Isabel, I haven't found it yet, found the source of the virus. I worked half the night—"

"Talk to Jacob, Simon. He'll listen to you. He can send us, Oa and me, and Jin-Li, too."

"And me," Adetti said hurriedly. "She may need medical attention."

"If we leave now, right away, maybe we can intervene before there's another tragedy."

"Isabel—until we know—you can't go. It's not safe."

"But we must, Simon, don't you see that? There's no time to waste arguing about it! Please, Simon. Talk to Jacob."

She was right, of course. He wanted to offer more objections, present arguments. His weary brain struggled through them, discarded them one by one.

"It's too dangerous," he said weakly. "Until we identify the vector . . ."

But Isabel was shaking her head, pulling him to his feet. "That doesn't matter now, Simon," she said tightly. "It just doesn't matter. Please hurry. Jacob is waiting in his office."

ISABEL THOUGHT SHE would go mad with tension as Simon and Boyer and Jin-Li discussed details, planned equipment. They were trying to hurry, she knew, but still two hours passed before the flyer lifted off.

Isabel had tried to explain the situation to Oa.

"Gretchen goes to the anchens?" Oa had said.

"Yes. I'm afraid so."

Oa had answered with intensity. "Oa, too. Oa is afraid."

They were on their way to the hangar at last, Jin-Li with a portable for recording, Jacob Boyer as pilot. The flyer was stocked with food and water and an emergency medical kit. Boyer had one of the dreaded shock guns tucked in his belt. Isabel had wasted precious moments trying to talk him out of carrying a weapon, but in this case the normally mild Boyer had been adamant. Isabel herself came almost empty-handed, leaving her tent and all her equipment stored in the terminal. She didn't want to take the time to transfer it to the flyer. And she thought, as the flyer lifted off with a clatter of whirling blades, that all she could really bring to the anchens was herself. If there was anything to be done for them, any way to protect them, it would come from her goodwill and determination. She had nothing else she could offer.

As the flyer banked and turned to the southwest, she held her cross in her fingers, and bent her head. The moment was at hand, the moment for which she had traveled months in twilight sleep, for which she had risked being in Simon's company again, the moment that would lead, she hoped, to the solution of the mystery of Oa. Silently, fervently, she prayed.

SAINT MARY OF MAGDALA,
PATRONESS OF THOSE WHO ASK,
GUIDE ME TO SHINE LIGHT IN THE DARK PLACES . . .

OA CLUNG TO the seat belt and pressed her face to the window to watch the play of light on the face of Mother Ocean. Anxiety twisted in her stomach like a live thing. She felt tears well in her eyes at the intensity of it.

Would they be there, Po and Ette and Bibi and Usa and Likaki? And if they were, what would pale Gretchen do to them? She remembered Gretchen seizing her half-eaten meal, crumbs of it glued to her painted lips . . . the people pushed the anchens away, discarded them, but Gretchen wanted to capture them, to use them. To devour them.

Jacob Boyer wore a shock gun. If Po still lived—what would he do when he saw it?

Oa remembered the din of the first flyer as it landed on the island of the anchens. It had been a peculiar, startling noise. They ran out of the forest, all of them, just in time to see the craft land in the grassy hollow below the kburi. Its side opened like a great mouth stretching wide, and two strange pale men came out. The anchens huddled among the trees, whispering to themselves, wondering, confused.

They stayed there while the men in their curious clothing stood in

*front of the kburi. The men circled it, touching it with their hands,
chattering together in words the anchens couldn't understand. And
then one of them bent to the base, pointing. The other man joined him,
and they squatted before the layered stones.*

*The anchens had chosen each rock with care, had built the kburi to
protect and preserve Raimu-ke. The kburi was meant to save Raimu-ke
until the time she could make the miracle happen, and all the anchens
would become people. Raimu-ke would give them souls.*

*Raimu-ke had been the first of the anchens, ancient and venerable
child, precious to each anchen who came after her. An anchen lost
everything, parent and sibling and home and hope. They had nothing
in the world except each other and Raimu-ke. When the strangers had
begun to disassemble the construction the anchens had labored over,
they were attacking the anchens' only true ancestor.*

*And when Po and Nwa and Oa cried out to them to stop, the men
turned and stared, openmouthed. They didn't care that the anchens
pleaded with them. One of the men had a stone in his hand, a stone he
had stolen from the kburi. Po shouted at him to put it back, and when
he didn't respond, Po brandished his knife, which only minutes before
had been innocently digging pishi from the sand. The man dropped the
stone at his feet, and pulled his ugly black hand weapon to point it at
the anchens.*

*And poor Nwa, little Nah-nah, always determined to show that
though he was small, he was brave, charged at the men, throwing his
knife as he ran.*

*It had been a beautiful day, with small puffy clouds very white
against the blue of the sky, Mother Ocean mild and welcoming as
they splashed in and out of the surf, digging for the pishi exposed
by the receding waves. The day turned dark as Nwa threw his knife, and
the man's weapon made a sickening noise, a sort of hissing crackle.
Nwa fell where he was, even as his knife struck the man. Nwa was
silent, but the strange man screamed, a strange, inhuman noise like
the cry of a seabird. The other man fired his weapon, and Oa, running
after Po, felt a sharp tearing in her thigh. Her leg failed her and she
collapsed, tumbling helplessly through the yellow grass of the steep
meadow.*

Oa struggled to sit up, to see what was happening. Her wound didn't hurt at first, but the horizon swung wildly around her and she struggled to draw a breath. Po turned back to help her, but the man lifted his weapon again and pointed it at Po's naked back.

Oa screamed at Po to run.

He obeyed her. There was nothing else he could do, and they both knew it. The anchens raced down the slope to vanish among the trees, their bare feet flashing up the buttress roots and into the concealing thickness of the canopy. Oa lay where she was, watching her blood stain the grass. She listened for Nwa to make a sound, to moan, to cry out, but she heard nothing. The world faded around her, and she felt herself slipping away.

Po would sorrow over her. The anchens would mourn her, and place her body in the kburi with Raimu-ke. She remembered thinking, with distant sadness, that she had lost her chance to find her soul. She closed her eyes, and prepared to die.

Would she find the anchens alive? A hundred things could have happened to them. They could, like Lili, have become people and left the island. They could have fallen, like Ulan, or drowned as Tursi had. Young men from the people's island could have come in their canoes, leaving hurt and broken bodies behind them. Or perhaps Gretchen would hurt them. Could Gretchen use one of the shock guns? Oa didn't know.

A whimper of fear escaped her.

Isabel's hand found hers, and Oa turned to bury her face against Isabel's shoulder.

JIN-LI, IN THE copilot's seat, squinted against the light reflected from the ocean, peering ahead for the first glimpse of the island. Jin-Li Chung had reason to know how cruel people could be, with or without intention. The streets of Hong Kong had been lonely and dangerous for unprotected children. The thought of Gretchen Boreson in pursuit of the old children of Virimund was a terrifying one.

Jin-Li leaned forward, wishing the flyer could go faster. The flight should take no more than forty-five minutes. But Gretchen Boreson had a long head start.

The noise of the rotors defeated conversation. They quickly left the power park behind, and green ocean stretched all around them. Adetti, in the back, sat with his arms folded, his jaw set. In the middle seats, Isabel held Oa in her arms. Boyer pointed to the horizon, and Jin-Li leaned forward.

A small peak rose in the distance, dark against the blue of the sky. Clouds were rolling in from the east, casting deep emerald shadows here and there on the water. Jin-Li glanced back at Isabel. Their eyes met, and Jin-Li gave a small nod. They would be there soon.

The Magdalene touched her cross. No doubt she was offering prayers. Jin-Li hoped they would help.

SIMON WATCHED THE flyer take off, every instinct rebelling against letting Isabel go without him. But he had work to do.

The biologist had located a nest of forest spiders. She had been unwilling to try to capture them live, but with the help of one of the off-duty hydros she had brought two ugly black corpses to the surgery and prepared them for analysis. They waited there for Simon, their forward eyes dull, their remarkably long legs splayed and limp. Simon had no particular fear of spiders, but these were particularly nasty specimens. He could understand why Oa hated them. The biologist and the hydro made it clear that the Port Forcemen and women agreed with her.

As the flyer clattered off to the southwest, the biologist said mournfully, "I hope we won't have another incident."

"That's why Isabel is going," Simon said. He hoped he sounded reassuring, but he was worried. Unlike Isabel, he had supported Boyer's arming himself. "And Jin-Li is with her. Jin-Li has a lot of experience."

They turned toward the terminal, facing into a breeze from the east that drove a bank of clouds before it. The biologist said hesitantly, "What is it she wants, Dr. Edwards? Administrator Boreson, I mean."

"Her disease is degenerative," Simon said grimly. In the circumstances, he felt no compunction about privileged information. "She wants the virus."

"But—" The biologist lifted her hands in confusion. "What will she do with it?"

"A good question. A damned good question."

26

"VOLCANIC," JIN-LI SAID.

Isabel looked down on the tiny island. It hardly seemed possible that this benign planet had ever had volcanoes spewing lava and ash and hot rock above its peaceful seas.

The peak of the ancient cindercone formed the center of the island. Black waves of lava had frozen in their flow down the northern slope. On the southern side of the island, a boulder-strewn meadow of the long yellow grass fell away to a wide strip of forest. Crescent beaches gleamed white between the dark green of the forest canopy and the emerald of the sea. As they completed their circle, the storm clouds piling across the eastern sky dulled the waters to olive. Gusts of wind buffeted the flyer.

Oa huddled in her seat, tense and silent, her teddy bear clutched to her chest.

On their second circuit, the flyer skimmed the treetops. The upper branches shifted in the wind created by their passage. Boyer banked over the lava field, and flew up and over the ageworn volcanic dome, down to the southern meadow.

"Oh, damn," Adetti groaned. "There it is."

Boyer said grimly, "Doesn't look good."

Jin-Li bent forward to see past Boyer, jaw tightening.

The flyer lay on its side, canted against a sloping boulder. Boyer turned and hovered above the field. The spin of the rotors blew a ragged circle in the grass around the other flyer. One of its struts splayed skyward, the other dug into the ground. Boyer flew a few meters below it, and settled to a landing. Even before the doors opened, they saw that the impact with the boulder had shattered the flyer's windscreen.

Boyer turned off his motor. The blades slowed and stopped, and silence filled their ears.

Oa spoke for the first time since leaving the power park. "Gretchen?" she whispered, not taking her eyes from the crashed flyer.

"We don't know yet," Isabel said through dry lips. She touched her cross.

The door retracted, bringing in a wave of cool air scented with the promise of rain. Jin-Li jumped nimbly out, striding to the crashed flyer, climbing up on the bent strut to look inside.

"Is she there?" Adetti called.

"No." Jin-Li stood on the strut to scan the patchy meadow. A hundred yards downhill, the edge of the forest looked impenetrable, a fortress with tangled walls of green and brown. Above the meadow, a cairn of black stones sprawled at the top of the hill. "I don't see any sign of her."

Adetti and Boyer climbed out, and went to look inside the flyer. "She left her wavephone on the console," Adetti said.

Boyer looked from Adetti to Jin-Li, and then to Isabel. "Don't know what to do," he said glumly. "Or where to look."

Isabel climbed out. The long grass scratched at her bare legs. Insects buzzed, then quieted as a roll of thunder jittered across the sky. Oa, still in her seat, stared fearfully at the crashed flyer, and then over her shoulder at the forest. "Oa, I'll help you out," Isabel began, and then stopped.

A wail sounded above the rising wind, a screeching as of a wounded animal.

"Where's that coming from?" Adetti demanded. No one had an

answer. The wind against the rocks made the sound seem to circle them, to bounce from random directions.

Isabel held out her hand to Oa, and Oa took it, leaping lightly to the ground, her knees bending as easily as the yellow grass in the wind. The cry came again. The fine hairs rose on Isabel's arms.

Oa whirled to look down the hill at the forest as the eerie sound thinned and faded on the whine of the wind. She said something in her own language.

"What was that?" Isabel said. "Oa, I didn't understand."

Oa babbled something, out of which Isabel caught only "anchens" and "Gretchen." She released Isabel's hand, and then she was off, racing down the grassy hill to the treeline.

"Oa!" Isabel cried. "Oa, no! Wait . . ." A chill crept up her side, the side where moments before Oa had stood so close. It seemed the child had left a hole in the very air, a vacuum that could be filled only by her presence. "Oa—wait for us to—Oa, don't—"

There was no answer. The last glimpse Isabel had was of Oa's bare pink soles twinkling up into the forest canopy.

Now she could hear nothing but the strengthening wind of the coming storm. She took a few futile steps, and then halted, standing uncertainly, bereft, in the rocky meadow.

OA HEARD ISABEL'S calls, but the words seemed to mean nothing, as if they were words she had never heard before. As if no time had passed since she and Po and Ette and the others had first heard the whip of flyer blades, saw the men's hands reaching for the stones of the kburi, since they had watched Nah-nah fall under the sibilant crackle of the men's weapons. Oa's feet sought the path to the forest as if she were coming home. Isabel was part of an illusion of soft beds and good food and kind people. Isabel was a dream, too good to be true. The habits of her years on the island of the anchens were real, hard and simple.

She reached the wall of trees, the familiar thicket of roots and broad trunks, the vines that trailed to the forest floor. She might have heard feet pounding behind her, voices shouting, but they were not real. What was real was the canopy above that would lead to the nest deep

in the forest, where the anchens might be hiding from the terrors of the
pale strangers, their flyers that brought fear and destruction and death.

Oa leaped to the nearest buttress root.

The slick surface of the wood was familiar under her long toes. She
shinnied up it to the lowest branch. The thready bark met her knees
with a familiar clutching. Her fingers grasped its layered fibers, her toes
locked into its texture. The scent of the nuchi leaves filled her nostrils,
and the canopy, dark and thick and vine-hung, called her home. All that
was left was to discover if she was the only anchen left to inhabit it.

*Oa remembered a night long, long ago. She had passed no more
than three or perhaps four tatwaj. She had startled awake, in darkness,
finding herself outside the protective walls of shahto. She hadn't known
where she was, or how she had gotten there, or where Mamah or Papi
were. She was too frightened to move, too frightened even to cry. It was
every child's worst nightmare come to pass. She was lost, and alone.*

*The familiar forest filled her with dread. The night threatened un-
seen dangers. Vines rustled and night animals chittered. Oa huddled in
her sleeping dress, her bare knees deep in the root mat that covered the
forest floor, her arms over her head.*

*It was the sting at her ankle that pierced her into action. She
screamed, leaping up, kicking at whatever had bitten her. She saw the
forest spider as it fell, its legs a-tangle, its forward eyes gleaming dully
in the starlight. Its venom flared up her leg, and she screamed again, a
shrill of pure terror.*

*Her mamah and papi reached her in moments. Her mamah swept
her up, clutching her with frantic strength while her papi smashed the
forest spider with a canoe paddle. Other people came out, and children,
wukened by the ruckus, wailed from their sleeping mats. Someone lit a
torch, and exclaimed over the flattened carcass of the forest spider, but
Papi kept beating it until it was indistinguishable from the moldering
leaves and fungi of the forest floor.*

*Mamah and Papi carried Oa safely into shahto, and snuggled her
between them in their own bed, stroking her hair and her back until her
tears stopped and the burning of the spider bite eased enough for her to
sleep. She had walked in her sleep, they said, pulled aside the wall mats
and wandered out into the forest. After that her papi made a great*

show of tying the mats tightly at night. And an elder of the people came to her in the morning with a poultice for her spider bite, and all the uncles and aunts and cousins made a great fuss over her.

Only later, when she was an anchen, did she remember the terrors of that night. It was not the forest spider that made it horrible, though that was bad enough. The insurmountable fear, the one every anchen faced as the elders left them standing on the beach of the island of the anchens, was the fear of being alone.

The anchens clung to each other for comfort, Oa and the others, curling together in their nest to sleep in a tangle of arms and legs, even their breath mingling in the closeness of their refuge. It was all they had for comfort in the wide, fearsome darkness. Oa didn't think she could bear it if she were the only one left.

Oa worked her way through the canopy, finding thick branches to support her weight. A long, angry cry sliced the thick air of the forest. She knew who made that sound, who raged now through the trees, searching. It was not a sound she had heard before, but she recognized the call of a predator. A hunter. And it—she—had given up on Oa, and was hunting for the others.

A vine gave under Oa's hand, and she caught herself by hooking one foot around a nuchi branch. A trec lizard slid along a vine near her face, its legs flashing as it disappeared among the leaves. Her breath came short, and perspiration dripped down her ribs. If Gretchen found the anchens, terrible things could happen. They would not know, Po and Ette and Bibi and the others, what Gretchen was. And if Gretchen had one of the weapons—would she kill one of the anchens for its flesh? Or carry it back to the infirmary, put it under the spider machine to be taken apart, as Doctor had tried to take Oa apart? They hadn't found what they wanted in Oa, but perhaps, in one of the others . . .

She gasped for breath, and hurried faster. Her feet slipped on the wood, her soles gone soft from wearing shoes. The bark abraded the skin of her hands, the insides of her knees, where her old calluses had vanished in the soft baths and sweet creams of Isabel's care.

She called silently to Raimu-ke to protect them, Bibi and Ette and Po and all of them. And for herself she prayed, Let them be there, please, Raimu-ke. Let them still be there.

*   *   *

THE POWER PARK on its deforested island had given little indication of the true nature of Virimund's forest. Here on the island of the anchens, the great trees stood wide apart, the crowded root buttresses flaring like closely set pillars to create a dense landscape. The broad leaves, almost black in the shadows, narrowed to needle tips. The twisting stems of vines looped low to the forest floor, and the root mat was deep, soft with the detritus of decaying plants, alive with tiny insects. The birds had fallen silent under the threat of the thunderstorm. Some slender creature slithered up a tree trunk so fast Jin-Li almost missed it. In other circumstances, Jin-Li would have found all of this fascinating, but Isabel's frantic worry and Adetti's and Boyer's grim faces made the trek tense.

Isabel had dashed after Oa, but by the time she reached the forest edge, the girl had vanished into the canopy. For long minutes, Isabel called after her. She received no answer. Jin-Li had seen the wild look in Oa's eyes, fear and fury together. Oa would not be called back.

Isabel turned to Jin-Li, pale-lipped and desperate. "Oh, lord," she said in a thin voice. She held Oa's shoes in her shaking hands. "Jin-Li—where did she go?"

Adetti and Boyer came panting up behind Jin-Li just as the banshee call sounded again, this time clearly coming from the forest. "That's Gretchen," Adetti said to Jin-Li.

"I know."

"She's gone mad," Isabel said faintly. "We have to do something."

Adetti reached into his pocket. A shock gun appeared in his hand, black and ugly.

"Put that away!" Isabel cried. "What are you thinking?"

"Oa could hurt Gretchen!" Adetti's face was tight with anger. "You can't control her, that's obvious."

"She's just a child . . ."

"Rot! And what about the others? We don't even know what's out there."

Boyer said, "Paolo, this is what caused the first tragedy. I'm not having another. Give it to me."

The two men faced each other in the fading light. Another roll of thunder, deeper and more insistent this time, rattled through the clouds, and a patter of rain began. Boyer put out his hand, and Jin-Li was impressed by the look of authority on his long face. "I'll protect her if necessary," he said in a hard voice. "Hand it over."

Adetti gave up the shock gun. He whirled and glared at Isabel as if it were somehow her fault. "You can't blame Gretchen," he said. "She's ill."

Isabel's hand was at her throat. "I know, Paolo. I know she is." She turned to Boyer, straightening her slender shoulders. A few raindrops filtered through the canopy to gleam on her bare head. "Jacob, what can we do?"

"We have to start by finding Gretchen," Adetti said.

"Shall we split up?" Isabel asked.

"I don't think so," Boyer said. "Better we're together."

They all turned in the direction they had last heard the cries. Jin-Li spotted a clear space, marked by a lichen-covered stone. A step closer showed a path, rutted and narrow, carving through the root mat. "Isn't she likely to have followed this?"

WHEN ISABEL FIRST put her feet on the path, she felt a shiver of recognition. The anchens had broken this trail. How many years ago? And did they still walk its narrow circuit, dodging these vines that hung everywhere, forging this thicket of roots? These furrows would just fit long-toed bare feet like Oa's. Her own feet, sandaled and inexperienced, moved awkwardly in the ruts. The path wound around copses of trunks, finding the easiest way, the most open space. The canopy hung overhead, mysterious, dense, daunting. And Oa was somewhere up there, had run from her as if their time together had never been. The word "reverted" came to Isabel's mind, but she thrust it away. She would not think it, would not believe it.

The wailing cry came again, resounding through the shadowed jungle. Isabel stumbled. It was like trying to run in a nightmare, her feet heavy, her way blocked at every turn.

"We're getting closer," Adetti said.

"What's happened to her?" Boyer asked, as they negotiated a cramped twist of the path. "She sounds crazy!"

"She's desperate," Adetti said.

"It's more than that, Paolo," Isabel said. She stopped for a moment to shake leaf and moss fragments from one sandal. Everyone else stopped, too, and a heavy silence settled around them, the forest creatures disturbed by their passage. Occasional raindrops found their way through the nuchi leaves to patter against the forest floor. Isabel spoke quietly. "It's Gretchen's nature to go after what she wants. It's not part of her character to submit to defeat—and in her mind, the enemy is death. Or worse, perhaps, at least to her, disability."

"We'd better find her," Adetti said, and pushed past Isabel to lead the way down the path.

Isabel followed. She tipped her head back, peering into the darkness of the canopy, yearning for a glimpse of Oa's bare feet, her legs flashing above.

Their way grew steep in places. They had to climb past horizontal roots and slide down banks where the surface of the ground was slippery and loose. Thunder shivered above them. Isabel began to feel chilly in her shorts and shirt.

They stopped at a branching of the path. Adetti turned one way, and then another, cursing under his breath. Isabel held Oa's shoes against her breast, much as Oa might have held her teddy bear. Briefly, foolishly, Isabel wondered where the toy was. She couldn't remember, and somehow that made her feel guilty. She stared down the branching path, left and then right, both ways leading sharply downhill. Surely, if you followed either branch, it led ultimately to the ocean, to those pastel beaches. But which way led to Oa?

And then, deep in the tangle of the forest, she caught sight of a pale figure, fronds of disordered silver hair, the face a white, distorted oval. It was Gretchen Boreson, struggling on her knees through the thicket of buttress roots and matted vines, trying to reach the path. In the filtered light she seemed unreal, a ghost. When she caught sight of the searchers, she wailed in a thin, mewling voice, "They're not here! They're not here!"

Adetti cried, "Gretchen!" in a tone of pure horror. Isabel leaped forward to help pull the distraught woman from the thicket. Her clothes tore on some woody prominence as she fell again to her knees on the path.

Gretchen Boreson's face was as wild as her hair. She lurched to her feet. Her sharp-nailed hands grasped at Isabel's shoulders, digging through the thin fabric of her shirt and into her skin. "Not here," she croaked. "She's the only one! Where is she? She's the only one!"

27

BORESON'S EYES ROLLED, and her hands fell nervelessly from Isabel's shoulders. Isabel couldn't catch her before she collapsed on the forest floor. Adetti leaped forward, and bent to lift her face from the dirt. He turned her gently, supporting her neck with one hand, brushing some sort of crawling insect from her hair. Boyer strode forward with a dry splash of dead leaves and twigs to kneel on her other side.

Isabel shuddered, and passed her hand over her scalp. It prickled with goose bumps.

Bits of moss clung to Boreson's white hair, and her face and hands jerked spasmodically. Adetti pulled an ampoule out of his pocket. He pulled back Boreson's sleeve to press the drug to the inside of her elbow. Her eyelids fluttered, showing nothing but whites.

"Will she be all right?" Jin-Li asked.

"In a minute," Adetti said shortly.

Boyer straightened, leaving Boreson in Adetti's hands. "So where did the girl go?" He peered into the forest. Some small creature buzzed around his face, and he batted at it.

"She's looking for the others," Isabel said. "Just like Gretchen." Her legs trembled suddenly, and she leaned against a root buttress.

Jin-Li's steady hand touched her shoulder. "Isabel. She lived in this forest for a century. She'll be all right."

Isabel drew a slow breath. "I'm trying to remember that." At her feet, Gretchen Boreson stirred, and her eyes opened, the pupils darting from side to side. Isabel forced herself to stand upright. "Come, Paolo. Let's get Gretchen to the flyer. Did you give her a sedative?"

"Didn't expect to need one," he said. His voice was edgy, but Isabel saw that his hands were gentle, lifting Boreson to her feet, supporting her slight weight with his arm.

"There's a medical kit on board," Boyer said. "Come on, let's all get back there. It's going to be dark soon."

"I've got to get Gretchen back to the power park," Adetti said. "She needs the medicator."

Isabel stiffened. "I'm not leaving the island without Oa."

Boyer squinted at her. "Look, Mother Burke . . ."

Adetti snapped, "The girl can take of herself. You know that."

Isabel whirled to face him, her anxiety swelling into anger. She could be angry at Paolo Adetti, and even at Gretchen Boreson, ill as she was. She could blame all of it on them, vent her fury on them, and not feel guilty about anything.

She folded her arms, gripping her elbows with her fingers. Anger would do no good. She could blame them for driving Oa back to the forest. But she had to credit them with bringing Oa into her care.

"Isabel." It was Jin-Li. Again Isabel felt that muscular, steady hand on her shoulder.

Isabel closed her eyes, and let the strength flow from Jin-Li's hand into her own body. "Yes," she murmured.

"Mr. Boyer and Dr. Adetti can take Gretchen to the power park. I'll stay with you. We can use the crashed flyer for shelter. Oa knows where it is. We'll wait for her together."

Isabel opened her eyes, and looked into Jin-Li's long dark ones. "Thank you, my friend," she whispered. She offered a silent prayer of gratitude as she turned away, and led the little group back up the tortured forest path.

*   *   *

THE NUCHI BRANCHES beneath her bare toes were like old friends to Oa. She listened as she climbed, heard Isabel calling her name, heard the low tones of Jacob Boyer, of Doctor, the neutral sound of Jin-Li's voice. She heard nothing else, but that didn't matter. If the anchens were there, they would make no sound. Hiding. If they weren't there, she would climb as far as she dared, until the darkness lightened, and the top branches were too thin to hold her, and she would swing from branch to branch, looking.

They should have hidden in the nest that day, she knew that now. When they heard the clatter of the strange flying thing, they should have climbed up into their lair and stayed there, waiting until the strange men went away.

But if they had? Would the men have taken away Raimu-ke? Nah-nah would not have died. But Oa would not have met Isabel.

There was an old song about the two sides of the wind, which brought evil and good together. Oa thought if she could have another evening on the northern point with the anchens, she could remember all the words . . . the words would come back to her, and then she might understand.

She swung through the canopy, knowing her destination, growing warm with exertion. Her muscles burned. She had not climbed anything in a long time.

She worked her way inward to the crisscross of branches that formed the anchens' nest. It was a rough bowl shaped by roots and low branches and slanting trunks. They had reinforced it over the years, carrying armloads of moss, grass, twigs, slabs of bark they softened in the surf and beat as smooth as they could. It was littered with the few things the anchens possessed—rags, battered sleeping mats, the baskets they wove, little piles of cutting stones, and their two precious digging knives, black now with rust.

She was almost there. She paused, needing to know, but afraid. She thought of turning back, climbing back down to let Isabel and Jin-Li take this burden from her. They would do it, she knew. They would search for the anchens with their scanners, and deal with Doctor and

Gretchen. They would allow Oa to be a child. Even now, they believed she was one.

But she was not a child. She was an anchen. Raimu-ke lay above her on the hill, and if Oa were the only anchen left to care for the kburi, she must know.

She listened. Gretchen's wails had faded. Even Isabel's calls had died away. The thunder had passed to the west, and raindrops pattered against the canopy, caught by leaves and vines before they could reach the forest floor.

She dropped now, climbing down the old familiar ladder of branches. Wood creaked beneath her weight. The nest lay only a little farther, beyond the veil of vines.

She flared her nostrils, searching for that old scent of salt water on skin, of hair full of leaves and moss, of familiar bodies. And for the lingering essence of long, long memory.

She shimmied forward across the branch, her Earth-material shorts catching on the bark, her hands sticky with resin. She pulled at the vines with her fingers, separating them, peering between their twisted cords.

ISABEL PACED BEFORE the flyer, the yellow grass catching at her knees, her hands clenching and unclenching, her brow creased with anxiety. "Where could she have gone, Jin-Li?" she asked for the tenth time. "Why doesn't she come back?"

Jin-Li said, again, "She'll be back. We'll wait. She'll come back."

And when Isabel protested again, Jin-Li repeated, "Try not to worry."

There was nothing more to say. Neither of them needed platitudes.

An hour went by, and another. They watched the storm pass, the sky clearing from east to west as the light faded. Isabel, exhausted with tension, sat on the bent strut, her head in her hands. Jin-Li stood scanning the gentle slope of the hill. Nothing moved. The brief rain had charged the air with the scent of ozone. The volcanic rocks that dotted the meadow shone in the evening's glow, freshly washed by the rain. Stars began to glimmer above their heads, and the song of evening birds filled the air.

"It's getting dark," Isabel said. "She won't be able to find her way back."

"She's spent many nights in the woods. She's at home here. We're not."

"But the—what if they're not here? What if she's alone out there—all night?"

"That's what Oa needs to find out." Jin-Li hesitated, questioning the appropriateness of giving advice to Isabel Burke. But there was no one else to do it. "Sometimes," Jin-Li finished softly, "you have to let them do it on their own."

"I know," Isabel said sadly. "I know. But nothing has ever seemed so hard."

28

JIN-LI HELPED ISABEL climb up into the damaged flyer. They slid on its slick floor, catching themselves on the tilted seats. Jin-Li touched the button for the door, and it creaked forward, not closing completely, but almost. "Enough to keep the bugs out," Jin-Li said.

With one hand on the seats for support, Jin-Li worked back to the cooler and pulled out two ration packets and a foil bag of water. "Here, Isabel. Let's eat, and then try to sleep. There's nothing we can do until morning, and Simon will come back with Boyer then."

"I can't sleep," Isabel said. "Not with Oa out there, somewhere. She'll think we've abandoned her."

Jin-Li struggled back across the slanted floor, and handed her a ration packet. "Eat, at least. You may feel a little better."

Isabel slit the opening on the ration pack, and pulled out a wedge of something that looked like dried cheese. She nibbled at it obediently, but she had no appetite. She glanced up at Jin-Li. "You're not very hungry either," she said.

Jin-Li sighed. "I remember what it is to be alone in a jungle. Mine was an urban jungle, but still . . ."

Isabel put down the wedge of cheese. "I'm so sorry," she said. "I've been thinking only of Oa. And of myself. It was Hong Kong, wasn't it?"

"It was. But I was never as alone as Oa."

Isabel pushed away the ration packet. "Maybe she's not alone, Jin-Li. Maybe they're still here. Maybe she found them."

"I hope so."

"I do, too. But if they are here, why didn't they show themselves?"

"After what happened the last time? I doubt they've forgotten so soon."

"If they're like Oa, they never forget anything." Isabel took her cross in her hands and held it, seeking comfort from the familiar texture of its carved wood. Please, dear God, she prayed silently. Watch over my Oa. Send her back to me, safe and sound.

She sighed, and slipped into the familiar comfort of litany:

REGARD NOT OUR SINS, BUT THE FAITH OF YOUR CHURCH . . .

THE STARS ABOVE the island of the anchens sparkled coolly, diamonds scattered on a shroud of black velvet. Isabel stared at them through the window of the flyer until her eyes burned. She didn't believe she could sleep, but it seemed, in the end, she dozed. She startled awake to find that the sky had paled, and the stars were beginning to dim.

She had heard something. There was a soft sound outside the flyer, something that wasn't the ever-present murmur of the ocean, or the soughing of the breeze through the fringes of the forest canopy. She straightened, making no sound herself, and strained to listen.

For a long moment, she thought she was imagining it. It was a murmur, like the murmur of Mother Ocean. It was the sound of soft voices, the whisper of bare feet through dry grass. Pushing on the back of the seat in which she had uncomfortably reclined, she managed to stand. Beside her, Jin-Li woke, and sat upright, dark eyes gleaming. Isabel, gripping the seat backs, moved to the partly open door.

The fading starlight made the scene outside the flyer into one of half-seen images, ephemera that drifted in the morning twilight, seeming as much imagination, as much the magic of a wish fulfilled, as it did reality. Midnight-dark faces, eyes flashing white in the gloom, hesitant movements, slender arms and legs and full lips, a cluster of old children sidling cautiously toward her. Isabel's heart pounded in her ears and her lips parted. Behind her, she heard Jin-Li take a sharp breath.

"Isabel." The sweet, familiar voice was like air to someone who was suffocating. "Isabel. Oa finds the anchens."

OA REACHED FOR Isabel's hand, to help her down from the broken door of the flyer. The scent of fear was sharp in the air, coming from the anchens, but also surrounding Isabel.

"Oa! Are you all right? I was so worried!"

"Oa is sorry," she said. "The anchens are afraid, Isabel."

"Yes, of course, sweetheart." Isabel put an arm around Oa's shoulder, pressed her cheek to Oa's hair. "They must be frightened. I'm just so glad to see you safe."

"Gretchen?"

"Gretchen has gone back to the power park, Oa. She's very ill."

Oa gave a sigh of relief. She regretted causing Isabel concern, but it had taken most of the night to tell her story. The anchens could not comprehend what had happened to her. They had believed for a long time that Oa was dead, and when she put her head through the curtain of vines that shielded the nest, they thought Raimu-ke had sent them a ghost.

There were no words, in the Sikassa language, to explain huge not-canoes that flew through space, towering shahto that loomed over the cold gray waters of another world, the icy marvel that was ice cream, the terrors of a spider machine. And Isabel—Oa wanted so much for the anchens to understand Isabel.

The anchens hung back now, staring openmouthed at Isabel. When Jin-Li jumped down to the ground, they turned as one to face this new threat, pale brown skin, long heavy-lidded eyes, the brush of black and silver hair. As the sky brightened, the anchens watched the newcomers. Their bare feet shifted, their hands touched each other, and Oa knew that at the slightest disturbance they were ready to flee. Or to fight. Po's knife hung at his braided-vine belt, and his face was tight with suspicion.

Po asked Oa if the flyer was the transport, and she tried to explain to him how much larger a space-going vessel was. She reminded him of the stories of the ancestors, but he shook his head in confusion.

Bibi asked why Isabel had no hair. Oa tried to explain, pointing to the Magdalene cross on Isabel's breast. Isabel, sitting on the bent strut of the flyer, watched and listened. She kept her empty hands open on her knees, palms turned up. Jin-Li leaned against the hull of the flyer, arms folded, submitting to the searching gazes of the anchens.

When a little silence fell, Isabel asked quietly, "Oa, are they all here? All safe?"

"No, Isabel," Oa said sadly. "Kikya is not safe."

"I'm so sorry. What happened?"

"Kikya does not eat. Kikya stops—stopped—eating."

Isabel's eyes darkened, and she touched her cross.

"Kikya is in kburi. With Raimu-ke." Oa pointed up the hill. The others, Po and Ette and Bibi and Toki and Malo, stiffened. Oa hastened to repeat to them, waving her hands for emphasis, that Isabel would never hurt Raimu-ke, that she would never hurt anyone or anything. She had said it all before, but she said it again, forcefully, as persuasively as she could.

She had not slept at all. None of the anchens had. When at last they believed she was really Oa, really alive, they had touched her, had sniffed her, and then they had all clung together, laughing and crying at once. But it was so hard to make them understand where she had been, what she had learned. Even now she was not sure they understood, and she had found herself lapsing into English over and over again, winning blank and suspicious looks. They had little news to tell her. There had been no smoke from the three islands, no new anchens, in all the time she had been gone. She explained that the scanners could not find the people, and together, they tried to think how long it had been since there had been a white pillar of smoke marking the tatwaj. The tatwaj had been their only marker, the only way they could measure the passing of years.

It was Ette who told the story of Kikya's death. Kikya, the oldest surviving anchen, had simply stopped wishing to live. It was Kikya who had claimed he remembered Raimu-ke, and the anchens allowed Kikya to tell all the Raimu-ke stories. And now he lay with Raimu-ke in the kburi. Kikya would tell no more stories, and that saddened Oa.

But finally, she could show Isabel the kburi. Now Isabel could know Raimu-ke.

THE MORNING LIGHT was brilliant, gilding everything, grass, treetops, green water, the polished black stones of the kburi. It imbued the scene, at the top of the island's gentle cone, with a sense of theatrical presentation that was intensified by the silence of the anchens. Their bare feet rustled the grass as they climbed the hill. Once or twice they murmured to each other in treble voices.

Isabel gazed at them in wonder. Like Oa, they appeared to be children. Their dark, smooth faces wore no sign of age, but many smudges of dirt. Some were bruised. One or two were taller than Oa, appearing to be twelve, perhaps thirteen years old. Several were smaller. One had a misshapen arm, as if it had been broken and never set. Another's cheek was marked with a ridged scar, a jagged pale line against the dark skin. All were bone-thin, hollow-eyed, their curling black hair hanging about their shoulders. They wore ragged bits of clothing, little more than loincloths, all of some rude material Isabel suspected was pounded bark. The girls' chests were flat. The boys had no hair on their bodies, only the slender, slightly swaybacked physique of prepubescent children. She counted fourteen of them, besides Oa.

The kburi was a mound of rocks, a sort of cairn of volcanic stones. Each had been placed with care, the largest at the bottom, diminishing in size toward the top, about five feet from the ground. It sprawled to the sides, a hillock of ancient stones, worn in places as if stroked by a thousand reverent touches. She thought of the statue of the Virgin in the cathedral in Seattle, its gilded toes worn completely away by the hands of the faithful. And she saw the faces of the anchens around her, their dark eyes solemn, their lips moving in some litany as they approached the kburi. They stretched out their hands in a gesture that was clearly ritual, but their eyes shifted to Isabel and to Jin-Li even as they circled the little monument.

Oa put one hand out in the ritual gesture and touched the stones. "Isabel," she said softly. "This is the kburi of Raimu-ke."

The anchens stroked the piled stones, murmuring. One of them laid a small, closed shell and a few morsels of some white fruit into a hollow depression in the center of the kburi. It was, Isabel understood, an offering. A votive sacrifice.

Jin-Li stood outside the circle, watching. Isabel noticed with gratitude that Jin-Li had not produced a wavephone, or in any way interfered with the moment.

And it was a moment, Isabel thought. It was a moment of revelation, like the one her patroness had experienced so long ago. Mary of Magdala had raised her eyes from the ground to see that He who was dead had risen from the tomb, that hope was restored. Isabel Burke looked upon the kburi of Raimu-ke, and understood, in a way that was soul-deep and inexplicable, that it represented hope to the anchens. Their only hope.

Isabel knelt before the kburi. Oa's hand slipped into hers. Isabel closed her eyes, and let sensation flood her, not only through Oa's fingers, but from this place that was sanctified by the prayers of the anchens. She felt love, and longing, and respect, and trust. She felt a powerful and desperate hope. And she felt, in a blinding rush like the moment she had first heard the call, faith.

Time slipped away from her. She knelt on rocky ground before a crude tomb erected by a community of impossibly old children, and her heart swelled with gratitude. She felt the hand of God in hers, touching her through Oa's slender fingers. She didn't realize until she opened her eyes that tears were streaming down her face. The anchens gazed at her with wide eyes. Only Oa seemed to understand, to share the emotion that filled her whole being. Oa leaned close, touched her shoulder with her cheek, smiled with tremulous lips.

When Isabel stood up at last, she found Jin-Li close behind her. "What is it, Isabel?" Jin-Li asked quietly. "What is the kburi?"

Without hesitation, Isabel answered. "It's a reliquary."

29

"HOW DID YOU know?" Jin-Li asked.

"It was a hunch." Isabel's smile was peaceful. Her eyes glowed crystal-bright in the morning light. "Or a leap of faith."

The anchens had led them down from the kburi by a winding path that followed the jagged rim of the lava field, skirted the woods, and ran along a low sandy ridge above the beach. Oa walked with Isabel, chattering occasionally with one of the anchens who looked back at her. She had named them for Isabel and Jin-Li, Po and Ette and Bibi and Likaki and Usa and others Jin-Li couldn't remember. It was a much easier walk than the tortured one they had taken through the forest the night before. Jin-Li saw how deeply rutted the way was, and marveled at how many feet, for how long, had worn away the ground. The beauty of the morning was stunning, the sky clear and blue, the air sparkling, the moving water glistening as if strewn with emeralds. Sea birds cried their morning calls, dipping and soaring overhead.

They sat now on the southern shore of the island, in the shade of a nuchi tree that tilted to the west, slanted by decades of eastern winds, its wide, horizontal roots making perfect benches. Oa sat with them, watching her old companions dig in the sand with their rusted knives. They brought out shellfish—pishi, Oa said—and dropped them into woven baskets.

Jin-Li flicked on her portable, and gazed at the screen again. The stereotaxic image was fuzzy, but the outline was clear. At the base of the kburi, in a sepulcher of stone, was a small, perfect skeleton. Raimu-ke.

"But why would they pray to her?" Jin-Li asked. "The offerings . . . the ceremony?"

"The Sikassa practiced ancestor worship. Raimu-ke was the first anchen—the ancestor to the anchens." Isabel lifted her face into the morning sunshine. "Most religions, Jin-Li, have a central, sacrificial figure. Raimu-ke is that for the anchens."

Oa, crouching beside them with her arms around her knees, stared out at the anchens on the beach. She said quietly, "Anchens are asking Raimu-ke to become persons. To become like the people."

"But, Oa," Jin-Li said. "How is an anchen different from a person?"

Isabel turned, a look of surprise on her face. Jin-Li wondered if the question was somehow offensive. But before the words could be retracted, Oa responded, still gazing out over the peaceful scene on the beach.

"Persons," she said gravely, slowly, "have soul. Because persons—people—" Her hand grasped air as she searched for words. "Because babies are coming to the people. In the birth time. But babies are not coming to anchens."

Isabel put a hand to her forehead as if something had struck her there. "Oh, my lord," she breathed. "Of course—oh, Jin-Li! *You* asked the right question. You've asked the question I should have asked." She ran the hand over her bare scalp, and her eyes darkened to the color of stone. "I was stupid—too close, I suppose . . . emotionally involved. Not very scientific of me."

Jin-Li closed the portable. "Dumb luck, Isabel. I'm not an anthropologist."

"I wonder how long it would have taken me?" Isabel mused. "It's so obvious. There were only three hundred of them, of the original colonists."

"You're thinking of the gene pool."

"Yes, of course. And I should have thought of it before."

Oa said, "Co-lo-niss?"

Isabel repeated the word. "Colonists. Your ancestors."

"An-ces-tors."

"Ancestors. Your mamah and your papi, and their mamah and papi, on back to the beginning."

"Back to Raimu-ke?"

Isabel smiled. "Yes, sweetheart. Back to Raimu-ke." And to Jin-Li, "The gene pool was too small. They needed babies, and lots of them, for the colony to survive."

Jin-Li looked out at the anchens working on the beach. "Those poor creatures. Never reaching puberty, never becoming fertile."

Isabel took Oa's hand. "Yes. The anchens were . . ." She hesitated, and when she finished her thought, her voice was full of pain. "The anchens were useless to the Sikassa."

Oa leaned her cheek against Isabel's knee. "Anchens are not people," she said sadly. "Now you are understanding."

"I understand a little better, Oa. Someday you will, too. Anchens are people to me, and to Jin-Li, and to Doctor Simon. Precious people."

IT WAS NOT going to be easy, Isabel thought. The old children were distrustful. Po was especially vigilant, watching Isabel's and Jin-Li's every move. He was the tallest and seemed to be a sort of leader. Oa chattered with him, her eyes flashing, and then she turned to Isabel to translate. "Po sees the flyers. He is thinking more are coming. More . . ." She squinted and tipped her head to one side, searching for words. "More of the bad men."

"Oa, they weren't bad men," Isabel said. "Only frightened men. They didn't know you anchens were here, and they didn't understand about the kburi."

Oa chattered more, and Po answered her, avoiding Isabel's eyes, staring at his long-toed bare feet. He, and all the anchens, were bone-thin, their ribs showing, their cheekbones sharp. Even the aboriginal children in the Victoria Desert had not been so thin. But if they didn't trust her . . . they certainly wouldn't trust a flood of people, Gretchen Boreson, Paolo Adetti, Jacob Boyer. Simon.

"Oa," Isabel said. "Doctor Simon wants to come to the island. Will that frighten Po, and the others? One flyer, with a pilot, and only Doctor Simon."

"Oa likes Doctor Simon."

"I know, sweetheart. Can you explain to Po?"

Oa nodded and turned away, pulling Po's arm to make him follow her. She led him down to the water's edge, where the anchens were digging with their long black knives. Isabel knew that one of those knives had caused the death of a Port Forceman. She saw how deft the anchens were with them, and she shuddered at what might have happened to Gretchen.

A child would thrust a knife beneath the surface of the sand, and then leap back while two or three others, waiting on their knees, scrabbled through the sand with their fingers. They came up with something small in their hands that they threw into a waiting basket, then poised themselves for another thrust of the knife. When Po and Oa reached them, they stood up, gathering in an uneven circle to listen to Oa.

Isabel watched her talking to them, her little hands flashing in the air. She looked very different from Bibi and Ette and the others. She had grown plumper, her cheeks full, her skin glossy. Though her shirt and shorts were torn and dirty from her trek through the forest, her hair shone in the clear light. Good food, rest, and nurture, Isabel thought. These were the gifts she had to offer the other old children, if they would accept them.

The rising midday heat seemed to mean nothing to the anchens, but Isabel was glad to be in the shade. Po and Oa left the circle and trudged back up the hot sand. The rest of them closed the lid to their basket, and two of them carried it between them, following Po. They squatted on the sand before Isabel and Jin-Li, Po and Oa in the forefront.

"Isabel, anchens are liking Doctor Simon," Oa said. "But anchens are not liking—" She made a shape with her finger and thumb.

"Shock gun," Isabel supplied. "You want Doctor Simon to come without weapons."

Oa nodded vigorously. "Wea-pons. Yes, Isabel. Doctor Simon is coming, only Doctor Simon. Not weapons are coming."

Jin-Li said, "I'll call Doctor Simon on the wavephone. I'll tell him."

Oa turned to chatter to the anchens. Isabel watched their faces, trying to remember the names she had learned. The small, quick one was Bibi. Ette was a girl with one blind eye, the pupil gray and blank. Simon might be able to repair it, if the child would allow him to treat her. Usa had use of only one hand. Likaki hung slightly back from the others, shy and quiet. All were marked with the rows and rows of tattoos.

Jin-Li tucked the wavephone away. "Isabel. Simon found the vector."

Isabel caught her breath. "He did? Are you certain?"

"Not positive. He sounded guarded. I'd guess Adetti was there, so he didn't want to say too much. He said he could be here in a couple of hours. I don't think he'd leave the work half-done."

"No. He's very disciplined, our Simon."

Isabel turned thoughtfully back to the anchens. The girl called Ette was kneeling beside a flat rock. She laid an ovoid, brown-shelled fruit on the rock and struck it with a triangular stone. Another of the anchens, a naked boy whose name Isabel had missed, squatted beside Ette with another of the fruit shells in his hand, apparently dried and hollowed. When a grayish juice spilled out of the fractured shell, he caught it deftly in the hollow one, and passed it to the others. They drank, one by one, handing it from one to the other. In the end, it came to Oa, and she took a sip, and turned with the shell in her hands.

"Isabel. This is nuchi, very good. You are drinking?"

Isabel accepted the shell. Jin-Li murmured, "This should be okay. They use it in the meal hall."

The juice of the nuchi had a mildly sweet taste, rather like watered milk. It dried Isabel's tongue but was not hard to swallow. She smiled at Oa. "It's good."

"Yes," Oa said. "Is very good."

Jin-Li, too, drank, and passed the shell back to Oa with a nod of approval. Oa's white smile flashed as she pointed to the lidded basket. "Now you are having pishi!"

Jin-Li laughed aloud. "Who knows what this will to do us?"

"Oh, well. I have to try it."

Ette was dicing the flesh of the nuchi with the triangular stone, and handing out bits of the white fruit to the anchens. Bibi lifted the lid of the woven basket, and Po bent to spill a dozen or so reddish shells out onto the sand. The anchens each took one, using stones to pry them open. With their thumbs and forefingers, they scooped out the meat inside, and dropped it into their mouths. They chewed unself-consciously, mouths open, eyes on Isabel and Jin-Li.

Po, all arms and legs and long, thin neck, opened a shell with one deft slice and held it out on his palm, offering it to Isabel.

She glanced at Oa, and Oa grinned. "Is good, Isabel. Is pishi." She took one for herself, popped open the shell, and slid the inner flesh into her mouth. She chewed, speaking around the mouthful, patting her stomach through her shorts. "Oa likes it."

Isabel smiled at Po, and accepted the offering. As Oa had, she slid her finger under the morsel inside the shell, and it popped out, quivering pinkly on her palm. Not giving herself time to reconsider, she put it in her mouth and bit down.

The texture, she thought, would take some getting used to. But the flavor was salty and rich, almost buttery. She chewed, and swallowed, and then smiled at Po. "Thank you, Po," she said. "I like it."

Oa chattered a translation. Po held out another pishi to Jin-Li. Jin-Li ate without hesitation, nodding appreciation. "Oysters," she said to Isabel.

"Sort of, I guess." They both ate a little of the nuchi fruit as well, which had a bland, starchy taste. The anchens watched every movement. When one of them spoke, they fell silent, listening, and they gazed openmouthed at Oa when she spoke English.

Isabel realized after a time that the anchens were inching closer to them, almost imperceptibly. They still squatted or knelt in the sand, but they fidgeted, moving their feet or their knees, and soon she found herself in a little knot of them, their nostrils flaring, their eyes sliding back and forth between herself and Jin-Li. Isabel smiled around at them, and Jin-Li squatted beside her.

It was the sparrowlike Bibi, moving with darting, precise motions, who first touched Isabel. She put out a short-fingered hand, the nails chewed to stubs, and stroked Isabel's bare calf. Isabel held very still, hardly breathing. Another of the anchens, Likaki, touched her arm. Po laid a hand on Jin-Li's short hair. All the anchens were sniffing, heads turning this way and that like puppies, as if the scent of the two strangers was the most important element in understanding them. They crowded closer, tumbling gently over each other, stepping on each other's bare feet, reaching to feel the strangers' skins with their fingers, snuffling whatever scent it was that rose from them to inform the anchens of what they were.

The anchens had their own scent as well. Oa, soap-washed and dressed in synthetic fabric, no long smelled that way. But Isabel could smell the bodies of the anchens, the scent of salt water on their skin, the acrid tang of their scraps of clothing. Po stroked Isabel's bare scalp with his palm, and said something to Oa. Isabel caught the words "priest" and "Mary Magdalene" in her answer.

"Do you have a word for 'priest,' Oa?"

"No. Po is not understanding."

"Ah. It will take time, I think."

"Yes. Oa thinks, too."

A few minutes later, the anchens stirred, and rose as one, like a school of fish, or a flock of wide-eyed birds. Isabel knew she would have to work to see them as discrete individuals. For now, they were almost interchangeable, one body with many parts. They were the answer to her prayers, and they were a puzzle to be solved. And it seemed, as several of them glanced back to make certain she and Jin-Li were following, that she had passed her first test.

She rose from her makeshift seat and followed as the anchens started up a path into the forest. She touched her cross, and breathed thanks to her patroness. She had been right to come.

OA COULD ALMOST believe her long months of captivity had never happened. She was one with the anchens again, her bare feet treading the familiar paths of the island, digging into the warm sands of Mother Ocean. Only Isabel's presence proved that her newest memories, of the ship, of the Multiplex, of the cool rainy place called Seattle, were true rememberings. Isabel's hand in Oa's was real. Jin-Li, walking behind them, was real. And Isabel understood now what an anchen was, and still she did not repudiate them. It was not the blessing Oa had spent so many years begging of Raimu-ke, but it was almost as great a thing, in its way.

And now they would lead Isabel, and Jin-Li, to their hidden place. They had changed it only once in all of Oa's years on the island of anchens, only after the time the young men of the people discovered them sleeping, and killed Micho. The memory rose in Oa's mind, but she pushed it away to remember another time. Now was a time for showing Isabel the nest. And Doctor Simon would come, and there would be more showing. This could not happen without Oa to translate, to explain, to intercede.

Oa watched the anchens walking ahead of her on the path, their long-toed feet fitting into the old, old grooves, their hands and arms touching, their bony backs moving in and out of the dappled shadows. They seemed strange to her somehow. She had not remembered how thin they were, how dirty, how ragged their clothing, how tangled their hair. But of course, it was not Po and Bibi and Usa and Likaki who had changed. It was Oa.

Despite the reassurances of Jin-Li and Isabel, it was true that she did not quite fit in either world. She was an anchen of Virimund, but no longer like them. She was of Earth because of her ancestors, but she was an anchen.

She sighed a little. Changes could not be unchanged. And it seemed change could not be controlled. She supposed she must give up yearning for the change that never came.

30

OA HAD CHOSEN the right word, Isabel thought. It was a nest. A covert.

Buttress roots, some horizontal, some vertical, formed an irregular bowl, a rough circle through which the anchens had woven vines, patches of moss, the broad dark nuchi leaves. Rags were dropped here and there, and wooden and stone tools. The forest canopy hung close, making a sort of low ceiling that held in warmth and the miasma of bodies and breath and decomposing vegetation. In other circumstances Isabel might have found the smell repellent. But she saw how the anchens clambered in, how they curled together in the noisome space like kittens in a basket, and she gave thanks that they had at least this, and each other. They had little enough else.

She and Jin-Li did not fit so easily, nor their bodies bend so lissomely as the old children's, but they tried. They moved on their knees, finding places to settle where they could lean their backs against some support, where they could see the anchens, and each other.

"We'll hear the flyer," Jin-Li assured Isabel.

She nodded. She wondered what Simon would make of this place. She had never seen anything like it, not in her experience nor in her studies. But then, there was nothing in the universe like the anchens of Virimund.

SIMON HAD BEEN shocked by Gretchen Boreson's appearance when Adetti brought her back to the power park. By the time she reached the infirmary, the medication had worn off, and she was babbling again, her limbs jerking and writhing spasmodically. Adetti and Simon, between them, laid her gently under the medicator. She twisted and fought, and they had to strap her down before they could apply the syrinxes.

When the medicator began its assessment, Simon glanced up at the readout, and shook his head. "She's in bad shape," he said. "Not just the Crosgrove's. She's made herself ill with exposure and stress. Did you know she was this close to the edge?"

"No, of course not. I would have . . ." Adetti's voice trailed off, and he made a helpless gesture. "I don't know what I would have done, Edwards. Look, I'm sorry. I'm over my head here. And nobody can tell Gretchen anything when she's made up her mind."

"I suppose, to be the General Administrator of the Multiplex, requires a strong will. And more than a little arrogance, I expect."

"She was good at the job."

"So I understand."

Boreson began to breathe more evenly, and the twitching of her body subsided. Adetti, with a gesture that surprised Simon, put his hand on hers, careful of the syrinx now attached to her thin white wrist. "Doesn't seem fair," he said gruffly.

"You mean, that she should be ill?"

"Yes." Adetti looked up at Simon, his chin jutting in the old way, but his eyes bleak. "She didn't have anything but her work," he said. "Like me. No family, no home to return to . . . only ExtraSolar Corporation."

Simon thought of Anna, his own home, a place he had no desire to go. "You should talk to Isabel about that," he said wryly. "She's better at the really hard questions."

Adetti glanced up at the readout, and then down at Boreson's form, still now, her eyes closed. A faint pulse beat in her neck, just below the jaw. "You think there's something wrong with people like that?" he said unexpectedly.

"Sorry?"

"I mean . . . people who have faith. Who believe in something better."

Simon leaned against the wall, watching Adetti with bemusement. He didn't know if he was being naive, or insulting. "I know there's nothing wrong with Isabel," he finally said in answer. "She puts her faith to the test, and she does good work in its name."

"Yeah. I guess." Adetti pulled a light blanket over Boreson, and tapped the screen to order a fresh dose of dimenasphin. "But I don't understand it."

Simon had said the same words, too many times. Hearing them in Adetti's mouth made him wish he had never spoken them.

When Jin-Li called the next day, Simon was again in the infirmary. Boreson was stable, and she seemed rational, but Simon had assigned the medtech to stay with her. He and Adetti were both in the surgery when his wavephone buzzed. He spoke cautiously, eager to know what they had found, wary of giving away too much. He would have liked to warn Jin-Li, warn Isabel, but he hesitated. He glanced down at Boreson. Her pale face was a mask, eyes closed, lips folded, but he had the distinct sense she was listening to everything he said. He made his promises with no mention of his discovery of the night before. When he broke the connection, Adetti pounced.

"They found them," he said.

"Yes. Oa found them."

"Can we go now, then?"

"Look, Adetti—" Simon began.

"Don't tell me!" Adetti snapped. "They want you, and not me."

Simon shrugged. "Not my decision. Isabel's. And Oa's."

"I'm not going to stand for it!" Adetti strode from the surgery, out into the tiny reception area. His lips were pressed thin, and his eyes, so bleak before, blazed with fury. "I came all this way to see those—those creatures—and I mean to do it!"

"You will," Simon said mildly. He stepped out of the surgery, and closed the door gently. "But not now. Isabel wants time, and Oa says they're afraid."

"I don't give a damn what Isabel wants," Adetti said. "So they're afraid! They'll get over it. No one's going to hurt them."

"Someone has already hurt them," Simon reminded him.

Adetti slammed a fist against a doorjamb. It made a dull thud, and his mouth twisted. "Damn it, Edwards, this is too important for such posturing!"

"Posturing?"

"You know what I mean. We need that virus, need to get started."

Simon forbore to lie to him, and he let the "we" pass. There would be time, later, to explain the work he had done, the vaccine that was almost ready to be tested. "I have to go alone. This is Isabel's request, as guardian. I promise, Paolo, after I've seen the anchens—"

Adetti made a sour face.

Simon chucked. "It's a real word. You might as well accept it. This is an anthropological issue. We may face ethical challenges, and we certainly can't afford more mistakes. We have to correct the ones already made, and we need to move slowly. You'll get your chance at the virus, and your research, but you'll have to wait."

The argument went on, Adetti dogging Simon's steps as he sought out Jacob Boyer, made his arrangements, secured a flyer and a pilot, and assembled a medical kit. Not until he had set out across the airfield to meet the pilot did Adetti subside. He stood glowering next to Boyer while Simon shook hands with the pilot and climbed into the flyer.

Simon couldn't resist giving him a jaunty wave as the flyer lifted from the tarmac and banked to the southwest.

IT WAS NO wonder Oa was afraid of them, Isabel thought. This one was enormous, at least ten centimeters long, its arching legs furred and its eyes shining an iridescent black with layered depths of green and bronze. It sauntered up the path, straight toward the spot where Oa stood frozen, staring at it.

They had heard the flyer as they were climbing out of the nest. Jin-Li spoke to Simon by wavephone and told him to wait beside the crashed flyer. The light was dimming, the sky darkening to a faint violet above the ocean. Oa said the forest path would be faster than the beach path. She led the way, with Isabel and Jin-Li behind her. The anchens came, too, but warily, touching each other's hands, glancing at each other. They placed their bare feet cautiously, and lagged far behind.

Isabel murmured to Oa, "Can we get out of the woods before it's dark?"

Oa walked faster, and Isabel had to hurry to keep up.

It was steep going. Oa scrambled with monkey-agility, but Isabel often had to pull herself up banks and over tangled vegetation, using vines and roots, sometimes almost on her hands and knees. When they reached the edge of the meadow, she was perspiring and her sandals were full of grit. She stopped for a moment to pull stickers and burrs from her socks. Oa waited with her while Jin-Li went ahead to signal to Simon that they had arrived.

The anchens hung back among the trees. Several took to the canopy, nestling among high branches where they could see the meadow. Only Po and Bibi held their ground. Po stood stiff-legged at the turning of the path, his rusty long knife hanging at his waist. Bibi shifted from foot to foot as if at any moment she might leap onto the nearest root and vanish above the canopy. Oa spoke to them, but they didn't answer, only stared fixedly forward.

Isabel put her socks and sandals back on, and straightened. "Shall we go to meet Doctor Simon, Oa?"

Oa nodded, and they started out into the clearing. The long grass looked brown in the dusky light, and a few faint stars had begun to glisten. Jin-Li had reached the flyer, and stood talking with Simon and the pilot, gesturing back toward the forest.

Po was following Oa, his hand on the long knife.

Isabel stopped. "Oa. Can you ask Po to put the knife down?"

Oa's eyes rolled to Po, and back to Isabel. "Po is being afraid," she said softly. "All the anchens are being afraid."

"I know, sweetheart." Isabel looked up at the flyer, and saw that Jin-Li and Simon had started down through the scattered boulders of the meadow. "But look, Oa. Doctor Simon and Jin-Li are coming alone

to meet the anchens. Doctor Simon would never carry a shock gun, or
any other weapon."

Oa's tongue touched her lips. She turned her head and spoke swiftly
to Po. He gave a hard shake of the head, and clasped the hilt of the old
knife.

"Po is remembering," Oa said quietly to Isabel. "The anchens are
remembering the—the shock guns. They are remembering that Nwa is
falling, and Oa. They are being afraid."

Isabel hesitated. She looked above Oa's head to Po, the old child be-
having like a man. Protecting his people, defending his territory. She
lamented the incident that brought them to this. Had the hydros only
come without weapons! "Violence begets violence," she whispered.

"Oa is not understanding."

"No, sweetheart, I know. Listen—" Simon and Jin-Li had almost
reached them. Bibi's courage was tested beyond its limit, and she swung
herself neatly and swiftly up onto the nearest branch. The other anchens were already invisible, hidden by the darkness of the canopy.

"Isabel!" It was Simon's voice, ringing across the meadow.

Po pulled his knife out of his belt, and held it at the ready.

"Just a moment, Simon," Isabel called.

Simon stopped, with Jin-Li beside him. "Something wrong?" He
was still thirty yards away, a dark silhouette against the brightening
stars.

Oa chattered at Po, and Isabel caught, "Doctor Simon," and her own
name. Po spat something back at her. Oa and Isabel were just beyond the
edge of the forest, where the grass shrank and died, leaving a flattened
verge between the meadow and the first trees, an open space where the
path widened into the open. Oa turned back to Po. He stood straddle-
legged, fierce, eyes blazing with ancient fury in his youthful face.

It was an impossible position for Oa. She hardly belonged to the
anchens anymore, and yet she needed them. Isabel supposed her speech
and her appearance made her old companions distrustful and suspicious. And the anchens had no reason to trust Isabel, or Jin-Li, or Simon. She felt their eyes on her from the gloom, and gooseflesh prickled
her arms and her scalp.

When the forest spider appeared, the poor light made it seem larger even than it was, marching out of the shadows of the forest and across the bare dirt of the verge.

Everything seemed to happen at once. Later, grief-stricken, sifting through her memories and impressions to think what she might have done differently, how she might have prevented the tragedy, Isabel found she couldn't put events in any sequence. Po's lifting of the knife, Oa's shriek at the sight of the forest spider, her own leap to put herself between the spider and Oa, and Simon's lunge, swift steps that brought him to her side, his attempt to bat the spider away from her, all of it jumbled together in her recall so that the only person who truly saw what happened was Jin-Li Chung.

JIN-LI RECOGNIZED THE fear and determination, the sheer courage, it took for Po to stand, as he believed, between the anchens and danger. It was Po's fear that made the situation explosive. It was at best an uneasy truce that had existed between the anchens and Isabel and Jin-Li—and even Oa—all day. The arrival of a third flyer, after the weird behavior of Gretchen Boreson, disrupted the precarious balance. Jin-Li saw Oa step forward, exhibiting her own brand of courage, trying to prevent a confrontation. Whether she could have defused the situation without any injury, no one would ever know.

Jin-Li and Simon saw the knife raised above Po's head, and they began to run. They were too far away, of course. If Po had decided to use his knife, they could not have stopped him.

The forest spider appeared on the verge between the boulder, where Oa stood, and the edge of the forest, where Po stood ready to die for Bibi and Ette and Likaki and Malo and the rest.

Oa screamed at the sight of the spider. Isabel misunderstood and cried, "No! Po, don't!"

Po whirled to face the imagined threat of Isabel, brandishing the knife above his head.

Isabel's leap was to shield Oa from Po. Isabel had not yet seen the spider.

Running hard, Jin-Li and Simon saw the spider a moment after Isabel did.

Simon called Isabel's name. They were within a few strides of the verge, Oa cowering against the boulder, Po rigid with tension as he saw Simon and Jin-Li rushing toward him. It was nearly dark, and things were moving fast.

The spider's stately motion became a flash of long black legs and ovoid body. Isabel's leap to protect Oa turned into a sprawl as she lost her footing and fell onto the verge, her arms outstretched, one sandal lost in the grass, the other dangling from her foot. And Simon, with a choking gasp of horror, bent to bat away the spider just as it reached Isabel's exposed arm.

When he straightened, he wore a look of incredulity on his narrow face. The black spider clung to his hand. Jin-Li strode forward to release it from him, and Simon pulled back, choking out, "No! Jin-Li, don't touch it! It's . . ." Even in the dusk, it was possible to see how his face paled.

Po saw the spider now, too, and lowered the knife slowly. Oa burst into wild sobs. Isabel scrambled to her feet, crying Simon's name, stepping forward to help him. He staggered away from her, crying again, "No! No!"

He shook his hand, hard, and pushed at the forest spider with his other hand. The creature tumbled, at last, to the ground. Po used the rusting knife to spear it where it fell. But it was too late for Simon.

31

OA STARED IN horror at the awful scene of Doctor Simon, gentle, kind Doctor Simon, falling to his knees and staring at the spider bite on his hand. It swelled immediately, but Oa had seen that before, had felt it on her own skin more than once. She remembered the vicious fire of it. But Doctor Simon looked stricken in another way, beyond simple physical pain. He turned stiffly to face Isabel, and said hoarsely, "The spider is the vector."

Oa didn't know what "vector" meant, but Isabel looked as stricken as if the spider had bitten her instead of Doctor Simon. For a long, awful moment everyone froze where they were, hardly breathing. Then Doctor Simon straightened, holding his bitten hand stiffly away from his body. "I'd better get back to the infirmary as quickly as possible."

Jin-Li strode forward, and put a long, strong arm around Doctor Simon, lifting and supporting him, saying in a hard voice, "You're sure?"

With a ghost of a chuckle, Doctor Simon said, "Unfortunately, yes. The forest spiders are the carriers."

"Oh, my lord." Isabel trembled, coming out of her trance. "Simon!"

Jin-Li said, with swift pragmatism, "Let's go. You have an antiviral?"

"Started on it. In the medicator." Doctor Simon straightened, staring down at the spider Po had killed. His eyes, when they came up to Oa's, were dark with shock. "Oa, don't let anyone touch that."

"No, Doctor Simon." Oa's voice was a whisper. She trembled all over. The anchens dropped, one by one, out of the canopy, and Doctor Simon's eyes widened in wonder at the sight of them. Po left his knife where it was, pinning the now-dead spider to the ground. He stood stiff-legged, watching and waiting. None of them said a word.

"Simon," Isabel said in a shaking voice. "Is that what killed the hydro? A spider bite?"

"Afraid so."

The three of them, Isabel and Jin-Li and Simon, turned to start up the hill. Jin-Li spoke into a wavephone, and Jacob Boyer, waiting beside the flyer, climbed up into the cockpit. Oa heard the motor start, and the rotors began to spin.

"Ice," Simon said.

"In the flyer," was Jin-Li's terse answer. "What else?"

Again the faint, hoarse chuckle. "Not much till we reach the infirmary."

They walked quickly up the hill, Jin-Li on one side of Doctor Simon, Isabel on the other. Oa trailed after them, casting a glance over her shoulder at the anchens, then looking forward, to where the flyer's rotors spun faster.

"Isabel. Oa comes with you."

Isabel spoke without looking back. "Yes, Oa, come with us. But tell the anchens we'll be back."

Oa called to Po. He stood, his arms hanging at his sides, his face creased with confusion.

"Do they understand?" Isabel asked. They had reached the flyer, and Jin-Li jumped inside, turning to give Doctor Simon a hand.

"Oa doesn't know." Oa climbed into the flyer, too, and went to one of the rear seats. She strapped herself in, not waiting to be told. Jin-Li dug through the medical kit for an ice pack as the flyer lifted from the meadow and banked over the old lava flow to the northeast. Isabel sat next to Simon, bending toward him, her hand on his uninjured wrist. She murmured something Oa couldn't catch.

Jin-Li came forward with the ice pack, and knelt before Doctor Simon to apply it. Oa hugged herself, and wished she had her teddy bear.

ISABEL TRIED TO smile reassuringly at Oa. She kept Simon's uninjured wrist in her fingers, and the wave of anxiety and physical pain that flowed from him made the bones of her hand ache. "I don't understand, Simon," she said in a low tone. "Other hydros were bitten, but only one got sick. The anchens—they carry the virus—but they don't get sick, either. They certainly don't die—just the opposite!"

His breathing was quick and shallow. "Venomous spiders can have dry bites," he said hoarsely. "The biologist at the power park brought me three, all dead, and they were all carriers. Sometimes—" He swallowed, and turned his eyes out to the vista of dark water. "About half of defensive bites . . . are dry. No venom."

Jin-Li secured the ice pack and took a seat across the aisle.

Simon put his head back against the seat rest and began to speak faster. Jin-Li took out the portable to record Simon's words, and the simple action filled Isabel with dread.

"I've been at it for a whole day," Simon said rapidly. "I knew so little about spiders. Stupid of me . . . Australia has bad ones, but I . . . let the medicator deal with those, when it was necessary. The hydro who died had an immediate onset of migraine, even before . . . necrosis set in. An hour before other symptoms . . . by then the virus had taken hold. Wouldn't have mattered . . ." He paused for breath, and rushed on. "Nothing the medicator could do. I put together a serum, but it isn't tested yet, and it may be that it has to be used prophylactically, or immediately upon envenomation."

"Simon, maybe you should rest. Try to breathe calmly."

"I'm calm, Isabel. I need to get all this out, in case . . . in case I don't have another chance." She saw that his eyes slid to Jin-Li, holding the portable. He gave a small nod of approval, and then turned his eyes back to the ocean, where reflected stars sparkled on the shifting surface. It was dark in the flyer, the only light coming from the amber glow of the instrument panel. Boyer had said nothing, Isabel suddenly realized. And she knew he, too, was frightened.

"You'll have another chance, Simon." But she saw the squinting of his eyes against even the dim light that reached them, and she knew the headache had started. She put her free hand on her cross and began to pray.

By the time the power park came into view, Simon was recounting his symptoms in a low, matter-of-fact voice. "Visual disturbance," he said. "Consistent with migraine, but fairly pronounced. Dry mouth, upset stomach. Probably have diarrhea in a couple of hours. The deceased hydro was dehydrated when he came to the infirmary. Expect the joint pain will start later."

The flyer settled to the tarmac before the Port Force terminal with what seemed to Isabel agonizing slowness. Boyer had called ahead, and the medtech was waiting with a stretcher and two men to carry it. Simon kept talking all the way to the infirmary, and Jin-Li, staunch and impassive, trotted beside the stretcher, recording everything.

Paolo Adetti had the medicator ready in the smaller surgery. The larger surgery was empty. Gretchen Boreson must have been discharged. Simon, his voice growing scratchy, gave instructions as the syrinxes were patched to his wrists and ankles and temples, and the click and whirr of the machinery began.

"Edwards, why didn't you tell me it was the damned spiders?" Adetti said, bending to secure a sensor to Simon's throat. "I could have kept working on the serum. This doesn't look to me like it's ready."

"Not," Simon gasped. "Out of options."

Adetti glanced at the readout, and he spoke to the medicator, too. Isabel, standing impotently in the doorway of the little room, saw that Simon breathed a little easier, but his color was terrible, a gray-blue cast that she couldn't blame on the poor light. Adetti ordered something else, and tapped the screen, but it didn't seem to Isabel that Simon looked any better. He still talked, breathless now, his voice faint.

"Subadults could be most predatory. Food-getting bites . . . see archival research on arachnidism . . . Try using regen in serum for reversing effects of virus . . ."

His voice trailed off. Isabel found she was gripping Oa's hand so hard it must have hurt. She forced herself to relax her fingers. Oa said, her voice almost as faint as Simon's, "Re-versing? Re-versing?"

Simon was beyond hearing her. Isabel knelt where she was, her cross in her hands. "Oa, pray with me," she said softly. "Please."

"Oa prays with you." The girl sank to her knees beside Isabel, so close Isabel could feel the warmth of her in the chill night. She could think of nothing to say. She fell back on ritual, on litany. She whispered, "St. Mary Magdalene, patroness of those who ask . . ." When that was finished, she said the Pater Noster, and after that the Nineteenth Psalm. The medicator's click was louder than her whispered prayers, and no one spoke to interrupt her, or to reassure her. She came to the end, and only knelt with her head bowed, her cross in her hand, Oa leaning against her shoulder. Isabel didn't know who was supporting whom, but she was grateful for the contact. When her own prayers died away, Oa began, in her own language, murmuring petitions to Raimu-ke. They knelt for a long time, and when their knees could hold them no more, they moved to the little reception room and sat together on the floor, their backs against the wall. Eventually Oa slept, her head in Isabel's lap. Isabel sat stroking her hair, watching the stars' cold light glimmering beyond the window.

The stars were fading when Jin-Li came to get her. The gray light of early morning made the air seem colder even than it was.

"Paolo says you should come into the surgery," Jin-Li said to Isabel.

"Is he better?"

Jin-Li's long eyelids dropped briefly, that characteristic cautionary gesture. "He's conscious, Isabel. But he can't move his legs."

Isabel felt a chill certainty in her chest that she was about to say good-bye to Simon. She wriggled carefully out from beneath Oa's head, and Jin-Li handed her a pillow to place beneath it. Isabel stood up on uncertain legs.

"The serum's no good, then," she said.

"I don't know. He's been working on it all night."

Isabel hurried into the small surgery, and went to Simon's bedside.

The head of the bed was raised. Simon looked ghastly, but his fingers were tapping at his computer, and he was muttering commands, both to it, and to Adetti, who was working at his own computer. The medicator's readout screen was a mass of numbers and symbols, not, Isabel felt certain, Simon's vital signs.

"Simon, what are you doing?" she asked gently. "Not still working?"

His eyes flicked to her. She was shocked to see how sunken they were, how weak his ghost of a smile. His voice was thready. "Make it count," he said. And then, to Adetti, "Input regen factor." Adetti nodded, and spoke to his computer. Jin-Li's portable was still recording, resting on the counter beside the little sink.

Isabel looked across the bed at Adetti. "Paolo, what's happening?"

He met her eyes, his black ones frank for once. He spoke gently. "Simon's systems are shutting down. The virus is lethal in a mature adult, the telomerase too much for a body with a functioning reproductive system. There's nothing more we can do, and Simon wanted to work on the antiviral."

"Almost got it," Simon whispered. "One more step."

"Then can you take it, Simon? Get well?"

"Nope." He tapped once on his computer, and then let his head fall back against the pillow, his eyes closed. "Got away from me, Isabel. Sorry."

Her heart missed a beat. She took Simon's hand in hers, and found it ice-cold. "Try, Simon," she whispered. "Try."

"Sure," he gasped. "But— 's too late. 'S gone too far." He took another breath, a rasp of air through collapsing airways.

She gripped his hand to her breast, and cast a look of appeal at Adetti. "Paolo, please!"

The other physician left his computer and came to stand beside her, his dark features drawn. "I've just ordered it," he said wearily. "The medicator's administering it now. But I'm afraid Simon's right."

"Hydros," Simon croaked. "Isabel."

"Yes," Adetti said. "Everyone will be inoculated. Isabel, too." He smoothed the blanket that covered Simon, an unexpectedly paternal gesture. "Simon, you've done everything you could. Now rest."

Isabel watched his kindnesses to Simon with despair, certain that only his conviction that Simon was beyond help could have pierced his usual self-preoccupation. Perhaps Gretchen had fled, unable to deal with this disaster.

But she, Isabel, was a priest of the Order of Mary Magdalene. She had duties to anyone who stood at the door to eternity, even he who was a nonbeliever.

"Paolo," she said. "Could I be alone with Simon? If there's nothing more you can do for him right now?"

"Yes. I'll wait outside with the girl."

"Thank you. Anything I should watch for?"

"The medicator will let you know." He hesitated, then gave the blanket a last pat, and turned away. Jin-Li picked up the portable and followed Adetti out.

Isabel squeezed Simon's fingers. "Can you hear me, Simon?"

His lips were as white as the pillow, and they barely moved. "Yes."

"Is there anything you want to say to me? A message for Anna?"

His voice was only a thread, and she bent closer to hear better. She could feel his breath, so fragile, so ephemeral, on her cheek. "Sorry," he said.

"Shall I say that to her, Simon?"

"Yes-s-s."

"I will. I'll tell her." Isabel ignored the pain in her throat, the incipient ache in her chest. She stroked his nerveless hand, and searched for words. "Simon . . . can I do anything else?"

There was a long pause that made her glance up anxiously at the medicator screen. It was once again monitoring Simon's heartbeat, his respiration, his temperature. The indicators were low, but they were, for the moment, steady.

When she looked down again, she saw that Simon's pale lips were curved slightly at the corners. "What is it?" she murmured.

"Mother Burke . . ." He drew a breath that whistled in his chest. "Know where . . . I'm . . . going?"

"I think I do, my dear friend. I think there's nothing to fear."

"Not . . . afraid."

Isabel put both her hands over his. "No, you wouldn't be, Simon. You've carried out an act of great courage. The antiviral serum will bear your name, I promise you."

Another curve of the icy lips. "Adetti . . . won't like."

"He may surprise us." She waited, watching his chest. Its rise and fall were almost imperceptible. "Simon," she said.

"S-still . . . here."

"I know you don't pray, Simon . . . but you won't be disturbed if I do, will you?"

"N-no." Another slow, shallow breath. "Pray . . . for me . . . Mother Burke."

Isabel's eyes burned as she made the sign of the cross with her right hand. As she had done at other times, she pushed her personal feelings to a small part of her mind and soul, to be dealt with later. If it was harder in this instance than it had ever been, it didn't matter. Her obligation was doubled because Simon was close to her. And because, in this moment, she was all he had.

She began the litany, her words just audible over the steady hiss and click of the medicator. Simon's face relaxed, and she still covered his hand with her left one.

She liked the words from the King James version, the old, old ones that had survived since the Renaissance, survived subsequent translations, survived even the revisions of generations of self-conscious editors.

She quoted softly,

THE LORD IS MY SHEPHERD. I SHALL NOT WANT.

A small sigh came from Simon, a sigh of recognition, of acknowledgment.

The familiar words were like honey in her mouth, the images balm to her spirit.

H<small>E MAKETH ME TO LIE DOWN IN GREEN PASTURES.</small>
H<small>E LEADETH ME BESIDE STILL WATERS.</small> H<small>E RESTORETH MY SOUL.</small>

She watched Simon breathing. His closed eyelids flickered gently.

H<small>E LEADETH ME IN THE PATHS OF RIGHTEOUSNESS, FOR</small> H<small>IS NAME'S</small>
S<small>AKE.</small>

Simon's lips moved, ever so slightly, and Isabel saw that he knew the words, that he was following along as she said them.

Y<small>EA, THOUGH</small> I <small>WALK THROUGH THE VALLEY OF THE SHADOW OF</small>
D<small>EATH,</small>
I <small>WILL FEAR NO EVIL, FOR</small> T<small>HOU ART WITH ME;</small>
<small>THY ROD AND THY STAFF, THEY COMFORT ME.</small>
T<small>HOU PREPAREST A TABLE BEFORE ME, IN THE PRESENCE OF MINE</small>
<small>ENEMIES;</small>
T<small>HOU ANOINTEST MY HEAD WITH OIL; MY CUP RUNNETH OVER.</small>

His cold fingers lifted, and twined with hers.

S<small>URELY GOODNESS AND MERCY SHALL FOLLOW ME ALL THE DAYS OF</small>
<small>MY LIFE,</small>
<small>AND</small> I <small>WILL DWELL IN THE HOUSE OF THE</small> L<small>ORD FOREVER.</small>

Simon opened his eyes, and fixed them on her face. The pupils had expanded, and the blinking lights of the medicator screen twinkled in them, giving them false life. He took a rasping breath. "Isabel."

"Yes, my dearest friend."

"Love." A long pause, another rattle of air in lungs that had ceased to function on their own. "Forever."

"Yes, Simon. Forever." Every line of his face, every detail of the room, burned itself into Isabel's memory to be replayed later, when she could grieve. She thought she would always remember the amber and green and red lights on the screen, the dull white of the sheets, the paleness of Simon's narrow lips. She stood, and bent over him to kiss his forehead.

"Bye," he whispered.

"Godspeed," she answered, just as the medicator alarm began to trill, a high, slender sound that pierced her heart. Before Adetti reached the bedside, she had put her hand over Simon's eyes, and closed the lids, ever so gently.

32

OA WOKE TO find herself alone on the floor of the reception area. Some-one had slipped a pillow beneath her head, and covered her with one of the stiff white blankets from the surgeries. She sat up, alarmed at the si-lence around her. "Isabel?" she whispered. And then, a little louder, "Is-abel?"

"I'm here, Oa." Isabel's hushed voice came from the small surgery.

Oa scrambled to her feet. Perhaps Doctor Simon was sleeping. A shaft of morning light stretched across the tiled floor, just reaching the open door of the surgery. Oa followed it, and stood in the doorway to look in.

Isabel sat in a chair beside the bed, both of her hands holding one of Doctor Simon's. She looked up when Oa's shadow fell across the bed. Her face was a hollow-eyed mask. The air in the room smelled dis-tinctly of death.

"Isabel?" Oa said weakly.

Isabel stood up, slowly, almost painfully, as if her bones hurt. She released Doctor Simon's hand, laying it on the blanket with great care, and she crossed the room to Oa, putting out her arms, pulling her into a gentle embrace. Oa nestled against Isabel's breast.

"Doctor Simon died about an hour ago," Isabel murmured. She let her cheek rest on top of Oa's head. "There was nothing more we could do for him, sweetheart."

Oa clung to Isabel. She couldn't take it in. She didn't want to believe that Doctor Simon, so smart and strong and capable, could be gone. That the bright world of Earth, so powerful, so masterful, could crumble, no more in control of events than the world of the anchens. It didn't seem possible that Doctor Simon could die. And if Doctor Simon could die . . . could Isabel? It was a terrifying thought. Oa didn't know what to do, and so she held Isabel with her arms, feeling the sobs that shook her slender body, letting her tears soak her hair.

They stood that way for a long time, until Isabel's tears ceased. She released Oa, and stood wiping her cheeks with her fingers. "Simon was very dear to me," she said softly.

"Oa is sorry, Isabel."

Isabel traced Oa's cheek with her fingers, and she managed a tremulous smile. "Thank you, sweetheart. I'm so glad you're here."

Oa gazed at Doctor Simon. He didn't look injured, or ill. He looked as if he were sleeping, though his face was white, and no breath moved in his chest. It wasn't like Micho, who had been so battered. Nor like Ufu, whose drowned and swollen body washed up on the beach the day after he swam after the canoe of the people. Oa's nostrils flared. It was true, though. Doctor Simon, though he looked so peaceful, was dead.

"Isabel. Mary Magdalene did not hear your prayers?"

Isabel's eyes welled once again. "I don't know, Oa. Perhaps she heard, but she couldn't change things." She dabbed at her eyes with the back of her hand. "It may take a very long time before I understand."

Isabel moved to the little sink to splash water on her face. She straightened, wiping her face with a disposable towel.

"Isabel, what is re-versing?"

"I beg your pardon?"

"Re-versing. What is re-versing?"

Isabel blinked, and gave a little shuddering breath. "Oh, reversing . . . well, it means turning back. Or undoing, I suppose." She tossed the towel away. "Now there are things I must do, Oa," she said in a stronger voice. "I have to call Doctor Simon's wife . . ."

Oa didn't hear the end of Isabel's thought. The outer door of the infirmary banged open, and they both turned.

Gretchen, her eyes reddened, her silver hair coming loose from its chignon, stood unsteadily in the reception area, swaying on her feet. "Paolo? Paolo!" she called. She clutched at her head with her shaking hands, her long nails glinting in the light. "Paolo, you have to help me—my head hurts—"

Isabel reached Gretchen in three long steps, catching her before she crumpled to the floor.

JIN-LI HAD GONE to the barracks for a couple of hours of sleep. It had been hard to leave the infirmary, but it was clear Isabel wanted to be alone with Simon, and two nights of sleeplessness had begun to wear. At the first light of morning, Jin-Li hurried to the meal hall for a hasty breakfast, and then back to the infirmary.

There had been little doubt of the night's outcome. Jin-Li expected long faces, a pall of grief. The bustle in and out of the large surgery came as a surprise. Oa stood in the reception area as if nailed to the floor. Her eyes flicked up as Jin-Li entered, and then fixed again on the open door to the large surgery. The door to the smaller room, where Simon lay, was closed.

"Oa. What's on?" Jin-Li said brusquely.

Oa looked up again. "Gretchen," she said obscurely. She pointed to the half-open door.

Jin-Li stepped to the door and looked in. Gretchen Boreson lay on the medicator bed, with Paolo Adetti bending over her. Isabel stood at the foot of her bed, her hands clasped before her. Boreson moaned. Her head and her right hand, all Jin-Li could properly see of her, twitched and jerked, fluttering the tubes of the syrinxes patched to her temple and her wrist.

Isabel glanced over her shoulder at Jin-Li, and then came out of the surgery. Her skin was ashen, and her eyes hollow. "Jin-Li," she said. "Thank God you're here. Oa should go to the meal hall, eat something. Do you think you could take her?"

"What's happened?"

Isabel rubbed her face with her fingers. She spoke slowly, as if reluctant to say the words. Jin-Li understood that. Speaking something aloud gave it power. "Simon passed away early this morning."

Isabel's eyes were the color of gunmetal, the whites reddened, the lids swollen. Her lips trembled, and Jin-Li felt a surge of pity. "Isabel, I'm so very sorry. You look exhausted. Why don't you take Oa to the meal hall? You need to eat, too, and to sleep. I'll stay here."

Isabel hesitated, and then nodded. "You're right, of course. There are things that will need doing. Hard things." She took an uncertain step, and then stopped. Half to herself, she murmured, "Someone has to call Anna. Simon's wife."

"I can do that. Or Jacob can."

Isabel looked out the window into the clear morning sky. "I suppose that would be best," she mused. "I'm the last person Anna will want to hear this news from." She stood still, staring into nothingness.

Oa looked up. "Jin-Li," she said. "Oa takes Isabel to breakfast."

"Yes," Jin-Li said, patting the girl's shoulder. "You do that, Oa. Take care of her."

Oa nodded solemnly. "Oa takes care of Isabel. Yes."

Isabel's smile was wan. "Thank you both. I'll eat, and rest a bit."

"Is Ms. Boreson ill again?" Jin-Li asked.

Isabel put a hand to her throat. "Oh, my lord, Jin-Li. Of course you didn't know."

Jin-Li waited, eyebrows lifted.

"Gretchen . . ." Isabel shook her head. "Gretchen—while Simon was with us, on the anchens' island—she infected herself."

"Infected—you mean, with the virus? From the forest spider?"

"Yes. Apparently she went into the room where he was doing his work—there—" She pointed to the closet Simon had used as a lab. "She's a smart woman. She figured out what he was working with, and injected herself. She showed up here with the migraine, and now she's running a high fever and she's been vomiting."

Jin-Li looked into the large surgery. Paolo Adetti was working beside the medicator, tapping the screen, muttering orders.

"Simon kept working on the serum right up until . . ." The muscles of Isabel's slender throat flexed as she swallowed. "Oh, lord . . . I'm so tired."

"Go. You and Oa. Eat, and sleep. I'll stay with Dr. Adetti."

"Yes, please do. He's giving Gretchen the serum. It was too late for Simon, but maybe for Gretchen . . . Well, it's something to hope for."

She turned to Oa, and the girl shepherded Isabel out of the infirmary, one small dark arm circling her waist protectively. Jin-Li watched them go, thinking that Oa would be a great comfort to Isabel just now. A great blessing.

ISABEL FEARED SHE wouldn't be able to eat anything, but Oa's watchful eyes on her made her put a few bites in her mouth, toast and eggs. Oa ate, too, and drank a glass of juice. Then, together, they made their way to their barracks room, and both fell into a heavy sleep until noon. Gradually, Isabel came to consciousness, wishing she didn't have to return to reality. When she opened her eyes, the bright Virimund day seemed colorless and empty.

Oa lay on her cot, facing Isabel, waiting for her to wake.

Isabel tried to smile. "Did you sleep, Oa?"

"Oa sleeps. Slept."

"That's right, sweetheart. Slept." Isabel sat up, and swung her legs over the edge of the cot. She still wore the same shirt and shorts she had put on two days before. She looked down at her dirty feet, her scratched calves. "I need a shower," she said, wondering at the prosaic necessity on this day of tragedy.

"Oa, too." The girl tugged on her half-undone braids. She was even dirtier than Isabel, her face smudged, her clothes tattered.

Isabel roused herself, for Oa's sake. "Come on, then. We'll have a nice long shower, and put on fresh clothes. We'll feel better afterward."

They showered, and brought fresh clothes out of their valises. Isabel sat on her cot, and Oa stood with her back to her while she worked at the tangles and knots in Oa's hair, combing and smoothing it before she rebraided it. The ritual was soothing, somehow, requiring a coordination of mind and fingers that kept sorrow at bay for the moment.

"Isabel," Oa said, as Isabel tugged on a particularly dense tangle.

"Yes?"

"Anchens are having the virus? Doctor Simon's virus?"

"Yes. It's the same. The forest spider carries the virus, and its bite can infect someone."

"But anchens are not being . . ." Oa's hand grasped air until she found the words. "Are not being ill. Anchens are not dying."

"No, that's right. The virus has a different effect on children."

"Oa is not understanding."

"I don't understand completely, either. Not yet. But Doctor Simon thinks—thought—it had something to do with being young when you were infected. Not being grown up."

"Not being a person," Oa said.

Isabel put down the comb, and turned the girl to face her. "Oa. Listen to me. Doctor Simon believed that the virus, from the bite of the forest spider, makes anchens. It's the virus that made you, and Po, and Bibi and Ette and the others, into anchens. You are people, all of you. Human beings. But the virus arrested your growth—stopped you from becoming an adult."

Oa listened, but her face didn't change. She would never accept it, Isabel thought. No matter what she said, what arguments she put forward. The cultural bias went too deep. She had believed something about herself, and the other anchens, for more than a hundred years. It was, for the anchens, a kind of faith, and it was unshakable.

SIMON EDWARDS'S FUNERAL took place on the Memorial of St. Mary Magdalene, a day of glorious light. The ocean shone the viridescent green that had given the planet its name. The little cemetery was bright with flowers and waving yellow grass. The grave had been prepared beside the others, facing south, swept by the ocean winds.

Isabel wore her black stole and chasuble, and followed the procession from the infirmary, where Simon had lain until all was ready. She walked carefully. Her bones felt like glass. Her mind was frozen, focused on the task ahead, refusing to deal yet with the fact of her loss. Oa stayed close beside her, watching her as if she might fall.

"I'm all right, Oa," she said, trying to smile. "You don't have to worry."

Oa didn't answer. She adjusted her steps to Isabel's as they walked up the sandy path.

Isabel paused at the top of the little rise, looking down on the gathered Port Forcemen and women, on Jacob Boyer's lanky, stooped figure, on Jin-Li Chung, who stood with arms folded, a little apart from the others.

And there was Gretchen Boreson, weak, unable to walk without a cane, but recovering from her bout with the virus. She had said little when Isabel went to visit her in the infirmary. She seemed to have aged a decade in their brief time on Virimund, the lines on her face deepening into dry furrows beside her mouth, wrinkles pulling at her eyelids, folding her neck beneath her jaw. Isabel tried to draw her out, but she had little success. Boreson had lost hope.

Simon's coffin rested on the little patch of trimmed grass. It was the simplest of containers, put together of unused construction materials, gray and dull. Its plainness, its anonymity, moved Isabel in a way that most elaborate hardwood coffin could not have done.

She laid her hand on it. There was no feeling in her palm, no emotion that made her skin tingle or her bones ache. Simon was no longer there. She looked around at the gathering.

"In the midst of our sorrow," she began, "there is pride in a life well-lived. There is gratitude for the gift Simon Edwards was to those of us who knew him, and for the gift he left behind for all of those who will go on working on Virimund. Let us remember, as we say farewell to a fine man . . ." Her throat closed suddenly. She swallowed, and felt Oa move closer to her. The child's warmth strengthened and sustained her. The lump in her throat dissolved, and a feeling of calm overtook her. "As we say our farewells, let us remember the privilege it was to have known Simon Edwards."

She lifted her hand from the coffin, and made the sign of the cross.

A few in the gathering followed her example. Others bowed their heads, and one or two wiped their eyes. "Not all of you knew Simon," Isabel said. "But those of us who did are grateful for your presence and support. It's one of the great mysteries of being human that in times such as these—difficult times, sad times, challenging times—we see the face of God."

And as she said it, she understood with all her heart that it was true.

JIN-LI WAS AMAZED by Isabel's composure throughout the funeral ceremony. Isabel stood, a slender, erect figure in black, as the coffin was lowered into the ground and covered. The day was relentlessly bright. Birds twittered in the one tree that had been left standing near the cemetery, and the breeze teased at Isabel's robes. Paolo Adetti helped Gretchen Boreson back up the path, Boreson leaning on her cane, tremors rippling through her body. Oa never moved from Isabel's side.

Jacob Boyer came up to Jin-Li when everything was finished, and they walked back toward the power park together. Jin-Li looked back once, seeing that Isabel and Oa still stood, watching the hydros covering the coffin with dirt and sand.

"You were there with Dr. Edwards," Boyer said.

"I was. Almost until the end."

"And the antiviral is good, the one he designed?"

"Yes. It worked for Ms. Boreson. Dr. Edwards wanted everyone to be inoculated."

Boyer walked slowly, one hand on his long chin. "Did Dr. Edwards say why the virus wasn't fatal for . . ." He glanced over his shoulder. Oa and Isabel now knelt by the finished grave, and they were planting something in the fresh dirt. "For the girl, and for the others?"

"He had a theory. Dr. Adetti is going to carry all his research back to World Health."

"The theory is?"

"Simon thought that the telomerase produced by the pituitary tumor stops the reproductive system from maturing. But if the person who contracts the virus is already mature, then the telomerase disrupts the adrenal and nervous systems, and they break down."

They reached the tarmac, and crossed it on the way to the terminal. "We still don't know what happened to the colony," Boyer said.

"No. Mother Burke wants us to go back to the island of the anchens, and then to try to find the islands of the people—that is, the islands of the Sikassa colony."

"I don't think you'll find much," Boyer said. They stood before the door to the terminal, squinting against the light. The work of the power park had resumed. Carts rolled back and forth between the solar collectors and the storage facility, and machinery hummed in the distance. "The forest pretty much takes over anything left untended." He gestured with his long arm at the few trees left standing behind the barracks. "We have to go out there and cut back vines and those damned roots almost every week."

"Right. Well, we'll have a look. Let you know."

"Of course. I'll give you a pilot and a flyer."

"I'll tell Mother Burke I'm going." Jin-Li looked back in the direction of the cemetery, the view blocked by the rise of the hill. "But maybe not today."

33

CONTEMPLATING THE TRANQUIL face of Virimund was, Jin-Li thought, like a meditation. Shallow waves, like idle thoughts, foamed on the pale sand underfoot. The blue arch of the sky deepened to violet and then to indigo, a mood change. The stars flickered to life, one, then two, then a swirl of them, mirrored in the smooth face of the sea. Jin-Li sat crosslegged on the cool sand, and gazed out over Mother Ocean.

Loneliness was a familiar part of Jin-Li's life, a habit. But Isabel Burke's courage in the face of her loss was an inspiration. And here, on Virimund, Jin-Li thought that perhaps a new beginning was possible. Isabel would return to Earth, in time, to make her report to World Health, to advocate for the anchens. And the anchens would have need of a protector, someone present, someone informed. World Health would need someone to archive the changes that were certain to come. Jin-Li Chung could be that person.

The wind from the sea grew cooler. Jin-Li rose, and turned from the peaceful view to go back to the barracks. Tomorrow would be soon enough to propose the idea of being permanently assigned to Virimund. To put down roots, at last.

All the barracks rooms were dark. Most of the hydros were in the habit of going to bed early, with work beginning at first light. The table had been cleared of cards and glasses and readers, the chairs neatly stowed. Jin-Li crossed the room carefully, shoes in hand, trying not to disturb the silence.

"Jin-Li?" It was Oa's small voice. She stood in the door to the room she shared with Isabel, her sleepshift ghost-white in the gloom, her hair a cloud of black around her shoulders.

"Oa," Jin-Li answered in a whisper. "I thought everyone was asleep."

"Oa is not sleeping. Not asleep."

Jin-Li smiled. "Do you want to talk?"

The girl looked over her shoulder, and then back to Jin-Li. She moistened her lips with her tongue, and then, as if it took courage to do it, she stepped out of the room and closed the door behind her. "Isabel sleeps. Is asleep."

"You can't sleep?"

Oa shook her head. "No. Oa is thinking."

"Ah. Yes, that will do it every time." Jin-Li set the shoes down, and pulled two chairs out from under the table. "Come on. Sit here with me, and tell me what you're thinking about."

Oa's bare feet glided soundlessly on the polished tiles as she crossed the room. She sat down, and ran her fingers through the ends of her long hair, her great eyes fixed on Jin-Li.

"Jin-Li," she whispered. "What is re-versing?"

"Reversing? As in, to reverse something?"

"Reversing—to reverse. Yes."

Jin-Li thought for a moment. "I guess I would say reversing is to turn around. I could reverse this chair, for example, turn it the other way."

"What means reversing e-ffect?"

"Oh. Well, that could mean to undo something, I suppose. Why don't you tell me where you heard the word? I'll explain better in context, maybe."

Oa's eyes were pools of darkness ringed in silver. "Oa hears—Oa heard Doctor Simon say 'try re-gen for reversing e-ffect of virus.' You were—" She held out a cupped hand to show what she meant. "Being archivist."

"Oh! Oh, yes, I was recording. Recording what Doctor Simon said."

" 'Try re-gen for reversing e-ffect.' "

"Yes, I remember that he said that." Jin-Li leaned forward, and took Oa's hand. "Oa, what are you thinking?"

Oa turned her hand to grip Jin-Li's fingers with surprising strength. "Forest spider bited—bit—Oa. Gave Doctor Simon's vi-rus. Oa wants to reverse e-ffect."

ISABEL WOKE WITH a start from a dream of Simon waving to her from the top of the cemetery's little hill. She sat up amid tangled sheets. A sheen of perspiration dampened her throat and back.

Automatically, she looked across to Oa's bed. The covers were thrown back and the bed was empty. She threw her own blanket aside, and put her feet on the floor. The tiles were cool against her bare soles. Before she even reached the door, she heard the sibilance of a whispered conversation beyond it. She turned the handle slowly, so the catch would make no noise.

In the misty light cast by the stars, she saw Jin-Li Chung at the table in the common room. Oa sat there, too, a wraith in a white sleepshift. They were whispering together, their heads bent close. Isabel paused in the doorway, not wanting to shatter the fragile moment. It was the first time she had seen Oa confide in anyone except herself.

And their conversation looked very much as if confidences were being exchanged. When she looked closer, Isabel saw that Jin-Li's hand lay lightly over Oa's, and Oa had not drawn it away. Oa's eyes were on Jin-Li's face, and the archivist was speaking slowly, as if choosing each word with care.

Softly, Isabel closed the door again. Jin-Li and Oa were managing on their own. If there was something she needed to hear, she could hear it in the morning.

She went to the small window, and looked out into the mild Virimund night. Her objective mind knew it was a beautiful scene, the stars brilliant, the glimmer of the ocean just visible through the trees behind the barracks. But its beauty was lost on her, at this moment. Her solar plexus ached with missing Simon. She had lost him twice, she thought. And he wasn't even hers to lose.

She turned back to her bed, and pulled the blanket up to her chin. There was no point, now, in agonizing over what she might have done, or left undone. She would grieve, and in time she would come to accept that Simon was no longer in the world. She told herself she would make his legacy count, as best she could. It was the only way to make sense of the tragedy.

OA SLIPPED BACK into the room. Isabel lay on her cot, her bare scalp glistening faintly in the starlight, her face turned toward the wall. Someone had brought the teddy bear from Jacob Boyer's flyer. Oa got into bed, and held the teddy bear close to her chest.

Jin-Li had promised to find the place in the recording where Doctor Simon had spoken of reversing the effect of the virus. Where he had mentioned regen. Oa didn't know what regen was, but hope made her heart pound as she lay staring at the unadorned ceiling. Reversing effect. Undoing. Was it possible? She prayed to Raimu-ke that it might be so, and then she lay replaying her newest memory, the sad, beautiful memory of Doctor Simon's burial there beside Nwa, of Isabel in her black robes speaking on the little hillside, the Port Forcemen and women standing respectfully before her, listening.

Tomorrow she must ask Isabel about the grave. It was, she thought, Doctor Simon's kburi, though it was set deep in the ground. She wasn't sure. And would Isabel pray to Doctor Simon now? Did being dead make Doctor Simon into god?

Sleep surprised her, early in the morning when the sky was beginning to lighten, and when it came, it laid a heavy hand on her. It was full, bright morning when she opened her eyes to find Isabel's bed empty.

Oa got up slowly, feeling sluggish with the heavy, late sleep. She opened the door and looked out into the common room. Isabel was there, with Jin-Li. A pot of tea and two cups were on the table, with Jin-Li's portable between them. When Oa appeared, they both turned to her.

"Good morning," Isabel said. Her voice sounded as it always did, calm, warm, comfortable, but her eyes were dark. "Did you sleep well?"

Jin-Li held a chair for her, and Oa sat down. The barracks were quiet, all the hydros off to their work. Jin-Li touched the portable with one finger. "I found it, Oa. As I promised."

Oa's heart began to thud again. "Reversing effect," she said to Isabel. "Try regen, Doctor Simon said."

"Yes, I know, sweetheart." Isabel's eyes grew even darker. "Jin-Li explained it to me. And we listened to the recording."

Later, Oa would remember this conversation, and regret that listening to Doctor Simon's voice made Isabel sad. But now, at this moment, she could think of only one thing. "Oa wants reversing effect," she said. "Oa wants . . . to try regen."

Isabel put out her hand to Oa, as Jin-Li had done last night. "Oa. I don't know if you understand what it would mean."

"Oa understands! Oa wants reversing effect."

"Yes, I know you do, sweetheart. But it would . . ." Isabel hesitated, passing a hand over her eyes. Oa gripped her hand in both of hers.

"Isabel, please. Oa wants."

"I know. I know. But it would change you, Oa. It would change everything."

"Yes, Isabel! Yes! It would change Oa. Oa could be a . . ." Now that the moment was at hand, Oa found she hardly dared say the word. She paused, her tongue touching her lips, her breath coming quickly. Doctor Simon had spent the last night of his life at work on this very thing, this marvel. Doctor Simon had left behind a miracle. When Oa did speak the word at last, the wonder of it made her voice tremble. "Oa could be a—*person*."

ISABEL LET OA and Jin-Li go on to breakfast without her. They parted on the sandy path, and Isabel turned in the other direction, away from the power park. She walked slowly, the weight of decision bowing her shoulders, her cross in her fingers. She passed no one on the path, and when she reached the cemetery, she was alone. She passed the Port Forceman's grave, and the small mound with its new marker that now proclaimed the resting place of Nwa, child of Virimund. She crouched beside Simon's grave, her elbows on her knees. She and Oa had planted a rhododendron there, a biotransformed seedling imported from the Multiplex. It was a shrub that would put down long, strong roots, to wrap around Simon's coffin and dig deeply into the soil. In spring its riot of white flowers would blaze briefly, and then fall on the grave, a litter of snowy petals. Already the rhody was showing signs of new growth, tender green leaves peeking from the woody stems.

"Simon," Isabel said. "I don't know what to do."

She looked out over Mother Ocean. The water shone like green glass. A few transitory clouds clustered at the horizon, and then dissipated under the morning breeze. "If Oa takes the antiviral—your antiviral, Simon, the gift you left us all—if she takes it, what will happen? I worry it might harm her, of course, although I don't really think that. I guess I worry more that it will work, that it will do just what she wants it to do.

"Did you hear what she said? She wants Doctor Simon's 'reversing effect.' 'Try regen,' she said. I swear she remembers everything she's ever heard or seen. If the serum does reverse the growth of her tumor, Simon . . . that amazing memory could be only one of the many things about Oa that will change."

Isabel's knees began to ache, and she sat down in the sand beside the grave, her legs stretched out before her. She closed her eyes, let the breeze caress her weary face. "Simon, I know this isn't fair. This isn't about me. But I love her, you know that, I love her the way she is. And if the antiviral works, if she . . . becomes a person . . ." She laughed, and patted the grave as if she could touch Simon himself. "I'd like to keep Oa the way she is. But that's not fair to her.

"If we give her the antiviral, if it works the way she hopes it will, she won't be a child anymore. She'll grow up. She'll become a young woman, and then an old woman. And one day she'll die."

The impact of this hard truth brought tears to her eyes. She lay flat on her back in the sand, one hand still on the grave. "Oh, Simon. I, who have never had a child, who never will have a child . . . I love *this* child. And I have to let her go. It's her life, not mine." The tears ran from her eyes, past her temples, to fall into the sand. "You left her a great gift, my dear friend." She thought of Simon laboring throughout the night, his last night, to perfect the work he had begun, and her throat ached. "I have to find a way to be grateful."

PAOLO ADETTI WORKED hard in the infirmary over the next few days. Every Port Forceman and woman at the power park had their turn, lying down under the medicator to receive the antiviral that Adetti and the medtech had formulated according to Simon's last instructions. Boreson had been the first to receive it, of necessity. Adetti insisted on trying it on himself next, after refining it even further. Then came the medtech's turn, and when none of the three of them experienced ill effects—and Boreson did, in fact, achieve a reversal of the illness, the tiny pituitary tumor beginning to shrink almost immediately—they began inoculations for the entire population. Isabel and Jin-Li received theirs early, two days after Simon's funeral. Isabel planned to return to the island of the anchens, and Jin-Li, with a pilot, was going in search of the remnants of the Sikassa colony.

When Isabel rose from the medicator bed, she found Oa, her small face set and brow furrowed, waiting her turn.

Adetti, Isabel thought, had done a fair job of burying his disappointment at the frustration of his ambition. He had spent an entire day transcribing Simon's thoughts about the antiviral serum, and another day and most of one night working on the formula. He watched over Boreson's recovery, and personally monitored every hydro who received the serum. Still, he expressed doubts about inoculating Oa.

"We don't know for sure, Isabel," he said wearily, "what the effect might be on her. When Simon suggested adding regeneration catalyst, he was thinking of those who were infected recently, not one of these—" He glanced aside at Oa, who stood stiffly beside the medicator, her gaze fixed on it as if it were a mountain to climb. "Anchens," he finished, with a gesture of capitulation. "The anchens have adapted to the virus, have coped in their own way. At the very least, reversal might take months, or even years, if it happens at all."

Isabel touched Oa's shoulder. "Are you listening, Oa? Do you understand what Dr. Adetti is telling us?"

Oa didn't take her eyes from the medicator. She muttered, "Oa understands."

"You wouldn't have to do it now, Oa," Isabel tried again. "You could wait. We could go back to the island, spend time with the anchens. And then you could—"

Oa looked up, but not at Isabel. She lifted her little chin, and spoke directly to Adetti. "Doctor," she said. "Oa is ready." And without waiting for assistance, she climbed up on the medicator bed, and lay back, arranging her long braids over her shoulders, settling her head against the pillow. "Please may Oa hold Isabel's cross?"

Isabel sighed, and lifted the cross over her head. She placed it in Oa's hands, and stroked her fingers. "I'm right here with you, sweetheart," she murmured.

"Thank you, Isabel." Oa held the cross to her breast, and closed her eyes.

Isabel took a breath, and then another one. "Well, Paolo. You may as well begin. I think Oa has made up her own mind."

34

ISABEL CONVINCED JACOB Boyer to let her go back to the island of the anchens alone, with only Oa as companion. "Oa will translate for me, until I begin to learn more of their language."

"At least wait for Chung," Boyer said gloomily. "Some protection."

"Jacob," Isabel said with a smile. "I don't need protection from the anchens."

He shook his head, and frowned, but he granted her request. He promised to fly Oa and Isabel to the island himself.

Adetti came to say good-bye the night before they left. Like Boreson, he seemed to have aged, not dramatically, but in some obscure way Isabel couldn't quite put her finger on. She had the impression he wanted to say something more, but he stood beside the door of the barracks, staring off toward the sea as if having difficulty meeting her eyes.

"Would you like to take a walk, Paolo?" she asked finally. "Talk a bit?"

He glanced up at her, and gave her a rueful smile. "Yes," he said. "I would."

They strolled together down the sandy path toward the little crescent beach, listening to the night birds twittering from the nuchi trees.
Isabel tipped her head back to appreciate the brilliance of the stars, to
wonder if the anchens would have names for the constellations. Adetti
walked in silence beside her. He didn't speak until they stood on the
narrow shore of pale sand.

"Gretchen's going to be okay," he said finally.

"That's good," Isabel said, knowing this was not what he had come
to tell her.

"Well, except for the Crosgrove's. I can't help her with that. No one
can, I guess."

"It doesn't seem so."

Adetti shuffled his feet. "Look, Mother Burke . . ."

"Isabel."

He nodded, and cleared his throat. "Yes. Isabel. Look, I feel terrible
about Edwards. About Simon."

"I know you do, Paolo. We all do."

A silence stretched again, broken only by the distant birdsong and
the whisper of the waves against the shore. The starlight shone on the
dark planes of Adetti's face. Isabel put her hand on his forearm, and she
felt a rush of pain and something like shame pour through her fingers.
"Why don't you tell me what's bothering you?" she murmured. "Just
say it out loud? It helps, I think."

He gave a deep sigh, and hung his head like a sorrowing child. "If I
hadn't been greedy," he said. "If I hadn't wanted to make a name for
myself, somehow, someway . . ."

"Paolo . . ."

He lifted his head again to stare out over the water, misery in every
line of his body. "It never occurred to me that anyone could be hurt,"
he said in a gravelly tone. "And if I were a better scientist—even a better physician—I might have figured it all out first. And then Simon
wouldn't have died."

"No one knows why things happen the way they do." Isabel followed Adetti's gaze out over the calm face of Mother Ocean. "Perhaps
this was always Simon's destiny. And yours—to be part of this discovery."

He made a hard sound that was almost a chuckle. "Some destiny," he said bitterly.

Isabel patted his arm again. "Mistakes are part of being human, Paolo. I know Simon wouldn't want you to go on blaming yourself. You've worked hard these last days, tirelessly. Who knows how many lives you may have saved? And we could never have done it without you."

"You're being kind, Isabel."

She nodded. "There's nothing wrong with that. Everyone needs kindness from time to time. It's no different for you. Or for me."

He chuckled again, a softer sound this time. "Thank you, Mother Burke. Thanks for listening. And for your kindness."

AS ISABEL WALKED with Oa to the terminal, she thought how appropriate it was that it was the Feast of the Transfiguration. Oa herself was transfigured. There was no sign of any physical change in her, not yet, but her belief in the coming miracle was unshakable. She glowed with an inner light, an absolute conviction that her prayers had been answered.

Who am I to doubt? Isabel thought. She chided herself with St. Mark's gospel: "All things are possible to one who has faith." Oa's faith shone bright as Virimund's star.

The evening before, the two of them had visited Simon's grave, carrying water for the rhody, and a handful of wildflowers to lay at the base of his simple headstone. They stood before it, the evening breeze playing with Oa's unbound hair.

"Can you read it, Oa?"

"Yes. It says Doctor Simon's name. But there are numbers, too."

"Yes, those are dates. The day of his birth, and the day of his death."

Oa bent to lay the posy on the stone. When she straightened, she stood tugging on the ends of her hair. "Isabel?"

"Yes?"

"This is Doctor Simon's kburi."

"Is it, Oa?"

"Yes. Doctor Simon's kburi. Not like Raimu-ke's kburi."

Isabel held her breath. This was a train of thought she did not want to derail.

"Isabel—Doctor Simon is dead now. Is he god?"

Isabel took a long moment to phrase her answer. She wasn't sure that Oa's vocabulary, though it had grown so much, was up to abstract concepts. "Oa, my belief is that Simon is not God, but is with God. Is part of God."

"God is man?"

"I don't know what you mean, Oa."

"Oa means . . . Raimu-ke is god, but is not man. A man."

Isabel started to speak, but then stopped. The moment had a feeling of being crucial, of being pivotal. She said slowly, "There is a word, in English, for a god that is not male, Oa. Not a word I use much." She gave a deprecating shrug. "But a perfectly good word, for a god that is female. It's 'goddess.' "

Oa's eyes came up to her, wide, shining with intelligence. "Goddess. Raimu-ke is goddess, to the anchens. Raimu-ke. God that is female, but is anchen. A child. Like Christ child."

"Child Goddess, perhaps," Isabel said. "You could say Child Goddess, to translate Raimu-ke."

For the first time since Simon's death, Oa flashed her wide white smile. "Raimu-ke is the Child Goddess!" she said triumphantly. "The Child Goddess hears the prayers of the anchens!"

ISABEL AND OA unpacked the things they had brought with them, some food to offer the anchens, clothes, a small kit of medicines and other things Isabel thought might be useful. They stood in the long yellow grass with their jumble of cartons and cases around them, and Boyer reluctantly lifted the flyer to return to the power park. He had at least persuaded Isabel to carry a wavephone, and a backup in case anything should happen to it. Jin-Li would join them in a week. Isabel took a deep breath, relieved to be alone with the anchens at last. She could make a much-delayed start on the work she had come to Virimund to do.

They sat down on a nearby rock to wait. An hour passed before the anchens began to come out of the forest. Po came first, alone, bravely. He wore the rusty knife at his braided belt, and stood before Oa, firing questions at her. Oa answered, and then turned to Isabel. "Po is wanting—wants to know what happened to Doctor Simon. Oa is explaining." The two anchens chattered at each other a little longer, and Oa said, "Isabel, Po is being very sorry that Doctor Simon died."

"Thank him for me."

"Yes. And Oa is explaining antiviral, and re-versing e-ffect."

The exchange went on, Oa talking, translating, gesturing. It was hard to believe that Po could understand all that she had to say, but it seemed Oa was making progress.

Little, quick Bibi appeared next, trotting up through the scattered boulders. She was followed by Ette and Likaki and Kwima. Bibi grinned at Isabel, and made a stroking gesture over her matted tangle of hair. Isabel smiled back, and mirrored the gesture, passing her palm over her naked scalp. The rest came then, dropping down from the canopy, dashing up through the meadow. They stood in a semicircle around Isabel and Oa, talking with each other, with Oa, the whites of their eyes flashing at Isabel. It was Bibi who touched one of the cartons, and directed a question to Oa.

"Isabel, anchens are wanting to know what is in boxes. If there is being something to eat."

"Is this a good time, Oa, to share the food we brought?"

Oa's smile flashed, and she laughed, beautiful in her joy. "There are being no bad times for food, Isabel!"

Transfigured indeed, Isabel thought. Even to making jokes.

BY THE TIME Isabel's tent had bloomed on the sandy beach, to the awe of the anchens, and her cartons had been arranged inside, the light was beginning to fade over the eastern sea. Bibi and Ette were already trying out English words for things, brush, pot, fish, bread. Po stood watching everything with a fierce eye, as if daring Isabel to make a mistake, but when she offered him entrance to the tent, and a chair to sit on, he accepted. Oa stood by, translating a stilted conversation between Po and Isabel. The others poured in after a time, tumbling through the entrance in twos and threes, filling the tent with their unwashed body scents and their high, quick prattle.

The nest, Isabel had known, would not be possible for her to sleep in. The tent was large enough to admit as many of the anchens who wanted to come inside. As night fell, the old children were still there, exclaiming over her things, watching the blinking lights of her portable and reader and computer with avid interest. Isabel heard or saw no signal, but when the darkness was complete, the anchens stood as one and filed out of the tent.

"Are they going to the nest, Oa?"

Oa shook her head. "No. Is time for the remembering."

"Remembering?"

"Yes. Come now, Isabel. Come with the anchens."

Isabel gathered up her portable, and a light jacket, and followed Oa out of the tent and onto the beach path. The stars, and their light reflected from Mother Ocean, made the path easy to see. Oa stayed beside her as the others walked ahead in an uneven line. The air was cool and fragrant, and Isabel treasured the odd moment, the alien surroundings, her strange companions.

Their destination was a great black rock, an outcrop of lava flow, Isabel guessed, on the north side of the little island. Its glossy surface rippled toward the sea, leaving a great flat place well back from the edge. Waves splashed halfway up the height of the rock, but the top was mostly dry. The anchens sat crosslegged, and Isabel did the same, finding the stone warm against her bare thighs. Oa sat close beside her.

"Now the anchens are remembering," she whispered to Isabel.

"Remembering?"

Oa nodded, solemn-faced. The starlight softened the old children's thin faces, their bony arms and legs. The ocean murmured accompaniment for the anchens' voices, a deep, monotonous note beneath their lilting tones. Isabel listened, fascinated, to the strange music they made, almost forgetting to follow Oa's translation.

"Likaki is remembering a day when the wind is being very strong and three nuchi trees are falling."

"A storm," Isabel whispered.

"A storm. Yes. A storm."

Another of the anchens began to speak. "Kwima is remembering Mamah, and making pang with Mamah in shahto."

How old that memory must be! Isabel could hardly take it in. The ritual went forward, oddly formal, almost hypnotic in its practiced drama. Another anchen spoke, and another, and Oa whispered the stories into Isabel's ear. The anchens listened to each other with solemn and complete attention, neither wriggling nor coughing nor interrupting. Isabel began to feel as if she were dreaming, as if she would waken any moment and find she had imagined it all. The stories seemed to jump about in time, far back to the anchens' infancy, then forward to events that had happened recently. If there was a pattern, Isabel couldn't recognize it. She was startled when Oa said, "And now is the last, Isabel. Now Po is remembering the day Oa is coming back to the island. And the anchens are not knowing if Oa is Oa."

"What do you mean, Oa? They didn't recognize you?"

Oa's whisper tickled Isabel's ear. "The anchens are thinking Oa is dead," she breathed. "Anchens are thinking Oa is—" In the half-dark, Isabel saw the familiar gesture, the little hand grasping in air for the word.

"Ghost," Isabel supplied. "Or spirit."

Oa nodded slowly. "Ghost," she repeated. "Anchens are thinking Oa is ghost."

Clouds rolled in as they walked back over the beach path to Isabel's tent. Isabel stumbled in the darkness, but the anchens walked surely, their bare feet fitting neatly into the worn track. Isabel struggled to accept that the anchens had walked the path for a century or even more. She hadn't an idea, yet, who among these children was the oldest. She had not seen a single arm that was not littered with tattoos. In time, she hoped, they would trust her enough to let her count. And even then, she thought, it would take a scan to know for certain. Oa had said there had been no tatwaj for some time, and the children were vague about the passing of years. The white column of smoke, marking the tatwaj of the people, was all the calendar they had.

To Isabel's relief, Oa decided to stay with her in the tent, while the anchens set off through the forest to their nest. Isabel watched them go, feeling uneasy. She had to remind herself that they had slept in their nest every night for years, that they were not the defenseless children they appeared to be. They looked back at her, eyes shining in the darkness, and then melted into the forest.

Isabel and Oa went into the tent, and sealed the opening. Isabel brushed Oa's hair for her, wondering if the others would let her untangle their hair, if they would learn to bathe and brush their teeth, all the things Oa had learned to do. "We'll need a place to replenish our water," Isabel said.

"Oa shows. Tomorrow."

Isabel tucked Oa into her cot, and stroked her forehead lightly. Such moments might be numbered. Oa might grow up after all. Isabel touched her cheek with the back of her fingers, and then went to her own cot. She lay listening to Oa's light breathing, the slight creak and flutter of the tent's panels, and the comforting chuckle of the waves washing the beach.

"Isabel?"

"Yes, Oa?"

"Jin-Li looks for the people?"

"Yes. Jin-Li will try. But you understand, Oa, we don't think the people are there anymore."

"The anchens, too. The anchens are not thinking the people are there anymore."

IN TIME, ISABEL would want to see this for herself, Jin-Li knew.

There wasn't much left to observe. It took two weeks for Jin-Li, with Jacob Boyer piloting the flyer, to find any remnant of human habitation. On a heavily forested island about forty kilometers south of the island of the anchens there was a wide sandy beach where they were able to put the flyer down. Jin-Li and Boyer, struggling through the thicket of tree trunks and buttress roots and hanging vines, finally found what they were looking for. Boyer stumbled over something that appeared to be a root. Jin-Li bent to give him a hand, and saw that he had tripped on an ancient and desiccated length of braided vine. Carefully wielding a laser cutter on the overgrowth, they uncovered an outline, little more than a memory, but enough to tell them they had found one of the structures Oa called shahto. A Sikassa dwelling.

Jin-Li recorded what they found, while Boyer took a couple of samples and tucked them into vacuum envelopes. "If Mother Burke doesn't come to see this soon," he said dourly, "there won't be anything left to look at."

It was true. Any artifacts there might have been had been devoured by the forest.

If ExtraSolar wanted to underwrite the expense of underwater scanning and metal detectors on the island, searchers might find more evidence of the Sikassa colony. But the salient fact was that there were no Sikassa left. The old children were alone on the planet, the last of their people.

"What I don't get," Boyer said, on their last flight back to the power park, "is why the girl—Oa—why she would want to take the antiviral. She already survived the virus, could live forever, apparently. Why change that?"

"She's convinced she's not truly human. That the anchens are not human."

"Their people told them that?"

"Mother Burke believes the Sikassa developed a myth to justify their rejection of the anchens. Because they needed offspring, they needed children, for the colony to survive."

Reflexively, Boyer looked back over his shoulder, but the island had already disappeared in the brightness of the water. "Guess they were right, in a way."

"Yes. In a way."

"But to send their children away . . . That doesn't seem human, either."

"No." Jin-Li gazed down at the bright water. "I suppose they felt they had to choose."

"It was cruel."

"Societies are often cruel to those who don't fit in."

"I know." Boyer fiddled with a control, and then leaned back, sighing. "So what's going to happen now?"

"Mother Burke will spend time with the anchens, complete her studies. Report to the regents."

"And we can go on with our work? Expand the power park?"

Jin-Li shrugged. "I guess we'll find out."

35

ISABEL LIT HER little blessed candle and set out the crucifix on a flat stone before the kburi. The morning light paled the flame of her candle, and made the wood of the crucifix glow. Oa came to kneel beside her, and Isabel smiled at her. "Today is All Saints' Day, Oa."

"All the saints? Saint Mary Magdalene, Saint Teresa?"

"Yes, all of them, but especially the martyrs."

Oa frowned at the new word. "Mar-tyrs."

"A martyr is someone who gives her life for something she believes in. In my church, Christ is the first martyr. Here, on Virimund, we already have two."

Oa nodded. "Yes," she said gravely. Were there changes in Oa's face, a slight lengthening of her neck, perhaps a broadening of the shoulders? Or would that be her imagination? It had been almost six months since Oa received the serum.

"Doctor Simon is a martyr," Oa said "And Raimu-ke is a martyr."

"That's right. Because Raimu-ke died trying to protect other anchens." Isabel had heard this story from several of the anchens, sitting on the great boulder on the north side of the island. The tale varied depending on the teller, but the essence of it was always the same. Raimu-ke had been the first child to cease growing before her menses. Her people had not known what to do with her, Oa had said, translating, and had begun the tatwaj when Raimu-ke's younger sister became a woman, and the people realized something was wrong.

Isabel now had her own memory of Raimu-ke, as real to her as if she had witnessed the events herself. She pictured a slender dark child, rather like Oa, rejected by her parents and siblings, living out her days on the fringes of her community. When the tatwaj revealed a second old child, and a third, Raimu-ke stormed the village to destroy the inks and needles, to steal the drums that accompanied the ceremony, to try to stop the tatwaj itself.

According to one version, Raimu-ke was felled by a single blow from one of the elders. In another version, several of the elders attacked her, striking her with their fists. In some versions, she died instantly, in others she lingered a few hours, murmuring words of comfort and wisdom to the other anchens. It was this version Isabel preferred, because it made her think of Simon. In all the stories, Raimu-ke was put into a canoe with the other two anchens, and banished forever. The two survivors buried Raimu-ke beneath stones at the top of the old volcanic island. It became tradition for each new arrival, each newly sorrowing anchen, to place a new stone. Some of them were far too heavy for one child to lift, but the others helped, and over the years the cairn grew. If an anchen died, the little body was also buried at the top of the hill, to stay close to Raimu-ke.

The anchens squatted in an uneven circle around Isabel and Oa, waiting their turn. Together they had created a new ritual, one in which Isabel first made her morning devotions, and then the anchens made their own offerings. Isabel, too, made an offering to Raimu-ke. To the Child Goddess. She crumbled a bit of cereal in her fingers and laid it in the hollow votive stone. When she turned to look at the anchens, a rush of satisfaction filled her breast. A little miracle had been wrought here, on this tiny island. Six months of improved food, supplements designed and produced at the power park and flown to the island, a little basic medical care had brought a shine to the skin of the anchens, filled out their narrow bodies, strengthened their legs. There was more that needed doing, much more. Ette's eye required more skill than the medtech possessed. Isabel, recalled now to the Mother House, hoped to find a physician who would make the journey to Virimund to heal Ette, and perhaps to do something for Usa's crooked arm. Marian Alexander had already begun the search for a volunteer.

Jin-Li squatted with the anchens, showing respect to Raimu-ke. Jin-Li would be staying on Virimund. ExtraSolar had deemed it worth the expenditure of one archivist as advocate for the remnants of an Earth colony. Isabel had no doubt that ExtraSolar's motives were political, but they were useful. She was comforted by knowing Jin-Li would be here, that the mission would be in capable hands, and the work would go on.

The issue of Oa, however, was still unresolved.

WHEN ISABEL RETURNED to the power park, she was shocked to see how much Gretchen Boreson's chorea had worsened. They would travel together back to Earth. Boreson said she planned to be in twilight sleep the entire time. "No point in trying to exercise," she said. The older woman spoke without inflection, without any sign of resentment or sadness. A cane leaned against her chair, and her hands trembled uncontrollably. Her lips were pale and her eyelashes almost white. Isabel imagined her shaking hands could no longer manage to apply the artful cosmetics that had been such a part of her. Only her eyes were the same, ice-blue, still sharp.

"I'm very sorry, Gretchen," Isabel said. "I know you had hopes that the virus would provide a cure for you."

One of the trembling hands waved a dismissive gesture, and came to rest on the desk before her. Jacob Boyer had provided Boreson with a small office, outfitted with an r-wave installation and a computer, but Isabel doubted much work was being done. Gretchen no longer toyed with objects, as she had when they first met. She seemed to spend most of her energy trying to keep her body still.

"I simply want to be home," Boreson said. "Paolo tells me there's nothing more to be done for my condition."

"I'm sure I would want the same," Isabel said. "I'm eager to see my own home, now that my superior has recalled me. It's been a long time."

"I don't think I've had a chance to tell you how sorry I am about Dr. Edwards."

"Thank you. One of the things I'll need to do is to visit his wife, in Geneva. Anna."

Even at this revelation, Boreson's eyes did not swerve. No hint of compunction shone in her cool gaze. "That's generous of you."

"I hope she'll understand. There are some of his personal possessions to be returned, and I thought it would be better if they came from someone who cared about him."

"Paolo tells me you want to take the girl with you."

Isabel nodded. "Yes. I want to take Oa to the Magdalene Mother House, in Tuscany."

"I don't see the point of that. We're setting up facilities here, we'll bring a physician out to the power park. The children will be cared for. They should stay together."

Isabel leaned forward. "I agree that the anchens should stay together. But Oa is changed. She's different, because Paolo brought her to Earth, exposed her to all that Earth has to offer. How could she ever go back to living the way she did?"

Now Boreson's eyes did drop, and her cheek began to jerk in an arrythmic spasm. "The provision has expired . . ." she began.

"I've been in touch with Madame Mahmoud, and she's spoken to the other regents. They've agreed to extend my guardianship of Oa indefinitely."

Boreson pressed her hand to her cheek. "No one informed me."

"I will ask Madame Mahmoud to send you a transcript of the meeting."

A quiver shook Gretchen Boreson's body. She dropped her hand to the desk, where her tapering fingers twitched against the surface. "It was a waste," she said. The flatness of her tone had a bitter edge to it. "A total waste. We came all this way for a virus that's useless."

"Gretchen," Isabel said gently. "We came all this way to save the anchens. To restore these children to their birthright."

Boreson's eyes glittered with a little of their old, cold fire as she lifted her head. "That's why you came, Mother Burke," she said. The corners of her lips curved upward in a mirthless smile. "I came to find a cure for my disease. To find Paolo's delayed senescence factor. I came for my own purposes, and I failed."

Isabel sat back in her chair, stunned by Boreson's pragmatism, her naked honesty. In a way, Boreson had made a confession, but it was a confession marred by a complete lack of penitence. If she was unburdening her soul, it didn't seem to be a burden that troubled her.

Isabel didn't respond. She could hardly offer absolution to someone who neither asked for it nor believed in it. It would have been gratifying to see Boreson exhibit some sort of regret. But it would not have been in character.

As she left the little office, Isabel felt weighed down by the coldness, the utter selfishness, that drove Gretchen Boreson. It was terrifying to think what Boreson might have achieved, how she might have used the anchens, without Simon Edwards to thwart her. It was disturbing to think of what she still might accomplish, once she had resumed her seat of power at the Multiplex. At least the anchens of Virimund would be beyond her reach. Simon had seen to that.

ON THEIR LAST night with the anchens, Oa looked around at the faces of her old companions, marveling at how they had changed in only six months. Their skin was soft and shining, their hair painstakingly trimmed and untangled under Isabel's ministrations. The myriad cuts and bruises and rashes they so often carried about with them had been bandaged and soothed. But more importantly, their eyes had begun to lose the haunted look that Oa had always taken for granted. The anchens had grieved over the disappearance of the people, but they blossomed under the constant attention of Isabel and Jin-Li. And Oa.

Oa watched her own body for changes, wishing for them with all her might. Was she perhaps a little bit taller, her fingers a little longer? She couldn't say for certain. And of course it could simply be that she was eating good food every day, instead of starving most of the time. Po was still the tallest of the anchens. Oa knew the number of the tattoos she bore on her arms and neck. One hundred two. Add to that two years in space, and how many years more since the last tatwaj of the people? Eventually, ExtraSolar would figure that out, and Oa might know exactly how old she really was. Certainly, the number was a great one, and during all those years, she had lived with only the faintest hope, a ghost of hope. Now her hope was a tangible thing, a constant presence. She felt, on most days, as if she could walk on air. She closed her eyes against the sweetness of it, the beguiling power of anticipation. She tried not ever to think of Doctor Simon's serum failing her.

Isabel sat a little apart from her tonight, with Bibi on one side and Ette on the other. Likaki curled as close to Isabel's feet as possible. Jin-Li, too, sat in the midst of the anchens as they looked out over the darkening face of Mother Ocean and remembered.

Bibi told the story of the night her little sister was born, a younger sister who had grown to be a woman, who was now long dead. Likaki remembered the accident that blinded Ette, the bleeding of her eye, the screams of pain, and how the anchens gathered around her, holding her, crying together, not knowing how to help.

Po recited the story of Doctor Simon and the forest spider, and spoke of the sadness of Isabel and Oa at the death of their friend.

Darkness fell. Oa looked up into the blanket of stars, knowing that the stars of Earth would never be so brilliant. She felt sadness at leaving Virimund again, but it had been her own choice. She would go to Earth with Isabel, and she would grow, and learn, and then she would come back. The Child Goddess had told her so.

Po's eyes were fixed on her, reflecting the starlight in their dark pupils. She knew what he wanted. She nodded to him, and then she turned to Isabel.

"Isabel," she said.

"Yes?"

"The anchens want to take the serum. For reversing effect."

Isabel's eyes glowed in the darkness as if they were the stars themselves. "Have you explained, Oa? That we don't know yet if it will work?"

"Yes. Oa has explained."

Jin-Li said, "She did. I think they understand."

Isabel sighed. "Jin-Li, I don't know how you've learned the language so quickly."

"I already speak several. Each one gets easier."

"So I understand." Isabel passed her hand over bare scalp, and turned her face out to the ocean once again. "Oa, I'll talk to World Health about it. I don't know what they'll say."

"But Oa took the serum."

"Yes, but that was different."

"The anchens do not think it was different," Oa said stubbornly.

"No, I suppose they don't." Isabel propped her chin on one hand, elbow on knee. "Jin-Li, this is all so hard to think through. An anthropologist is supposed to study new cultures, not interfere with them. Not change them. If we inoculate these children . . ."

"If the antiviral works," Jin-Li said.

"Right. If it works. But there are no others like them. No other anchens in the universe."

"But can we withhold this from them, if they want it?"

"No. I don't think so. But I'm not certain it's our decision to make."

Oa said quietly, "Whose decision is it?" She saw Isabel and Jin-Li look at each other, and Jin-Li began to grin. In a moment, Isabel, too, was laughing. Oa lifted her hands, bewildered. "Oa is not being funny," she said.

Isabel smiled, her lamplight smile that could light even the darkest night. "No, sweetheart, of course not. It's just that you're right. You're so right, and we both see it. The decision belongs to you, to each of you. There's no point in my troubling myself over it!"

THEY LEFT VIRIMUND on the first day of Advent. A departure, Isabel thought, rather than an arrival. An ending, but charged with possibilities.

Two volunteers from Port Force, a man and a woman, had gone to the island of the anchens to assist Jin-Li in building a proper shelter for the children, and to acclimate them to more people. Isabel had a long conversation via r-wave with Madame Mahmoud, and it had been decided that inoculation of the anchens should wait until they knew how Oa's body reacted. Oa and Jin-Li explained to Po and the others that the serum would be theirs, if they still wanted it, after that time.

Boyer was busy overseeing the loading of the shuttle, the hydrogen containers in the cargo bay, Isabel's and Oa's things in the passenger cabin. Isabel was carrying copies of all Jin-Li's work, pictures of the anchens for the regents, and recordings for linguists to study. Simon's things had been carefully packed to be returned to Geneva. To Anna.

Before the flight, Isabel took a last walk to the cemetery. The bio-transformed rhododendron had grown quickly. By spring there would certainly be flowers on it. It stretched its branches over Simon's grave, its glossy leaves brushing his headstone. Isabel stood looking down on it, holding her cross in her fingers.

"Dear Simon," she said softly. "I suppose if I hadn't asked for your help, you wouldn't be lying here." She lifted her head to feel the caress of the breeze on her scalp. "But I have confused feelings about that, my sweet friend, because if you hadn't come to Virimund, there would be no antiviral for the anchens. And they want it so very much."

She knelt beside the grave, her knees settling into the pastel sand. The mound of the grave was covered now with a swiftly growing moss in the shade of the rhododendron. She touched the headstone, and it was warm under her palm.

Suddenly she longed for the touch of Simon's hand so much she almost cried out. She pressed the cross against her breast as if to soothe the pain. "Oh, my lord, Simon, I miss you. I will always miss you. I'm sure you would have been quick to point out that we weren't going to be together in any case . . . But I would have known you were there, to call, to think of, to wonder about. I have so much to be grateful for, and yet the world seems empty without you."

She knelt there for many minutes, her head bowed, her hand against the warm stone.

"Isabel?"

She looked up to see Oa standing at the head of the path. The teddy bear was in her arms, but she held it differently now, propped on one hip in a maternal fashion. Isabel felt her lips tremble as she tried to smile. "Is it time, Oa?"

"Mr. Boyer asked Oa to find you."

"All right. I'm coming." Reluctantly, she lifted her hand from the stone, letting her fingers trail over the mossy surface of the mound.

Oa came to stand beside her. "Are you saying good-bye, Isabel?" she asked quietly.

Isabel stood up, dusting the bright sand from her bare knees. "It's silly," she said slowly. "Simon isn't in there, of course. I know that better than anyone. Only his body is there. But the grave is a symbol, like . . ."

"Like the crucifix?"

"Yes. And like the kburi." Isabel put her arm around Oa's shoulders, and they turned together to walk back up the path. "But Simon's soul will always be with us, Oa, with you and with me. As long as we remember."

36

ON THEIR RETURN to Earth, Isabel and Oa spent only one night at the Multiplex. They boarded the sonic cruiser to Geneva the next morning, on the Feast of St. Blase. Paolo Adetti saw them off. There was no sign of Gretchen Boreson.

Isabel entertained Oa with the various stories regarding St. Blase, a physician from the fourth century. He was purported to have been protected by wild animals, and to have been martyred in various unpleasant ways. The story Oa liked best was about Blase saving a boy from choking on a fish bone, and becoming, in that roundabout way, the patron saint of singers. She made Isabel tell it twice, before her eyelids began to droop, and she slept.

Isabel drowsed, too, still feeling the effects of twilight sleep. Both of them woke just as the craft soared to its smooth landing in Geneva.

Isabel wore her usual black, with her Roman collar, and her black overcoat. Oa wore a jumpsuit of cream polysilk, her hair collected into a long ponytail that hung to her waist. Isabel glanced at her with pride, and gave her a coat to put on before they descended the metal stair of the cruiser. The air was cold, and heavy with snowclouds. Hilda Kronin, ExtraSolar's liaison to World Health, met them on the tarmac, and shepherded them into a long black car, a perfect copy of the one that had carried Isabel away from the Mother House.

"Mrs. Edwards is expecting you, Mother Burke," she said when they were settled in the car. Nothing in her demeanor indicated that she found this visit out of the ordinary. Possibly Boreson and Adetti had managed to keep their own counsel in the matter of troubling Anna.

"This is a sad duty," Isabel said carefully. "I thought Mrs. Edwards would prefer to receive her husband's effects from someone who knew him."

"You've never met her?"

Isabel turned her face to the street scene beyond the window, hiding the emotion that must show in her face. "No, we've never met. But Simon spoke of her to me."

"She's a quiet woman," Kronin said, and then fell silent herself.

The house was modest and solid. Isabel stood on the sidewalk outside, with Oa beside her, and looked up at the brick facade, the green-painted door. The tiny lawn was covered with a pristine blanket of white from the last snowfall. No footprints, large or small, disturbed it. Somehow the sight saddened Isabel. She bowed her head briefly, asking for inspiration and guidance, and then she led Oa through the little iron gate and up the walk to Anna Edwards's door. Hilda Kronin came behind with the driver, the two of them carrying the cartons of Simon's things.

The door opened at a murmured command, and Simon's wife appeared.

Isabel stood on the step, uncertain whether to offer her hand.

"You must be Isabel Burke," Anna said. Her voice was light, almost childish, at odds with her graying hair and slightly stocky figure. She wore no cosmetics, and shadows marked the sagging skin beneath her eyes and lips.

"I am," Isabel said quietly. "Are you Anna?"

"Yes." Anna Edwards stepped back to allow Isabel and Oa and the others inside. She closed the door, and gestured to a little sitting room off the hall. "Please."

Hilda Kronin and the driver set their burdens down in the hall, and Hilda stood back while Isabel and Oa went into the sitting room. "Anna," she said. "I think I'll wait in the car. Give you and Mother Burke a chance . . ."

Anna didn't look back. Her eyes assessed Isabel, shifted to Oa, and back to Isabel. "There's coffee in the kitchen, Hilda."

"No thanks, Anna. I'll call you tomorrow, make sure everything arrived safely."

Isabel waited until Anna came into the living room and took a seat before she sat down on the small divan beneath the front window. It was a pleasant room, unremarkable, but designed for comfort. In one corner a desk lamp illumined a stack of flexcopies. Books lined every available space, and a large reader was set unobtrusively into one wall, almost hidden by a vase with sprays of holly. Christmas, Isabel thought. She and Oa had slept through Christmas. Twice.

"I hope you don't mind if I call you Anna," Isabel began. "I feel as if I know you, through Simon."

The shadowed eyes blinked once, slowly. "Really," Anna said in a flat way. "I don't feel as if I know you at all."

The air was charged with emotion. Oa sniffed audibly as she tried to identify it.

"It's only natural for you to feel antagonism toward me, Anna," Isabel said quietly. "And I'm sorry. I'm deeply sorry for that, and for the sad circumstances that have led to our meeting."

"Why are you here?" Anna asked. She closed her eyes, and her lips trembled briefly. When she opened her eyes again, she said, "I have . . . resented you for a long time."

"I wanted you to know . . . to understand."

Anna's jaw tightened. "What is there to understand?"

"I want you to know that what happened in the Victoria Desert . . . Virimund was different. Nothing can compensate for the loss of your husband, I know—"

"I had already lost him," Anna said, leaning forward with a sudden energy. Oa took a sharp breath. "Long before he went to Virimund. He broke his vow to me. And you, I believe, broke yours."

Isabel nodded slowly. "You're quite right, of course. And I have done—am still doing—penance for it."

"Taking Simon with you to Virimund was doing penance?" The words were so bitter, Anna's mouth so tight as she said them, that Isabel felt a wash of sympathy.

"No, Anna. That's what I'm trying to explain. Why I came here." Isabel turned to Oa, who sat stiffly, as if ready to spring to Isabel's defense. "Oa," Isabel said. "Oa is why Simon was needed on Virimund. Oa and fourteen other lonely, abandoned children."

"He told me about it," Anna said. "He called me, from the transport, and from the power park. But I still don't see why it had to be Simon. You must know other scientists."

"But Simon was the one," Isabel said. "Because of his political influence, because of his ability to be both scientist and diplomat. Because of his great heart." She stood, and went to crouch beside Anna's chair, to look up into her face. She tried to see what it was in this face that Simon had once loved, what had drawn him. "Anna. I'm so very sorry you were hurt. It shouldn't have happened."

"The fault is not all yours."

"No, it's not. But I accept my share of it."

Anna clenched her hands with a sudden fury, and leaned forward, toward Isabel. "What was the point of it all? Why did Simon have to be a hero? What could possibly make it worth his dying?"

Isabel held her gaze. "That's far too big a question for me to answer. But I can tell you—I came to tell you—that Simon performed a great service. His name will be remembered, here on Earth and especially on Virimund. Even at the end, when he knew the virus was going to win, he worked on the antiviral serum, worked right through the night, until his last breath. Who else had such courage? Only Simon. Only your husband."

"I loved him." Anna seemed to wilt, the brief energy of her anger fading. Tears welled from her eyes, and she pulled a handkerchief from a pocket. "I loved him as a man—not a scientist, not a physician, not a diplomat—as my husband! It's been two years, and I still grieve."

"Of course," Isabel said. "You have every right to your grief."

Anna dropped her head, and sobbed silently into the white cloth. When her tears subsided, she sat on, her eyes covered, her head bent.

Isabel stood, and signaled to Oa. "We should leave you alone. But thank you for seeing me, Anna," she said softly. "I wish there were more I could do."

Anna lowered the handkerchief. She stood, too, straightening her dress, smoothing her hair. She lifted her head to gaze at Oa. "This girl . . ."

"Oa."

"She's had the antiviral? The one Simon created?"

"Yes, she has."

"Is it working?"

"We don't know yet. Simon thought it could take quite some time."

Anna took a deep breath, and when she spoke again, her voice was a bit stronger. "I'm a teacher," she said. "I've devoted my life to children."

"I know."

Anna Edwards met Isabel's eyes. Her eyes were still reddened from her tears, and the lids were a little swollen, but there was courage in her gaze, and perhaps, Isabel thought, the beginnings of acceptance.

Anna said, "There is something you can do for me, Mother Burke. You can let me know if Simon's scrum works for Oa. You can let me know if it was worth it."

IN THE SECOND week of Easter, the priests and novices and lay ministers of the Priestly Order of Mary Magdalene celebrated a special liturgy in honor of Oa of Virimund.

The Tuscan sun shone its benevolent light on the old stone chapel, warming the heads of those lining up for the procession. First the servers, then the ministers and novices, and lastly the priests, twenty-seven of them, their bare scalps shining, filed into the chapel. They wore albs of white, draped with chasubles of green. A children's choir from the village of San Felice sang, and several priests representing other orders were present. Marian Alexander presided, her face calm, but her eyes glowing with pride at the success of the Virimund mission. At Isabel's success.

Oa was already in the chapel, kneeling in readiness in a pew before the altar. In her hand she held a tiny stone, a bit she had carried away from the kburi, to have with her something of the Child Goddess. Isabel knelt beside her. She had designed the ceremony, with the help of Mother Alexander, and all that remained for her to do was shepherd Oa through her part.

The great moment, for Oa, had come during the Sacred Triduum, the three holy days before Easter. She had risen from her cot in Isabel's room, and gone down the corridor to the bathroom to wash. Isabel was already up, dressed, almost ready to go to the chapel for morning Mass. Oa had run back down the corridor, her sleepshift flying, a smeared towel in her hands.

"Isabel!" she cried, before she was even in the door.

Isabel, startled, put down her cross and turned. "Oa?"

Oa burst into the room, forgetting to close the door, forgetting the rule of quiet, forgetting everything as she held the towel out for Isabel to see. "Isabel! Look!"

"Oa, what—oh, sweetheart! Is this yours?"

"Yes, yes! This is Oa's! The blood of a woman—of a person!"

They had embraced, Isabel laughing, Oa laughing and crying at the same time, freeing herself to pirouette around the room, coming back to hug Isabel. The girl had grown at least three inches, and was almost as tall as Isabel. She was thin, of course, as all the anchens were thin, but her breasts had begun to bud, her childish hips to round. She was growing up. And now, for Oa, the proof. Her menses had begun.

Isabel had explained to Marian how important this was to Oa, and today they would honor the great event in a public liturgy. The press were invited, so that people could understand what had happened, what remained to be done for the other anchens. The children in the choir stared curiously at Oa, distracted from their music by this dark-skinned, slender girl over whom such a fuss was being made. Gretchen Boreson had sent a representative, the envoy Cole Markham, bearing gifts for Oa's special day, and bringing an archivist to record everything.

Isabel smiled at that. Gretchen Boreson, even ill as she was, would turn all of it into a public relations triumph.

The ceremony was solemn and simple. Candles were lit, scriptures read, prayers offered. At last, Isabel escorted Oa to the altar and Marian Alexander blessed her, saying "Oa of Virimund, you are one of the great mysteries, and the great miracles, which make us grateful to God for the wonders of being human."

Isabel saw Oa's eyes flicker, searching for her. She stepped a little closer, and put a hand on Oa's shoulder.

"We are, all of us, grateful to have you as part of our community, and we rejoice with you. We also honor the Child Goddess, your patroness, who sustained and strengthened you while you waited for this day."

Oa held out the little stone, the bit of volcanic rock carried all the way from the planet Virimund. Marian took it in her hand, and sprinkled holy water on it, and then gave it back. Isabel had had a necklace made, with a reliquary, and she helped Oa to fit the stone into its little locking compartment. Oa hugged her, and murmured her thanks to Marian.

Marian finished by saying gravely, "Oa of Virimund, on this day, here in the Magdalene Chapel, all of those present recognize and honor the existence of your immortal soul. May God bless and keep you always."

And then every Magdalene came forward, one at a time, to embrace Oa, to bless her with their hands on her curly head, their cheeks pressed briefly to hers. Through it all Oa's smile blazed white, and her eyes shone with joy.

Isabel closed her eyes, sending her thanks to Simon. And to God for providing him.

IT ALL SEEMED like a dream to Oa. Or was it the long, long years on Virimund that had been a dream? But each of these women who came forward, who brushed her cheeks with theirs, who blessed her, each of them knew the secret that now she knew, too, felt the sensations that she felt. Was she really different from the anchen she had been two weeks before? Or was it her belief that she was changed that made her feel different? It would be a long time, she thought, before she could think of herself as no longer being an anchen. Or maybe, in a way, she would always be one.

Isabel led her out into the sunshine, part of the procession, while the children sang their anthems and the birds of Tuscany answered with their own twittering melodies. In the courtyard of the Mother House, a great feast had been set out, fruits and breads and olives and nuts and lovely elaborate cakes. Oa stood at the head of one of the tables, taking the congratulations of people who were new to her, who shook her hand and chatted with her.

Marian Alexander brought a man to meet her, a gray-haired man in black, wearing a white collar like Isabel's. "Oa," Marian said, "I'd like you to meet Father Raymond. He's a physician, and he has volunteered to go to Virimund, to work with the anchens."

Oa stared at him. "You will go to Virimund?"

He smiled back at her, a pleasant smile in a gentle, wrinkled face. "I'd like to. Do you think your companions would welcome me?"

Oa glanced at Isabel, who stood close at her elbow. It was very strange, almost overwhelming, to think of this stranger going to the island, and not Oa herself, not Isabel. But she knew Isabel had a new assignment, and she herself . . . well, she had decisions to make.

"Oa thinks . . ." she began, and then stopped in confusion.

"Oa?" Isabel said gently. "I think you could use the pronoun now."

Oa took a deep, trembling breath. It was true. She was a person now. She had a soul. It had been proclaimed by Mother Alexander, in the chapel. She knew what Isabel meant.

"Yes," she said, nodding to Father Raymond. "I think the anchens will welcome you." She glanced again at Isabel. "I will go, too, Isabel," she said. "The anchens will need me."

AUTHOR'S NOTE

There has been much controversy regarding the Biblical and historical figure of Mary Magdalene, with little agreement even on the meaning of her name. Her identity is clouded by a confusion of translations, traditions, rejected gospels, and myths. There are several excellent websites devoted to research and study regarding Mary of Magdala, and also a number of books that interested readers may wish to investigate. Please visit the author's website at *www.louisemarley.com* for a list of resources devoted to this fascinating and mysterious woman, who is variously reported to be a prostitute, a priestess of an ancient cult, a mystical figure in eastern religions, or the very first apostle and an active, preaching disciple of Jesus Christ—a female disciple.